AF757205

E-LEARNING – LONG-DISTANCE AND LIFELONG PERSPECTIVES

Edited by **Elvis Pontes, Anderson Silva, Adilson Guelfi** and **Sérgio Takeo Kofuji**

E-Learning – Long-Distance and Lifelong Perspectives
Edited by Elvis Pontes, Anderson Silva, Adilson Guelfi and Sérgio Takeo Kofuji

Published by InTech

Janeza Trdine 9, 51000 Rijeka, Croatia

Publishing Process Manager Ivona Lovric

Technical Editor Teodora Smiljanic

Cover Designer InTech Design Team

Additional hard copies can be obtained from orders@intechopen.com

E-Learning – Long-Distance and Lifelong Perspectives,
Edited by Elvis Pontes, Anderson Silva, Adilson Guelfi and Sérgio Takeo Kofuji
p. cm.
ISBN 978-953-51-0250-2

For EU product safety concerns:
IN TECH d.o.o., Prolaz Marije Krucifikse Kozulić 3, 51000 Rijeka, Croatia,
info@intechopen.com or visit our website at intechopen.com.

Meet the editors

Elvis Pontes is professor at the University Estácio de Sá, at the Universidade Paulista, and at SENAC. He applied for Ph.D. at the University of São Paulo, holds MSc from the Institute of Technological Research of São Paulo; MBA from the Institute of Energy and Nuclear Researches; BSc from the Technological Institute of Osasco.

Anderson Aparecido Alves da Silva applied for PhD at the University of São Paulo (USP), Electrical Engineering Postgraduate Program. He holds MSc from the Institute of Technological Research of São Paulo (IPT), MBA from the Alvares Penteado's Foundation, and technological degree from the Educational Institute of Osasco. Currently he is full time professor at the Paulista University.

Adilson Guelfi holds PhD in Electric Engineering from the University of São Paulo. He is professor and researcher at the Institute of Technological Research of São Paulo, technical manager of the first Brazilian laboratory for testing and verifying the compatibility of systems, devices and equipments for the Brazilian Public Key Infrastructure standards.

Sérgio Takeo Kofuji holds Bachelor Degree in Physics from the University of São Paulo (1985), Masters in Electrical Engineering from the University of São Paulo (1988) and Ph.D. in Electrical Engineering from the University of São Paulo (1995). He is currently Professor RiDP Polytechnic School of the University of São Paulo.

Contents

Preface

E-learning is a model of apprenticeship which concerns courses for any branches of science (natural or social) with classes supported by electronic means and, lastly, addressing long-distance and in-classroom courses.

For decades, long-distance courses were offered only by TV or correspondence. But with the advent of computer systems, early E-learning models have been presented mostly as computer-based learning, automating old education and teaching styles, whereby the role model was for transmitting information and knowledge. Although they were electronically supported, those models lack interactivity for students and educators, as interaction is superficially or not approached at all. Intending to cover this gap, models based on computer-supported collaborative learning were proposed, encouraging the shared development of knowledge and, therefore, lifelong learning.

In this sense, real-time tools have become an important demand for E-learning and, consequently, nowadays long-distance courses feature mainly in online environments. Information and communication systems features (as multimedia and mostly the Internet) are employed for making available lessons and lectures, improving experiences of exchange and interactivity among educators and students. This way, with multimedia and online tools available in the Internet, it was possible to combine multiple approaches to learning, mixing the use of virtual and physical resources for what is generally defined as Blended learning (B-learning). The mobility characteristics are subsequently introduced for the learning environments as well, merging another important feature for online long-distance and traditional face-to-face education.

With all the characteristics previously mentioned, E-learning enables students to pace their studies according to their needs, making learning accessible to (1) people who do not have enough free time for studying – they can program their lessons according to their available schedule; (2) those far from a school (geographical issues), or the ones unable to attend classes due to some physical or medical restriction. Therefore, cultural, geographical and physical obstructions can be removed, making it possible for students to select their path and time for the learning course.

Students are then allowed to choose the main objectives they are suitable to fulfill.

This book regards E-learning challenges, opening a way to understand and discuss questions related to long-distance and lifelong learning, E-learning for people with special needs and, lastly, presenting case study about the relationship between the quality of interaction and the quality of learning achieved in experiences of e-learning formation.

The book is divided in three sections. In the first section, the reader will find chapters which discuss long-distance and lifelong learning, focusing on adaptive models, mobile learning and e-learning in developing/developed countries. E-learning for people with special needs, specifically blindness, is approached in section two. In the final section, case study is introduced on the subject of quality interaction and quality learning.

Professor Elvis Pontes,
Professor Anderson Silva,
Professor Adilson Guelfi and
Professor Sérgio Takeo Kofuji
Department of Electrical Engineering
Polytechnic School
University of São Paulo (USP)
Brazil

Part 1

Long-Distance Courses and Long-Life Learning

1

Adaptive Model for E-Learning in Secondary School

Todorka Glushkova
Plovdiv University "Paisii Hilendarski"
Bulgaria

1. Introduction

The application of ICT[1] in the classroom training process allows us to compare two basic stages - a computer based training and e-learning (Stoyanov, 2005a; Stoyanovich, 2001). These two concepts are similar but there are some differences between them. The computer based training (CBT) is an attempt to automate education, replace an educator, and develop self-paced learning. It is place-, time- and content-predetermined learning. E-Learning has its origins in CBT. The main focus of e-learning is not only to educate without barriers of time and distance, but to adjust to the user's goals and needs. It is a just-in-time, in the workplace, customized, on-demand method of learning. For the realization of this kind of training we need to develop appropriate learning resources and mobile services. E-Learning is the next stage of the learning process; it is a new educational paradigm. We consider the passage from CBT to e-Learning a step-by-step process from traditional education and use CBT to adaptive lifelong learning.

A system for electronic and distance learning DeLC[2] (Stoyanov, 2005b) is developed by Plovdiv University "Paisii Hilendarski"(PU) with Institute of Information Technologies (IIT), BAS- Bulgaria; Telecommunication Research Centre (TRC), University of Limerick, Ireland; Software Technology Research Laboratory (STRL), De Montfort University, Leicester, UK; Software Technology Group (SWT), Humboldt University, Berlin, Germany and the secondary school "Hristo Smirnenski", Brezovo, Bulgaria. In compliance with the main objectives of the project we establish a network of educational DeLC-portals that provide an adapted learning process to their customers and exchange learning resources and services.

The information society requires the application of new methods and approaches to the independent as well as the classroom education of students. According to the characteristics of education in Bulgarian schools DeLC-models and approaches will be applied, which focus primarily on the adaptability and some aspects of their application (Glushkova, 2005). The approach that we follow is related to the study of adaptability as a key feature of any e-Learning system. It can be seen from different viewpoints regarding the planned features, but we will concentrate our attention mainly on those aspects which stem from the pedagogical practice and experience. We will examine the adaptability in terms of:

---

[1] ICT-Information and communication technologies

[2] DeLC-Distributed e-Learning center

- students' knowledge at the beginning of each learning session;
- students' goals and plans in terms of their training;
- specifics of different school subjects;
- cognitive characteristics of students;
- emotional types and characteristics of students;
- students' habits and preferences;
- temporal characteristics of training;
- achievement of certain states in the learning process;
- training from anywhere;
- mode of access to learning resources etc.

We will explore the implementations of each of these aspects of adaptability in the basic models of the e-Learning system - the user, pedagogical and domain model. On the other hand, we will examine the main features of e-learning, according to the accepted definition above - a personalized learning process from anywhere at any time. Thus, drawn from the educational theory and practice, aspects of adaptability and the main features of e-learning will be implemented in the basic models by which the target adaptive e-Learning system will be created, which concentrates the theoretical and practical experience in it. (Figure1.)

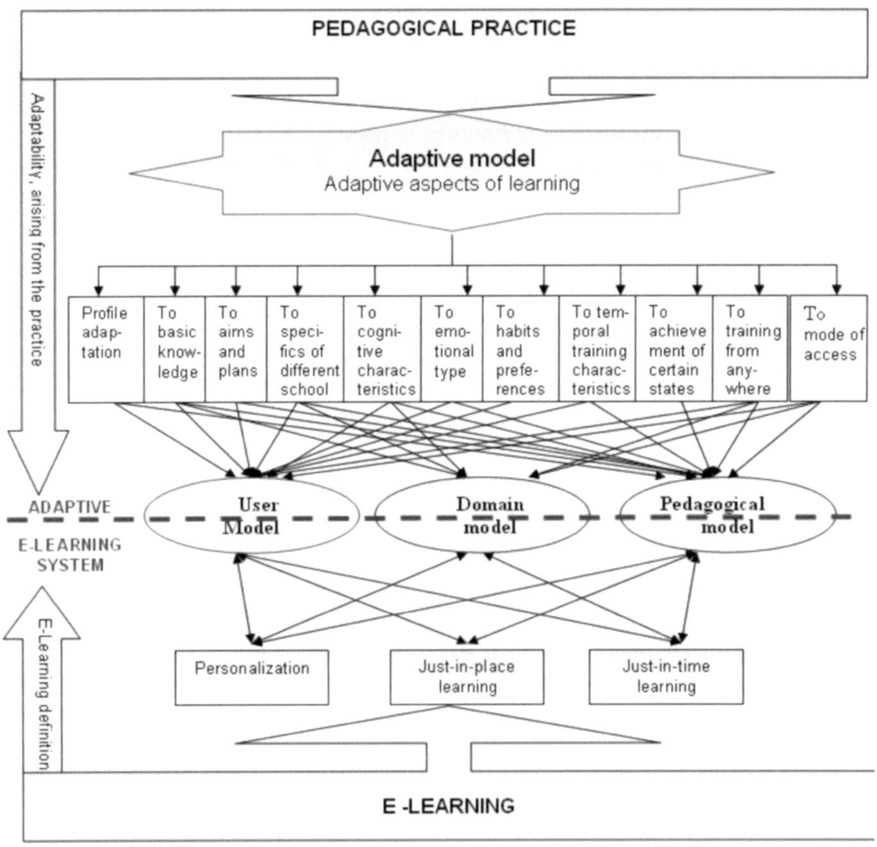

Fig. 1. Relationship between adaptability in the learning process, the basic models of the system and the key features of e-learning.

The three basic models - the user, domain and pedagogical ones, are in a dynamic relationship and dependency between them. Each one affects the status of the others and we need a mechanism for dynamic linking and reporting of relationships between them. Because adaptability in its various aspects is implemented to varying degrees in each of the three basic models, we could look at them as concrete expressions of adaptability of the system for e-learning. Therefore, the basic models are the result of the analysis of possibilities to realize the adaptability of the system and can be used as concrete forms to manage different adaptive aspects.

On the other hand, each of the base models provides mechanisms for the implementation of the key features of the e-Learning system - personalized access to resources from anywhere at any time. The user model provides the most direct property personalization of the learning process and greatly influences the provision of appropriate services and resources anywhere and anytime. The pedagogical model specifies both a customized learning process and appropriate educational process from anywhere, anytime. The domain model is connected with the characteristics of each school subject and provides a mechanism for a more effective personalized learning process, in accordance with the timing of training.

The structure of the manuscript corresponds to the described methodology. In section 2 "Adaptive model of the school e-learning system" discuss various aspects of adaptability associated with personalization of the learning process and access to educational resources from anywhere, anytime. Here are reviewed and adaptive levels of the system in horizontal and vertical plan. Section 3 "Adaptability in the basic models of e-learning system" describes the three basic models of system-UM, DM, PM, in which are implemented the described aspects and levels of adaptability. The results of the partial implementation of the proposed model of e-learning in secondary schools are encouraging. Work on the realization of the full adaptive model continues.

2. Adaptive model of the school e-learning system

Adaptability is an abstract concept which can have different specific forms of manifestation in e-Learning systems. There are different definitions of this concept according to the specific characteristics and goals of any such system. We will consider the adaptability as feature of the system that ensures maximum satisfaction of students and teachers in the e-learning process.

2.1 Adaptability and personalization

A key requirement of the e-learning system, according to the basic definition, is its personalization. This determines the key role of the user model (UM) and the adaptability, which implements it (Brusilovsky, 2001). There are different definitions specifying the UM as a source of user information and mechanisms for changing the behavior of the system according to consumer needs and desires (Kass,1988); as the basis of specific knowledge in dialog systems, which contain information and suggestions on various aspects of the user, related with their behavior during the dialogue with the system (Kobsa,2004) etc.

In its building the model will be based on the view that the knowledge and assumptions about the individual consumer must be able to be separated from other knowledge about the system, which is provided clearly, and can be managed, stored and changed. In terms of the personalization we will look at some basics about the nature of the system views.

2.1.1 Aadaptation to the role of the user

Users of the system can be differentiated according to their role as:

- Students from different classes and forms of education;
- Teachers - as authors of e-content or as trainers and consultants in the educational process;
- Parents who monitor the individual progress of their children;
- School Administration, which analyzes global trends in education for different groups of students, etc.

We will focus our attention mainly on the first two groups. To formalize this type of adaptation we will use a stereotypical approach (Figure 2.).

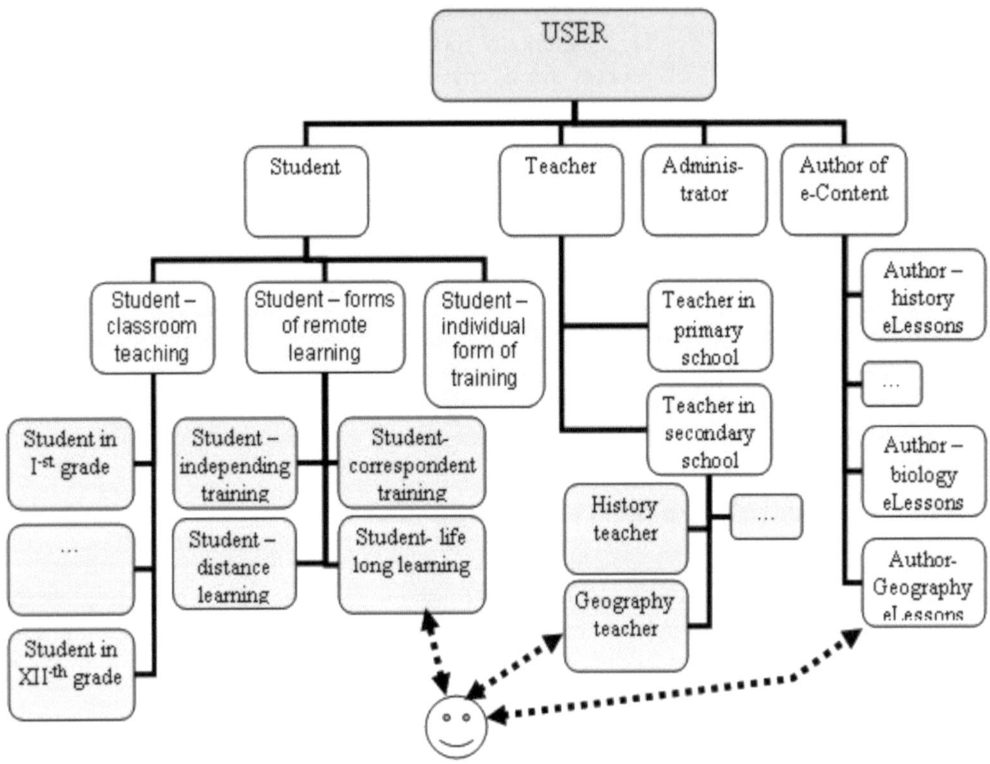

Fig. 2. Stereotypical hierarchy and association of users.

2.1.2 Adaptation to the base knowledge of the student

This aspect of adaptability is associated with defining the areas of consumer knowledge by measuring the level of understanding of various concepts in a subject area (domain) of the particular student. There are different approaches for the realization of this kind of adaptability. Besides the stereotypical approach, we can use the overlay model and the combined approach. The overlay model considers the user's knowledge as a subset of common knowledge, supported by the system. This model is among the dominant types of user models, usually represented as a hierarchical or semantic network of nodes directly linked to concepts from the subject domain. We can use a logical or numerical value for assessing the student's knowledge. The statutory curriculum in all subjects in school education is a prerequisite for creating domain ontologies, including basic concepts and relationships between them. To each concept there will be attributed a relative numerical value (in%), which shows the degree of certainty of the system about the student's knowledge. We use the initial test, including knowledge of various school subjects for the class to determine basic knowledge of the student who is new to the system. The test results are evaluated on three levels: as a general result for the student; as a comprehensive assessment of each school subject and as an evaluation of the level of knowledge about each concept. The evaluation of the first level is used to determine the stereotypical group of the student; the evaluation of the second level – to determine the student's sub-stereotype in their studies of this subject area, and the results of the third level - to realize the model of overlapping with concepts from the domain.

If a student is known to the system, it has preserved information about their past learning sessions and the results from tests in the respective school subject. These values are initialized by the system when the student is identified at the beginning of this training course and are used in the next training cycle. We assume that the student knows a concept if the system assesses their knowledge at a level above 50%. In an established hierarchical structure, the assessment of any concept is derived from the average score of its subsidiary concepts. We will therefore appreciate the level of knowledge of each term in the formula:

$$Mark\_Term = \frac{1}{k}\sum_{i=1}^{k} MarkSubTerm[i] \tag{1}$$

MarkSubTerm [i] is the evaluation of the i-th subsidiary concept; k-number of subsidiaries (1)

Each subsidiary of the concept itself can be regarded as a parent for its subsidiary concepts and receive the same assessment formula, etc. The assessment of student knowledge on each school subject can be calculated as:

$$Mark\_Subject = \frac{1}{n}\sum_{j=1}^{n} Mark\_Term[j] \tag{2}$$

Mark_Term[j] is the evaluation of the j-th basic concept; n-number of these concepts.

The evaluation of the test as a whole can be present by formula (3). This formula is calculated in% of student achievement, taking into account the weight of each subject in it.

$$MarkTest = \frac{1}{num\_test\_quest} \cdot \sum_{i=1}^{m} num\_quest[l].Mark\_Subject[l] \tag{3}$$

Mark_Subject [l] - assessment of students in l-th domain; num_quest [l]- number of questions on this domain, m - number of domains; num_test_quest -total number of questions in the test.

This model has many advantages, mainly related to its simplicity and small resource requirements. However, it is difficult to locate the unknown concept to the individual user, particularly if the school subjects are not represented by a hierarchical tree model but as ontological network structures. Due to the fact that this model should be applied to each individual student, this would hamper the system and would reduce its effectiveness. To ignore these shortcomings and to multiply the effect of using the above two approaches, we combine them. The combined approach is based on a combination of stereotypical and overlay models. The algorithm includes the following steps:

1. Users are associated to certain stereotyped groups in the hierarchy according to their profiles;
2. The system sets the initial value of 50% of all concepts from all subject areas taught in the previous class. This is determined by the Bulgarian Educational Standards (BES) that determine the minimum level of knowledge in each school subject upon completion of each class. Therefore, students know at least 50 percent from the previous class concepts. After doing the initial test knowledge of each student is valued on three levels:
   - as a common assessment test by formula (3), which is needed for its accession to any substereotype for the form of education and class - "beginner" (<60%), "good" (60% -80%) and "excellent" (>80%);
   - as general knowledge of the school subject. For each topic of the curriculum there will be developed lessons that are classified into three main groups providing "basic knowledge" (to 60%), "good level" (from 60% to 80%) and "high level" (>80%);
   - as an assessment of the level of knowledge about different concepts in the domain. These values are used by the system for selecting the most appropriate lesson containing the necessary information on the topic;
3. If a student is already taught in the system, it stores information about their knowledge of the answers to the questions and doing tests in previous training sessions, and initializes the level of knowledge of the concepts from the domain with these values;
4. The three levels of evaluation are constantly changing during the training, thus the system adapts dynamically to the respective user. If initially, for example, the student was assigned to the sub-stereotype "beginner" with knowledge of the history of "good level" and in the course of training gets higher and higher learning outcomes, he go into the next "high level" of knowledge in this subject area. Thus, the system will offer lessons from increasingly higher level of difficulty in the other subject domains. It will enable them to move to the next sub-stereotype of „good" or even "excellent".

2.1.3 Adapting to the goals and plans of the student

To provide the student with educational resources and services that are appropriate for them, the system needs information about the goals and plans for their implementation. Usually the student does not set them explicitly, which leads to considerable difficulties. The system must have mechanisms to detect them. This can be achieved by monitoring the behaviours of students during the learning process. Since the implementation of elementary, indivisible tasks is trivial, we need a mechanism for decomposing the goals and to create scenarios for the implementation plan of the user. The scenario is a sequence of elementary actions. The process of determining the plans is ongoing. They must be updated dynamically depending on the student's behavior. Periodically, the system must compare this behavior with predetermined conditions corresponding to the current plan. If there is a compliance it is assumed that the user wants the implementation of exactly this scenario and continues with its execution, otherwise they launch another, a more appropriate, one. In the e-Learning system a special model of the goals and objectives is developed, called Goal & Task Model (GTM), which can be considered as part of the pedagogical model. We will use the mechanisms that have user stereotypes and a cluster model. Originally, stereotypes are activated by static user groups and they define basic stereotype goals. For example, if the student is associated to the sub-stereotype "beginner", the system assigns a common group goal - "to obtain a minimum of knowledge". Then a dialogue starts, which can specify their personal goal. If the student clearly defines their goal, the system temporarily associates them with a particular cluster of users with similar personal goals; it chooses a plan and a scenario for its implementation. If a student does not clearly define its goals, the system defines a common goal for the sub stereotype and starts a scenario for its implementation.

A multiple repetition of the same objectives in turn could influence a change for the typical stereotype goals. So, while adapting to the personal goals of students, the system will adapt to the general objectives in stereotypical groups to which these students belong.

2.1.4 Adaptation to the nature and specifics of the school subjects

The organization of learning according to the specifics of different subjects is another aspect of the adaptability of the systems. For example, if the achievement of key objectives in mathematics education need to pay more attention to the application of theoretical knowledge obtained in solving practical problems through interactive methods and continuous interaction with the system, the training in geography will focus on cartographic material and additional knowledge; in history education attention will be paid to animated diagrams, charts and other methods that help the absorption of factual material. In a classical classroom training the school subjects are grouped in different cultural and educational fields, according to different global didactic goals. Based on this structure we can create a stereotypical hierarchy of educational subject areas, stereotyping them according to the specific teaching objectives and features of the methodological approaches in the learning process.

The topics for each course and for each class are predetermined by the curriculum, in which there are fixed both the level of knowing concepts and the mandatory minimum knowledge of relevant subjects. We will discuss the following groups of e-Learning resources:

- mono-lessons (related to only one domain)
- bi-lessons (linked to more than one domain);
- additional reference materials;
- educational games and other interactive and collaborative services.

The mono-lessons are connected to only one domain. They are developed by teachers in a specialized development tool SELBO[3] (Stoyanov,2008; Mitev, 2008) and include information on certain topics of the syllabus for the class. The authors plan this adapting during the creation of the lessons according to the specifics of the domain and global objectives of the course. Based on the stereotypical hierarchy of domains parent domain are originally initialized with default values, and then subdomains are specified. After specifying the specific domain and subdomain for a particular topic, SELBO initializes relevant ontology

[3] SELBO- SCORM Editor for eLearning Based on Ontologies

and proposes appropriate templates and tools for creating an e-Lesson. For example, if the teacher creates a lesson in Math, SELBO will propose not only the corresponding ontology, but also a structure of the lesson with the formal definition of the concepts, animated charts and diagrams to illustrate the causal links, examples and a large number of practical tasks in which at different levels the knowledge, obtained so far, is verified. The created e-Lessons are recorded in a special repository- Lesson DB and are provided to students for training in this domain. The bi-lessons are linked to concepts from two or more domains. The created lessons are stored in the e-Learning system. They will be provided to students as additional learning resources in some of these domains. The reference materials such as dictionaries, encyclopedias, reference books, etc. are developed as additional learning resources. The students can use them in the training process in various disciplines, regardless of their classes. These materials are mostly related to language education, as well as natural and social school subjects. Educational games can be used for training in all subject areas in a primary school; the interactive forms, online competitions, crosswords, training tests, etc. can be used mainly for training in languages, mathematics, and natural and social subject domains. The discussion forums, consultation and other synchronous and asynchronous communication services can also be used for teaching in all subject domains. The teamwork and project learning can be used largely for training in information technology and social sciences. The use of these kinds of learning resources is particularly important in the training of disabled students.

Therefore, adaptability to the relevant school subjects take place on several levels. Initially the domain in the hierarchy is determined. Then the appropriate subdomain is specified, which is connected with the class and form of education, and the system offers it the appropriate learning resources - e-lessons, reference materials and other interactive and collaborative services.

2.1.5 Adaptation to cognitive characteristics of students

Training in a subject area is an individual process of information search, navigation in space education, formulating hypotheses and making conclusions. To examine the level of cognitive activity we will use estimates of the student of the first two levels - as a comprehensive evaluation of a test and as an evaluation of individual school subjects. In addition to these values we will monitor the number of used training resources and visited navigation links, which in various combinations can provide a different presentation of educational materials. We will use three types of navigation links: "from general to the particular concept", "connection with parallel concepts for search of analogy and formulating hypotheses" and "random link". We will appreciate the learning resources according to their number and types - images, text, animations, videos, etc. The high number of visited images, animations and other support and help materials will be described as the presence of low levels of abstraction. The content will be determined in terms of detail, abstraction and structuring.

In building the model we will determine the direction of change in cognitive activity, the level of general and domain knowledge to students, as well as the observed values of the content, the number of connections and types of learning resources. The tendencies to raise the level of inductive thinking and from there the type of cognitive activity will be defined in the next Table. (+1 trend to increase; -1 - to decrease, 0 - no change).

knowledge in the domain		general level of knowledge		
		"beginner"	„good"	„excellent"
basic knowledge	number of links	+1	+1	0
	Number of info. resources	+1	0	0
	Learning content:			
	- detail	+1	+1	+1
	- abstraction	+1	+1	0
	- structuring	+1	0	0
Good level knowledge	number of links	+1	0	-1
	Number of info. resources	0	0	0
	Learning content:			
	- detail	+1	0	-1
	- abstraction	+1	+1	0
	- structuring	0	0	0
High level knowledge	number of links	0	-1	-1
	Number of info. resources	0	0	-1
	Learning content:			
	- detail	0	-1	-1
	- abstraction	+1	0	-1
	- structuring	0	0	-1

Table 1. Trends in changing of observed parameters and cognitive activity.

The table shows that the proposed model leads to the generation of nine 5-dimensional vectors (4.):

$$MarkTestMarkSubject=(numLinks, numInfRes, contentDetail, contentAbstr, contentStruct) \quad (4)$$

The adaptation to specific cognitive characteristics of students can be realized in the following algorithm:

1. If a student is new to the system, after solving the initial test formulas (1) - (3) determine the extent of its general and domain knowledge. If not - these values are initialized with the entry of the student into the system.
2. According to these values the system defines their general type - "beginner", "good" "excellent" and type it in the selected domain - "basic knowledge", "good level" and "high level".
3. The system initializes the values of vector (4). LMS[4] starts the lesson, which meets these values most closely.
4. The system also has additional resources such as dictionaries, picture atlases, reference books, etc., and additional domain-dependent services. We can create a few basic scenarios, corresponding to the values of the vector, and determine a sequence of presentation of learning resources (tutorials, additional materials and services), so that the learning process will correspond most completely to the type of cognitive activity of students and will help to improve their abstract and inductive thinking.

[4] LMS-Learning management system

For example, if a student from 5th grade is from the stereotype of "beginner" and the sub-stereotype "good" in Teaching Geography, the system sets the values of the five global variables, respectively (1.0, +1, 1.0) and runs a scenario which begins with an educational game (eg a crossword, which increases the interest and number of links). Then LMS selects a lesson and starts it in the topic, in which the information is detailed, and there are more opportunities for connections with additional reference materials or fun - type "curious" or "Do you know that ..." (Figure 3).

Fig. 3. Servises by type of cognitive activity.

Training can be completed with a test that is desirable to look like an educational game, which ends with encouraging results. If the game is the kind of "puzzle", "quest treasure" or "question game", where each step is connected with the right answer to a question from the lesson, this will increase the degree of abstractness of training.

2.2 Adaptability in accessing the system at any time

Learning is a continuous process of obtaining and processing information throughout life. Over a long period of twelve years students should be familiar with the concepts, tools for research and facts on various school subjects. Therefore, training should be done systematically and incrementally, by following the sequence in the training of various school subjects, and order of study of educational topics in each of them. This sequence is regulated by law in Bulgaria as a defined curriculum and syllabus for each class and form of education. This means that in a specific interval of time (class, term, etc.) in the e-Learning system there must be available only resources from certain school subjects and topics covered in accordance with the relevant curriculum.

Each school subject has its own peculiarities. On their basis we described a model for using different types of learning resources - tutorials, reference materials, educational games and other collaborative learning services. Some of these resources are largely independent of time training - such as reference books, dictionaries, atlases, etc. Others depend on real time (date, time) such as collaborative services, group work, discussion forums, real-time consultations with teachers, etc. The third set of resources, including mostly e-Lessons and tests, can be considered from various aspects in terms of time usage. On the one hand they depend on relative timing of training but on the other, they depend on real time, as these lessons and tests will be available only for a certain time interval (eg one month). This is due to the fact that the electronic lesson is a combination of three elements: structure, content and process. The first element doesn't depend on time; the second depends on the real time, to the beginning of which a student must have already acquired basic knowledge and skills;

and the third element depends on the relative progress of training time. Therefore we can describe the training period from two aspects (Figure 4.):

- as real-time with characteristics date and time or time interval;
- as relative time. It is characterized by the achievement of certain conditions.

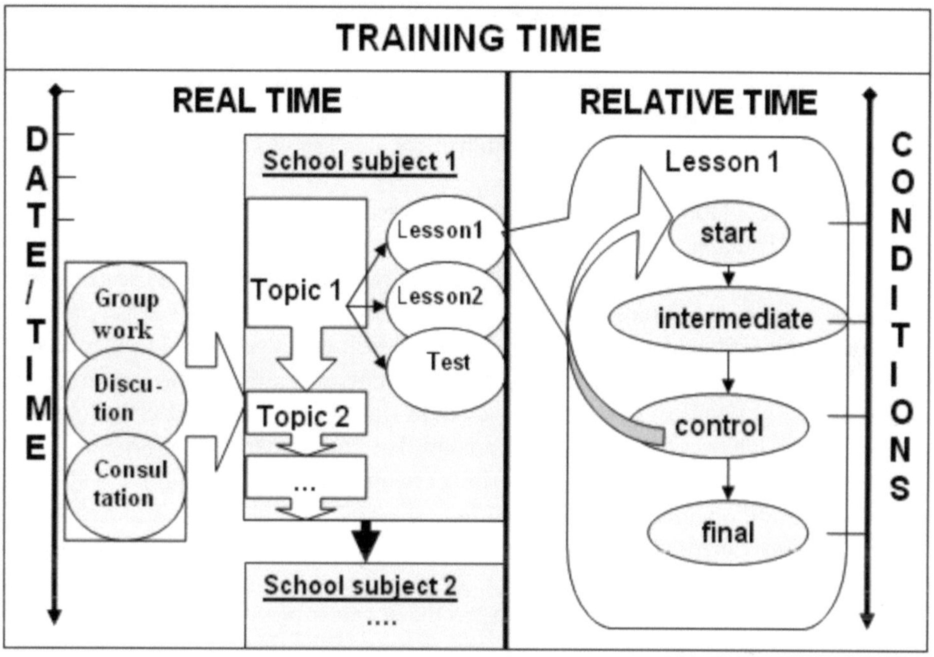

Fig. 4. Adapting the system in terms of training time.

In this sense, if a student from 5th grade wants to be trained in the system, he will have access only to the 5th grade school subjects and will not be able to study physics for example, because he doesn't have the necessary basic knowledge in mathematics. Therefore, the student must go through the topics successively and thus build a system of knowledge of this school subject. When he starts an e-lesson in the current theme, the content of this lesson will depend on the real time (eg, the time when the student is in the 5th grade). However, the learning process will depend on the relative conditions, through which it passes successively depending on the educational scenario and the behavior of the student during the session. When the training ends with a test, it can be performed with any group of students from the fifth grade, who study the same topic in this real period of time. Then it is necessary to set a specific date and time. The evaluation of the student can be done personally, in which case it is relative in time. When in the course of training the student wishes to comment on the learning material with other students from their stereotyped group, or to ask their questions to the teacher, they can do it in real time. In organizing the group work it is also necessary to plan and organize various activities in real time.

There are many mechanisms that provide opportunities for learning activities in real time. Therefore we will concentrate our attention mainly on the implementation of the personalized learning process in relative time.

In order to observe the changes in the educational system we must follow certain values of its parameters. The condition is the vector with specific values of the observed parameters. The adapting of the system in this aspect requires the definition and classification of meaningful conditions. We can have a look at a few basic conditions:

- a start-condition in which LMS starts the e-Lesson and the learning process begins;
- an intermediate state - a key condition that determines whether the learning scenario is performed correctly;
- a control condition - when the system enters this state, the learning process must be interrupted and the current scenario must be corrected;
- a final state - a condition that determines the successful conclusion of the learning process.

This aspect on the adaptability of the system is directly related to the adaptation to user goals and plans. Dynamically, during the learning process the system checks the values of the key parameters and a predetermined combination of them detects the presence of some of the above types of conditions. Once you have determined the school subject and theme, the system identifies the educational goal - personal (if it is defined clearly) or the total for the stereotypical group. LMS initializes a start-condition and initiates the learning process, while continuously monitoring the change of the values of the observed parameters. If the process is in an intermediate state, this means that the scenario is appropriate for the particular student and the teaching and learning continue to the next state. If the system gets into a control condition, then the process stops and a new training scenario starts. When the parameters' values determine the final condition, we assume that the goal is achieved and the learning process is completed.

If the author of an electronic lesson determines the duration of an operation, the end of this time period will automatically initialize the control condition, which, if it meets the conditions for a successful completion of the training, passed to a final condition. Otherwise, the system returns to the initial state, and there is launched a process to search for a more suitable lesson on the same topic. If a student has not successfully completed the training due to lack of knowledge, a new easier lesson on the same topic is sought and launched and the student is associated to the lower sub-stereotyped group – e.g. from "high level" to "good level of knowledge". If the cause is related to the speed of the current learning process, the cognitive type of the student must be corrected.

2.3 An adaptation to the manner of access to learning materials

The adaptation to the manner of access to learning materials is another important aspect of the modeling system. If the user uses different standard or mobile devices to gain access during a learning session, it is necessary to develop a mechanism and describe the different basic scenarios for the realization of this task. Access can be realized in two ways: fixed or mobile. In the first case, access is obtained through the browser. Due to some differences in the functionality of the most popular browsers, as well as consumer preferences, it is necessary to use a mechanism for transmitting this information to the system in order to provide GUI[5], which is appropriate for the browser. If the user uses a mobile device, the system must keep information about the characteristics of this device and adapt to them.

[5] GUI- Graphical User Interface

This task requires the standardization of access and use of an intelligent adaptation to different types of mobile devices.

If the user is located near the school, they can use wireless mobile access. The Infrastructure model is based on the principles of the system DeLC for providing mobile services (Stoyanov, 2008b). When the user comes within the range of any of the info-stations in the area of the school, the system activates services for the supplying of information. Depending on the device for mobile access - GSM, PDA, laptop, etc., the Info-station establishes a connection to the info-center, initializes the parameters of communication and maintains them until the end of the session with this device. Since various events may occur in the training process, which are related mainly to the change of the mobile device or user location, we can consider the following basic scenarios:

1. The mobile device and user location are not changed to the end of the training process. In this case the e-Learning session continues by adaptation to the specifics of the device.
2. The mobile device remains the same, but the user's location is changed. At first the user is within range of one info-station, but in the session they move and go within range of another info-station. Since the session is established between a mobile device and an info-center by info-stations, a mechanism is needed to transmit the parameters from one info-station to another. This scenario is realized at an info-center.
3. During the learning session, the mobile device is changed, but the user's location remains the same. The replacement of the mobile device leads to filing of its parameters to the info-station, which must suspend the session, to replace the old values of the parameters with the new ones; to transmit these parameters to the info-centre; to adapt the transmitted training resources to the parameters of the new device, and then to resume the transmission of information. Therefore, if the info-station establishes a session break, it must wait a certain time to change the mobile device, prior to transmitting information to the info-center to end the session. This scenario is realized at an info-station level.
4. During the same user session both the mobile device and user location are changed. If initially the user changes the mobile device for training and then their location, as the system passes within range of another info-station, it starts with scenario 3, followed by scenario 2. If initially the user passes within range of another info-station, and then immediately changes the device, the system starts with scenario 2 of the info-center, followed by scenario 3 of the info-station. Formally, there is a third possibility, in which these changes occur simultaneously. To ensure the continuation of the user's session in this case it is necessary to develop a model for a dynamic communication between the Info-center and Info-stations. The user session will be stopped and there will start the initialization of the parameters of a new device to adapt the graphical interface according to these parameters. Finally the signal must be checked down from another info-station in order to pass parameters from the new device to this info-station and to connect and resume the session.

2.4 Adaptive levels

The main elements of the adaptive model are "condition-action" rules that change the parameters of the environment and realize the adaptation to a user's knowledge, goals, abilities, preferences, etc. The implementation of the model requires the consideration of various aspects of adaptability of horizontal and vertical principles. The first one we presented in the previous section. We discussed the different aspects of adaptability and the interactions between them. The second one is based on the classification of the species' adaptability to the level of implementation and realization in the course of the training. We will distinguish the following three adaptive levels:

1. **Elementary adaptive level (EAL)** – An adaptation to the static profile information of the student as name, class, type of training, the type of device to access educational resources (mobile or fixed), etc. At this level the adaptation is based on a stereotype approach. The teachers generate a set of e-Lessons for learning in typically school subject domains, based on typical teaching objectives, methods and techniques relating to a particular group of traditional users (eg. regular education fifth grade, math). The educational resources are common to all groups of students. The adaptability of this level is realized in the phase of preparation of the typical training materials before the beginning of work in the system.
2. **Static adaptive level (SAL)** – This level builds on the elementary level and is directly related to mechanisms to provide adequate learning materials for individual students according to their knowledge base, personal goals, plans and ambitions. Adaptation mechanisms are set in advance by the authors of educational resources and services, foreseeing the actions and behavior of the typical learner. This can be realized based on the log-information about past interactions between this student and LMS and a set of rules set by the authors of the educational materials. The basic knowledge of students is determined by initial testing or by the current results from already completed training sessions. According to the level of this knowledge the system classifies the student to some sub-stereotype - beginner, good, excellent. The system then compares individual goals and plans of the student with the global didactic goals and targets, according to the Bulgarian educational requirements. As a result, from the Lesson DB is extracted this, which most fully meets the basic knowledge, stereotypical characteristics, objectives and plans of the individual student. Adaptability of this level is achieved before the system operation or in its initial phase when the concrete training scenario is specified. Adaptability can be improved significantly if using intelligent agents as personal assistants for each student, which will monitor and guide the entire learning process.
3. **Dynamic adaptive level (DAL)** – This level complements and builds on the previous two ones. It is related to the dynamic interaction between students and the system during the training (in run-time). After selecting the most appropriate e-lesson in the previous adaptive level, LMS starts the learning process as a sequence of actions set by the author of e-content and the behavior of the individual student. Based on the intermediate results during the training and information from previous sessions, the system adapts dynamically to the changing characteristics of the learning environment, generates new "condition-action" rules and continues the training process or starts a new more appropriate e-Lesson. At this level, in the process of dynamic interaction between learners and the training system it is essential proactive to use intelligent proactive agents, who interact with the system and with each other, so as to provide a flexible change of training scenarios, depending on the behaviors and actions of the individual student.

3. Adaptability in the basic models of e-learning system

The examined aspects of adaptability are not independent of one another. They are in constant interaction and interdependence among themselves. Each of them is implemented to varying degrees in the basic models of the e-learning system – user model, pedagogical model and domain model.

3.1 User modeling

The user model is an important element of any educational system in order to be personalized and tailored to the individual characteristics, knowledge, goals, preferences and requirements of learners. We will separate the information about students from the rest of the knowledge in the system and will describe it on three levels - elementary, static and dynamic. The first level includes the profile information with individual user characteristics such as name, grade, form of education, birth date, e-mail, global goals, preferences, etc. The next level describes the stereotypical hierarchy where users with similar characteristics are combined and presented together in the system. The dynamic level includes specific information about the student in the process of working with the learning environment. It is related rather to the studied school subjects and the user's evaluation during a real session. This defines the relationship between the user model and the adaptability to the student's knowledge and the need for application of a combined approach (Glushkova, 2006).

The user model describes the concept of the system for a user's knowledge, interests and goals. This model must be continuously updated according to the dynamic changes in the accumulation of knowledge. The algorithm involves the following steps:

- Step 1. filling the static profile information. According to the form of training and student class, the user is associated to a certain sub-stereotype in a stereotypical hierarchy. The initial parameters of the model are completed in a dialog mode or are set the default values from the common stereotype model.
- Step 2. According to the stereotype, which the student joins, the system offers a comprehensive initial test. The results are used to initialize the individual user's profile and are grouped into three levels: as a general assessment, an evaluation of knowledge in each domain and an evaluation of each concept. (formulas (1),(2),(3)).
- Step 3. In the dialog mode the system determines the school subject, topic, personal goals and plans. Then it searches, offers and starts an appropriate lesson, according to the student stereotype ("beginner" , "good" and "excellent") and its level of knowledge in the domain.
- Step 4. Conducting of the individual learning process.
- Step 5. Saving the new values for the student's knowledge of the three levels - as a general assessment; level of knowledge in the domain and a valuation of each concept. The values are calculated by the formula (5):

$$\textit{New score} = \textit{average (continuous assessment, assessment from the last session)} \quad (5)$$

- Step 6. Updating of the student's profile information.

The dynamic level of the user model supports interaction with other models of the system. The student's basic knowledge is associated with the domain model. The pedagogical model is related to the GTM which is initialized by the user profile (Figure 5).

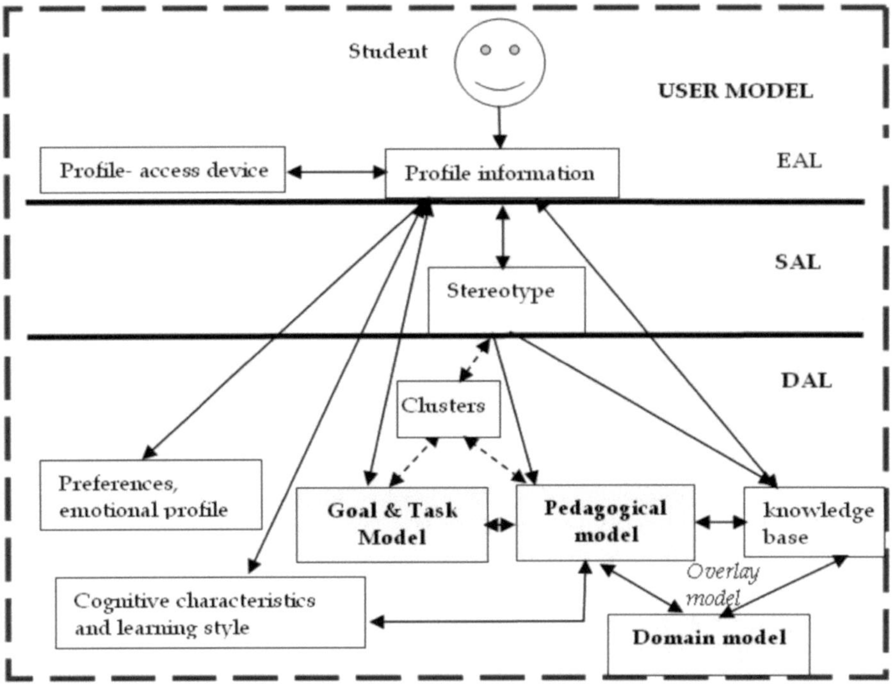

Fig. 5. Interaction of the user model with other basic models of the system.

3.2 Domain model

The domain model (DM) is one of the logical models for each e-learning system due to the need for structuring, clear presentation and processing of knowledge in different subject areas. The model presents the various domains in the system, regardless of the other knowledge in it. The DM is a conceptual model describing the key for the domain objects and relationships between them. For formal description logical structures can be used as frames, semantic networks, ontologies, a system of rules, etc. The model can be realized in the process of software development: the concepts are presented as classes: their characteristics and properties such as attributes and methods. We accept this approach and use ontologies and UML class-diagrams to describe concepts and relations between them.

The process of creating DM goes through several stages. Initially, we define a hierarchy of subject areas according to the curriculum and describe it as a meta-ontology. In the classes, representing different groups of domains, there are described relations with the appropriate services or additional resources such as dictionaries, encyclopedias, reference books, etc. The next step is a presentation of the specific subject areas into the system. Each domain contains semantic information, which is formalized by the creation of domain ontologies. For each area we can create different ontologies for the representation of knowledge. The knowledge in each academic discipline is expanded and supplemented into each next class, as each concept or relation is studied at different levels. For example, the term "triangle" is originally defined in the third grade as a "closed broken line with three vertices" and connects with the terms "vertex" and "line". In the fourth grade the students study the types of triangles; in the fifth - the term "person of triangle", in the seventh - the triangle is already a part of the plane, in the ninth and tenth its metric and trigonometric relationships are discussed, and in the twelfth the methodology of analytic geometry is examined. This approach for accumulation of knowledge is used in the process of creating ontologies for different classes with "part_of" connections. Given the fact that across school subjects there are links and dependencies between them that will be reflected in the appropriate ontologies, we get a complex multi-layered network of ontologies and links between them.

3.3 Pedagogical model

The pedagogical model (PM) is key to any training school system. It interacts with other basic models, ensures the acquisition of specified knowledge and the achievement of specific didactic objectives. The model will be looked at from two aspects - during the creation of electronic tutorials and the training of students in the system.

As already mentioned, training resources and tutorials are created by teachers in a special domain-based development environment. Let us concentrate our attention on two basic characteristics of the lesson - the content and structure. The content of lessons is related to specific topics, which in turn are part of specific domains. Therefore, the e-lesson is a semantic structure of the knowledge contained in a particular area. Formally, it is an instance of a particular part of the ontology, describing the subject area, in which the individual concepts are associated with real information resources that represent them. The structure of the e-lesson depends on defined didactic goals and the characteristics of the subject area. The didactic goals, that are related to obtaining certain knowledge, determine the type of lessons (for new knowledge, practice, summary and testing). To formalize them we will use Bloom's taxonomy, according to which there are six cognitive levels - knowledge, comprehension, application, analysis, synthesis and evaluation (Bloom,1956). The author of the lesson can structure the learning resources in different ways depending on their goals. As a result of studies on the structure of the lesson came to the conclusion that there is similarity between different kinds e-Lessons and the cognitive levels of Bloom's taxonomy. I.e. formalization of the different kinds of e-lessons according to didactic goals can be realized by creating standard scenarios for training and templates, that describe them. Each template we will seen as a combination of: learning resources, structure and scenario for training

The created e-Learning resources are stored in online repository. They are associated with concepts of ontologies and provide itself into the development environment for creating e-Lessons. The structure of lesson is determined by the author using the parameterization of some of the basic templates. Thus creates an instance of the template in which no free parameters. To conduct educational process itself must determine the training scenario. It is directly related to didactic goals, basic knowledge and behavior of students. The authors of the lessons describe the various options and determine the rules under which will be held the learning process. Formalization of these scenarios can be realized also through the parameterization of the basic templates. Therefore, the e-Lesson will be presented in the system as a specific instance of some basic template, which (by setting values of parameters) is associated with specific learning resources. In this template are determined the structure and rules for training (Figure 6). Creation of educational resources(SCOs[6]) will not be examined in the model, as they are created as independent units, stored into special SCO-

[6] SCO – Sharable content object

repository. They are used for creation of e-Lessons and are associated with the concepts from different ontologies.

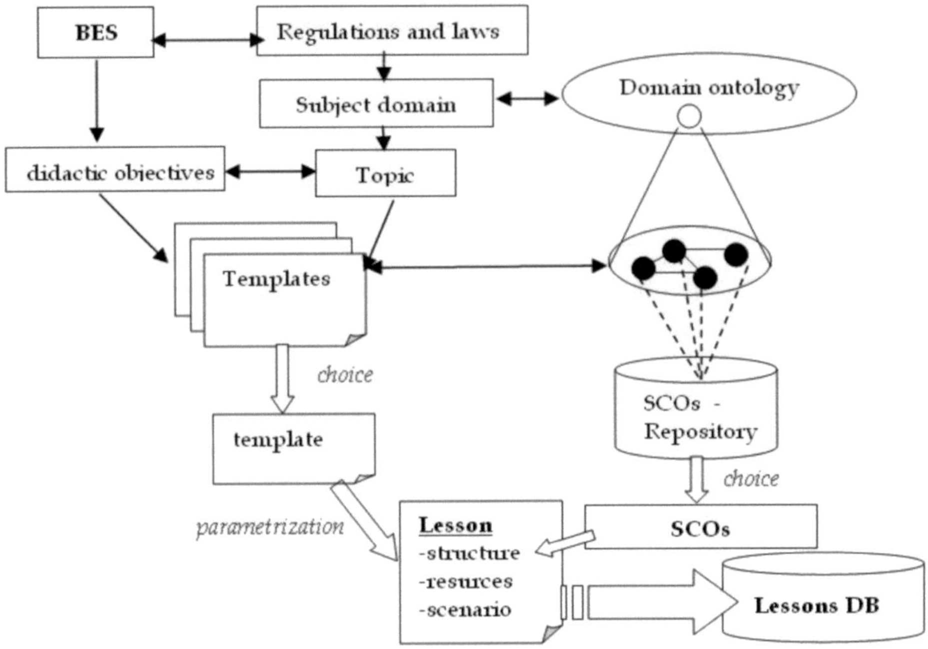

Fig. 6. The pedagogical model in the process of creating e-lessons.

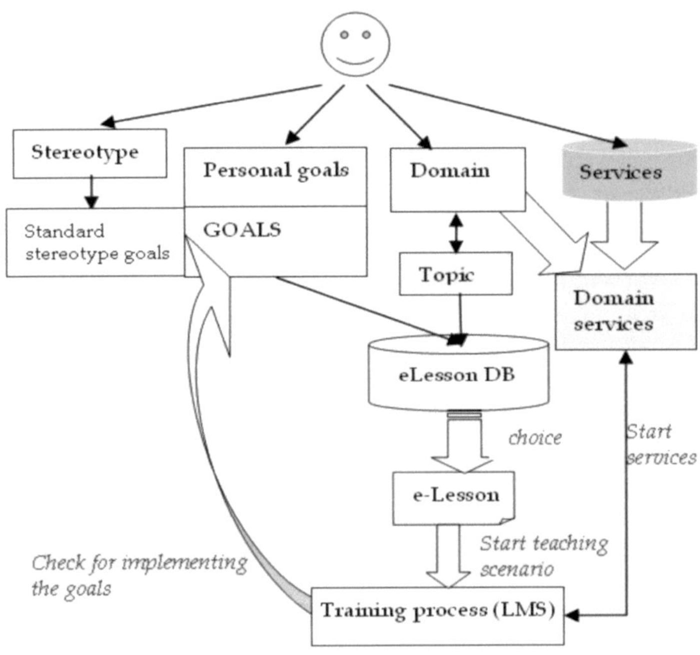

Fig. 7. The pedagogical model in process of learning.

The second aspect, which we will discuss the pedagogical model is a learning process in e-Learning environment. After identification, the student is associated with a particular Stereotype, which is connected to a system of standard didactic goals, pedagogical theory and practice. The student can determine their own goals that overlap with the standard ones and define the goals with which the student is present in the system. After selecting a specific school subject and topic, from the services available in the system, are selected ones which are suitable for the particular domain and theme. According to the didactic goals and theme from the Lesson DB will be elected the appropriate e-Lessons. Depending on individual student characteristics such as basic knowledge, cognitive type, emotional activity, etc., the system defines one of these lessons and LMS starts the training process. During the learning process the student can use the services defined by the educational scenario. The LMS monitors the level of implementation of goals and if it is established that they are inappropriate, it is updated and the process starts all over again (Fig.7).

4. Conclusion

The implementation of proposals in the manuscript adaptive model will allow for better training of students from independent form of training and distance learning, and pupils with special educational needs and disabled children. Based on figure 1 we designed an adaptive model on the basis of which is developed the first version of education e-learning portal of the secondary school "Hristo Smirnenski" Brezovo (Glushkova, 2007). According to the profile characteristics, form of education, basic knowledge and goals, students have access to resources and services, which are appropriate for their learning. E-lessons are created according to SCORM[7] standard *(http://www.adlnet.gov).* We use basic templates from SCORM Best Practices Guide for Content Developers (*http://www.dokeos.com/doc/thirdparty/ScormBestPracticesContentDev.pdf*) and parameterized them according to specific didactic goals and requirements of the authors. The authors create standardized electronic lessons through a special domain-oriented authoring tool (SELBO). It uses intelligent editors (a combination of component and agent) to manipulate the learning content and aid the content developer during the content creation. Ontologies provide developers with predefined resources covering a specific domain that can be used directly in the content. SELBO also utilizes education templates that define pedagogical goals and agents to govern them. Furthermore, the environment employs schemes for adapting itself to its user and for collaborating with the SCORM-learning management system (LMS). The establishment of educational environment is based on adapted nine-layer architecture of the corporate portal of Delphi group. For a particular realization of the educational portal is used portal framework Liferay (*http://liferay.com*), into which is implemented LMS of SCORM RTE[8]. There are many services that support the training process in different subjects and raise the level of interactivity in learning (Glushkova, 2008).

We continue the work on the implementation an agent-oriented version of e-learning system, as well as the realization of scenarios related to adaptability in mobile learning. The team elaborate model for management of the dynamic adaptive level by ITL and polices (Sloman, 1994).

[7] SCORM- Sharable content object reference model

[8] RTE – Run-time environment

5. References

Bloom, B.(1956). Taxonomy of Educational Objectives, Handbook I: The Cognitive Domain. New York: David McKay Co Inc.

Brusilovsky, P.(2001) Adaptive hypermedia, *User Modeling and User Adapted Interaction, Ten Year Anniversary Issue (Alfred Kobsa, ed.)*, Vol.11, No 1-2, pp. 87-110, 2001, ISSN- 0924-1868

Glushkova, T.; Stojanov, S.; Trendafilova, M.; Cholakov, G.(2005) Adaptation of DeLC system for e-Learning in Secondary School, *Proceedings of International conference on Computer Systems and Technologies - CompSysTech'2005*, pp. IV.15.1-15.6, ISBN 954-9641-38-4, Varna, Bulgaria, June 16-17, 2005

Glushkova, T.(2006) User modeling of distributed e-learning systems for the secondary schools, , *Proceedings of International conference DIDMATHTECH*, pp.117-123, ISBN-978-80-89234-23-3, Komarno, Slovakia, 2006

Glushkova, T.(2007). E-learning environment for support of secondary school education. *Cybernetics and information technologies*, Vol. 7, No 3, (2007), pp. 89-106, ISSN 1311-9702

Glushkova, T.; Stojanova, A.(2008) Interaction and adaptation to the specificity of the subject domains in the system for e-Learning and distance training DeLC, *Proceedings of International Conference "Informatics in the Scientific Knowledge"*, pp.295-307, ISSN 1313-4345, ISBN-13:978-954-715-303-526-28, Varna, Bulgaria, June 17-19, 2008

Kass, R.; Finin, T.(1988) A general user modelling facility, *Processing of the SIGCHI conference on Human factors in computing systems*, pp. 145-150, ISBN:0-201-14237-6, Washington, USA, 1988

Kobsa, A.(2004) User Modelin and User-Adapted Interaction, Publ: *Springer Netherlands*, Vol. 14, No 5, pp. 469 - 475, ISSN: 0924-1868 (Paper) 1573-1391 (Online) DOI: 10.1007/s11257-005-2618-3, 2004

Mitev, D.; Popchev, I.(2008) Intelligent agents and services in eLearning development environment Selbo 2 *Proceedings of the International Conference "Informatics in the Scientific Knowledge 2008"*, pp.275-284, ISBN-13:978-954-715-303-5, Varna, Bulgaria, 26-28 June, 2008

Sloman, M.(1994) Policy driven management for distributed systems, *Journal of Network and System Management*, Vol.2(1994), pp.333-360, ISSN 1064-7570

Stojanov, S.; Ganchev, I. ; Popchev, I. ; O'Droma, M.(2005a) From CBT to e-Learning, *Information Technologues and control*, No 4(2005), Year III, pp. 2-10, ISSN 1312-2622.

Stojanov, S.; Gancev, I.; Popchev, I.; O'Droma, M.; Dojchev, E. (2005b) An approach for development of agent-oriented Distributed E-learning Center, *Proceedings of the International Conference on Computer Systems and Technologies CompSysTech'05*, pp. IV-13.1-IV-13.7, ISBN 954-9641-38-4, Varna, Bulgaria, 2005

Stoyanov, S.; Mitev, D. ; Minov, I.; Glushkova, T.(2008a) eLearning Development Environment for Software Engineering Selbo 2, , *Proceedings of 19th International Conference on Database and Expert Systems Application (DEXA 2008)*, pp. 100-104, ISBN: 978-3-540-85653-5, Turin, Italy, 1-5 September, 2008

Stoyanov, S.; Ganchev, I. ; Popchev, I. ; O'Droma, M.(2008b) Service-oriented and Agent-based Approach for the Development of InfoStation eLearning Intelligent System Architectures, *Proceedings of the IS 2008 – IEEE International Conference on Intelligent Systems*, pp.6-20-6-25, ISBN 978-1-4244-1740-7, Varna, Bulgaria, September 6-8, 2008

Stojanovich, L.; Staab, S.; Studer, R.(2001) eLearning based on the Semantic Web, *Proceedings of the WebNet2001- World Conference on the WWW and Internet*, pp. 23-27, ISBN 1-880094-46-0, 2001

2

Electronic- and Mobile-Learning in Electronics Courses Focused on FPGA

Giovanni Vito Persiano and Sergio Rapuano
Università del Sannio,
Italy

1. Introduction

Distance learning is the practical and cost-effective solution to deliver education and training in places where University classes and professional courses are not offered due to lack of local expertise or low student enrolment. Its potentiality was recognized since Internet spread worldwide and became the main communication channel to reach students and workers at their homes. Therefore, nowadays a lot of lessons, seminars and simulation of experiments are available on the Web and delivered to students and professional figures, so that they can improve their degree of instruction or their competences with no physical and time constraints (Fujii & Koike, 2005; Grimaldi et al., 2005, 2006; Leiner, 2002; Rapuano & Zoino, 2006).

Thanks to the evolution of information and communication technologies, we have the chance to combine multiple approaches to learning, i.e. a "blended" use of virtual and physical resources commonly defined as *Blended Learning* (BL). Although it can be used in a wider sense, in today's prevalence of high technology the term BL often refers to the provision or use of resources which merge electronic (*E-learning*) and mobile learning (*M-learning*) with other educational resources (classroom, courses, etc.), "combining online and face-to-face instruction" (Bonk & Graham, 2004).

The key roles played by both *E-learning* and *M-learning* have been also recognized by European Commission, which have been developing several projects (Education Audiovisual Culture Executive Agency [EACEA]; Attewell & Smith., 2004) to promote the inclusion of Information and Communication Technologies (ICT) in all learning systems and environments. As *E-learning* and *M-learning* remove the physical, geographical and cultural barriers to the education and enable the learners to choose their own learning path and time, they are suitable to fulfil the main objectives of the mission to improve the education systems in Europe, as officially announced by European Union the with the declaration of Lisbon in 2000. There, basic and high instruction as well as adult training was recognized to be at the centre of the growth, innovation and integration processes in the democratic societies and much effort had to be made:

- to give to all citizens the same opportunities to gain an higher degree of instruction;
- to promote the institution of a life-long learning system to update the competences and to encourage new specializations of the adult people, thus increasing their capability of finding or changing their work.

Early web-based learning environments are grounded on fundamental instruction models that might result in out-of -date pedagogical approaches where learners play only a passive role (Batatia et al., 2002). More up-to-date pedagogical approaches, instead, are based on models of collaboration used in modern working life (Batatia et al., 2002; Blumenfeld et al., 1991), where teaching is provided through the development of projects that also involves the learners' performance and application of gained theoretical knowledge.

To pursue this goal, practical training is absolutely essential to ensure a good knowledge transfer from teacher to students and hence to educate good professionals. Thus, laboratory activity related to on-line teaching applied to scientific domains and remote control of instrumentation and the execution of real experiments via Internet have been becoming topics of interest for many researchers (Albu et al. 2004; Arpaia et al., 1996, 2000; Bagnasco et al., 2002, 2003; Benetazzo et al., 2000, 2002; Canfora et al., 2004; Daponte et al., 2002, 2004a).

The need of remote laboratories must be mostly met in teaching of electric and electronic measurement topics, both in academic courses and in industrial training industry, where learners should achieve an accurate practical experience by working in real conditions and on real instruments. Indeed, mainly due to their costs, both public and private electric and electronic measurement laboratories are not so widespread, thus complicating the life-long learning of specialized technicians especially in the field of process control, quality control and testing engineering.

In the case of university classes, for example, creating, maintaining and using an efficient laboratory in an undergraduate curriculum could become an unfeasible task (Cmuk et al., 2006). The main drawbacks are:

- the high cost of measurement equipments and, in general, of the experimental laboratories;
- the growing number of students;
- the reduced number of laboratory technical staff;
- the continuous evolution of measurement instrumentation involved, that makes it difficult and very expensive to keep the technical staff up-to-date.

As compared to remote lessons, seminars and simulation of experiments, interactive remotely controlled experiments have diffused more slowly, but there has been an increase in developments in this field since 2000. Projects for sharing real laboratories on the Internet have been realized and validated in different contexts. As an example, in the field of biochemistry, where access to an electron microscope provided to remote users offers them control over the only instrument features that they need to undertake their tasks. Therefore, they cannot damage the equipment (Cooper, M. 2005). In the field of electronic measurement learners are made able to remotely practice with measurement methods and electronic instruments, executing real experiments on analogue and digital circuits by using multimeters, function generators, and oscilloscopes (Rapuano & Zoino, 2006; Chirico et al., 2005). Also, in digital electronics learning environments provide simulated experiments at distance. A developed example of this type contains simulators that cover combinational and sequential logic networks, finite state machine design, and, being fully integrated together, they allow design and simulation of complex networks including standard logic, state machines and microcomputers (Donzellini & Ponta, 2003).

An interesting application of remote laboratory experiments is the hardware implementation of projects on Field Programmable Gate Arrays (FPGA), large-scale integrated circuits that can be programmed after they are manufactured rather than being

limited to predetermined, unchangeable hardware functions (Pellerin & Thibault, 2005). Owing to their flexibility, their possibility to be programmed several times in phase of design and low development cost, FPGAs are excellent alternatives to custom ICs (Quintans et al., 2005). They are commonly used in applications that are traditionally in the domain of Application-Specific Integrated Circuits (ASICs), even if they are slower and more power consuming. FPGAs constitute the base of many complex electronic systems with different applications ranging from automotive to multimedia market. Control engineers draw advantage from use of FPGA in automation applications that must be continuously adapted to new requirements and to different operating conditions. The flexibility of programmable logic reduces time, cost and risk of reconfiguration, done with specific software tools that allow to simulate, to test and to validate the project before leaving it to run on real machines. Software designers, instead, can obtain benefit from FPGA-based hardware implementation of computational intensive algorithms and the use of FPGA is considered as a good trade-off between flexibility of software and speed of custom ICs. Hardware implementation with VLSI design, in fact, represents a faster solution, but the long VLSI design time and its lack of flexibility lead to a fast obsolescence of such systems and, hence, to a less widespread use. In the literature, no effective remote teaching and execution of FPGA applications have been performed yet. Other distance digital electronics courses propose tutorials on FPGA and VHDL (VHSIC Hardware Description Language), but there is lack of complete learning environments, including on-line experiments, where users don't need any other resources but an Internet connection. Similar examples of remote experiments either allow control of FPGA based applications only from local network (Extebarria et al., 2001; El-Medany, 2008], or do not provide real-time interaction with hardware (Zuver et al., 2003; Sanchez Pastor et al., 2004. In this latter case, the remote learners have only the possibility to upload their placed and routed designs to a server, which batches together the jobs coming from different users, and sequentially programs an FPGA board, inputs test vectors, and generates a report that details the results.
In this chapter we show how to implement a complete web-based remote course (both *E-learning* and *M-learning*) on FPGA theory and laboratory practice. The course is based on an *E-learning* system, and its extension for *M-learning* operation, that includes a geographically distributed laboratory. This system is based on a thin client-server computing architecture, where a remote user can design, simulate, execute FPGA-based applications and have access to all of the resources of the distributed laboratory, by using a Personal Computer (PC) or a Mobile Device (MD) equipped only with an internet connection, a standard web browser and a Java Virtual Machine.
The development software for FPGA hardware, in fact, is located on the server and no installation on client's PC is needed. As a result, we have a complete web-based educational environment, where remote students can take familiarity with all the steps of FPGA-based project design by easily performing practical experiences requiring software tools and repeatedly interacting with hardware instruments. To this aim, the course is structured as follows:

- as a first step, students are taught the fundamental theoretical concept, about FPGA technology and VHDL language, using lessons available on the Web and accessible under the control of a Learning Management System (LMS) (Rapuano & Zoino, 2006);
- as a second step, remote users develop and simulate projects of digital circuits for ALTERA FPGA devices, using Quartus II software environment, made accessible for

learners thanks to the Microsoft Remote Desktop Protocol (RDP). The experiments on FPGA boards require to go beyond simulation and to test the designs in a real system, in order to face problems that generally do not appear in simulation like real effect of I/O pins assignment, insufficient current load from the power supply, selection of which device on the board will be configured, physical wiring of switches and LEDs with I/O pins;

- as a third and last step, users interact with the hardware, checking the behaviour of the real FPGA device (ALTERA MAX 7000S). The data transmission and the remote control of the board are made possible by specific software interfaces, i.e. Virtual Instruments (VIs) developed in LabVIEW, a widespread standard language from National Instruments. VIs are accessible from Internet portal of LA.DI.RE. (the acronym of the Italian LAboratorio DIdattico REmoto) "G. Savastano", a remote didactic laboratory distributed over a geographic area whose features will be described in the next section.

The chapter describes all the aspects of the developed didactical environment and is organized as follows. In Section 2 the main characteristics, services and architecture of the remote laboratory LA.DI.RE. realized at University of Sannio are presented. Section 3 describes how to develop a distance e-learning FPGA course: a few details of the theoretical elements are given, before considering use of Quartus II software and experiments (Persiano et al., 2007) on devices in FPGA-based applications. In this case, examples of distance-controlled binary to decimal converter, two-wheel vehicle and robotic arm are shown. The functionalities of the LA.DI.RE. have been extended to allow operation form a MD. The new functions along with an experiment of mobile control (Persiano et al., 2010) of a FPGA-based traffic control system of a railway station are described in Section 4.

2. The Remote Didactic Laboratory LA.DI.RE. "G. Savastano"

The topic of distance learning has been raising a growing interest in last years. It is often perceived as a group effort where content authors, instructional designers, multimedia technicians, teachers, trainers, database administrators, and people from various other areas of expertise come together in order to serve a community of learners (Ong & Hawryszkiewycz, 2003).

In order to reduce the complexity of their joint work, specific software systems have been developed to manage teachers and students activities (Learning Management Systems, LMSs) and, at a higher level, general contents (Learning Content Management Systems, LCMSs).

A LMS provides a support to teachers and learners involved in distance didactical activities. Its main role is to manage learners, keeping track of their progress and performance across all types of training activities. The LMS manages and allocates learning resources such as registration, user access control, classroom and instructor availability, instructional material fulfilment (such as publication of content), and online learning delivery.

The LCMS usually includes an LMS and adds an authoring system, providing an infrastructure that can be used to rapidly create, modify, and manage content for a wide range of learning to meet the needs of rapidly changing business requirements. The LCMS can retrieve detailed data on learner scores, question choices, navigation habits and use them to give content managers crucial information on the effectiveness of the content when combined with specific instructional strategies, delivery technologies, and learner preferences.

These software systems also provide support for interaction among learning space participants, a mechanism to deliver course materials over the Web, administrative components to allow instructor to tracks student records and to monitor their progress, and collaborative components like Bulletin Board, Chat, E-mail etc. (Ong & Hawryszkiewycz, 2003).

Most of the early proposals of didactic laboratories for electric and electronic measurement did not include the noticeable advantages that a LMS could give to teachers using a learner-centric approach. In these cases, students could not self-design their own learning process, nor could they carry out a collaborative or project-based learning; teachers, instead, could not track the activity of the students, nor could they carry out an interactive experiment in a virtual classroom.

These hindrances were overcome in the distributed platform based on a LMS proposed in (Grimaldi et al., 2005, 2006; Rapuano & Zoino, 2006). This platform integrates the advantages of an off-the-shelf LMS, which is compliant with international standards for web-based training, and an approach for providing remote experiments on measurement instrumentation. This approach, which is based on web services and the thin client paradigm, relies on Virtual Instruments (VIs) developed in LabVIEW and ensures that the students access the instrumentation without downloading heavy plug-ins.

Based on these fundamental aspects, the Laboratorio Didattico Remoto-LA.DI.RE. (Remote Didactic Laboratory), which is dedicated to the memory of "Prof. G. Savastano", has been designed, then financed by the Italian Ministry of Education and University (M.I.U.R.) within the National Operating Program (P.O.N.) 2000-2006, and at last realized. This geographically distributed *E-learning* laboratory provides the students of electric and electronic measurement courses with access to remote measurement laboratories, delivering different teaching activities related to measurement experiments. The activity carried out over the years led to a further project, financed by the Italian Space Agency and aimed to design a distance learning system that uses satellite networks as a backbone for providing web- based training to mobile as well as home/office learners located in the whole Europe (Daponte et al., 2004b)

The initial infrastructure of the LA.DI.RE. was composed of the laboratories at the University of Sannio in Benevento and at the University of Reggio Calabria "Mediterranea" under the patronage of the National Research Association on Electric and Electronic Measurement (G.M.E.E. standing for Gruppo Misure Elettriche ed Elettroniche) and the collaboration of about 20 Italian universities and specialized instrumentation, *E-learning*, and publishing companies such as National Instruments, Tektronix, Agilent Technologies, Yokogawa, Keithley, Rockwell Automation, Didagroup, Augusta publishing. Afterwards, several universities in Croatia, Greece, Slovakia and Ukraine joined (or are about to join) the LA.DI.RE. to develop common projects (Borsic et al., 2006).

2.1 Services delivered by LA.DI.RE.

The distance learning course in FPGA is delivered by the remote didactic laboratory LA.DI.RE. "G. Savastano". As said above it is a virtual learning environment devoted to the teaching of electric and electronic measurement that integrates an off-the-shelf LMS and a geographically distributed laboratory, accessible from the web by using a simple browser. The distributed laboratory is accessed through the LMS executed on a central server that delivers such functionality to users by means of a thin client-based software architecture (Grimaldi et al., 2005, 2006; Rapuano & Zoino, 2006), virtual instruments (VIs) controlling the instrumentation, and Java applets constituting a remote interface of LabVIEW VIs. In such a way it is possible to reuse already developed VIs for integrating existing instrumentation in a remote laboratory without developing new software (Rapuano & Zoino, 2006).

Content consumed by learners and created by authors is commonly handled, stored, and exchanged in units of Learning Objects (LOs). Basically, LOs are units of study, exercise, or practice that can be consumed in a single session, and they represent reusable granules that can be authored independently of the delivery medium and accessed dynamically, e.g., over the Web (Vossen & Jaeschke, 2003).

LOs are also used to enable remote users to get control of a measurement instrument transparently and to display the measurement results within the normal learning activities. To do this, specific LOs have been developed to add VIs written in LabVIEW to the LMS Inform@ from Didagroup.

At present, the measurement instruments of the LA.DI.RE are distributed in four laboratories belonging to as many universities (Sannio and Mediterranea in Italy, Zagreb in Croatia and Kosice in Slovak Republic). Access can be done at the web address: http://www.misureremote.unisannio.it.

The access to the measurement instruments is handled by a scheduling system which, transparently through specific scheduling policies, connects the user to a specific physical laboratory in which the required measurement instruments are available.

Different user profiles are managed by the system: administrator, teacher, and student (Rapuano & Zoino, 2006).

The administrator is responsible for the correct working of the overall distributed system and of handling the user profiles. The services delivered to the teacher are related to the remote handling of the available experiments (remote creation, modification, and removal of experiments, etc.).

The services delivered by the remote measurement laboratory module to the student are mainly the following:

- *Synchronous virtual laboratory* – this service allows the student to follow online laboratory activity held by the teacher. The student can see on his/her display the desktop of the server used by the teacher to control the measurement instruments involved in the experiment. The experiment is carried out by operating on the front panel of the LabVIEW VI controlling all the involved instrumentation. In Fig. 1 the control panel of a VXI oscilloscope is connected to the Measurement Server (MS) by means of an MXI-2 interface card. Of course, the students should be logged in the system during the scheduled lab session. The data stream from the physical laboratory to the students can be sent in multicast mode. No automated scheduling policy is foreseen for such kind of activity;
- *Experiment visualization* – this service allows the student to observe the automatic execution of the experiment to take practice with the experiment procedure (see Fig. 1). This kind of service can be delivered to the students at each time of the day and all the times they need it without supervision;
- *Experiment control* – this service allows the student to perform an experiment controlling remotely one or more instruments and, in some cases, observing them by means of a camera. The student can choose a specific experiment in a set of predefined ones and he/she can run it only if the required measurement instruments are currently available (see. Fig.2);

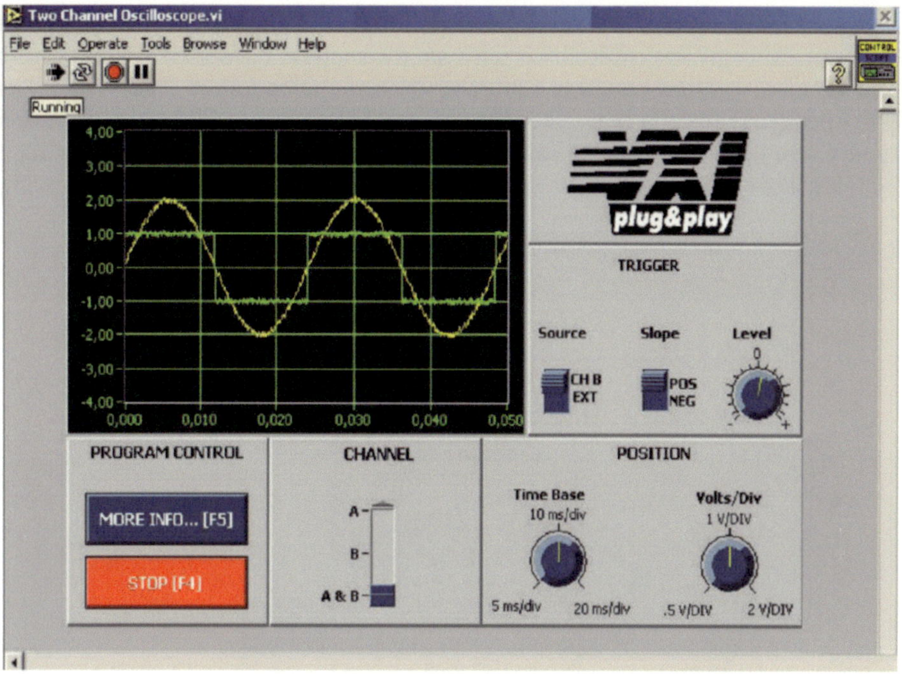

Fig. 1. Example of Synchronous virtual laboratory/experiment visualization.

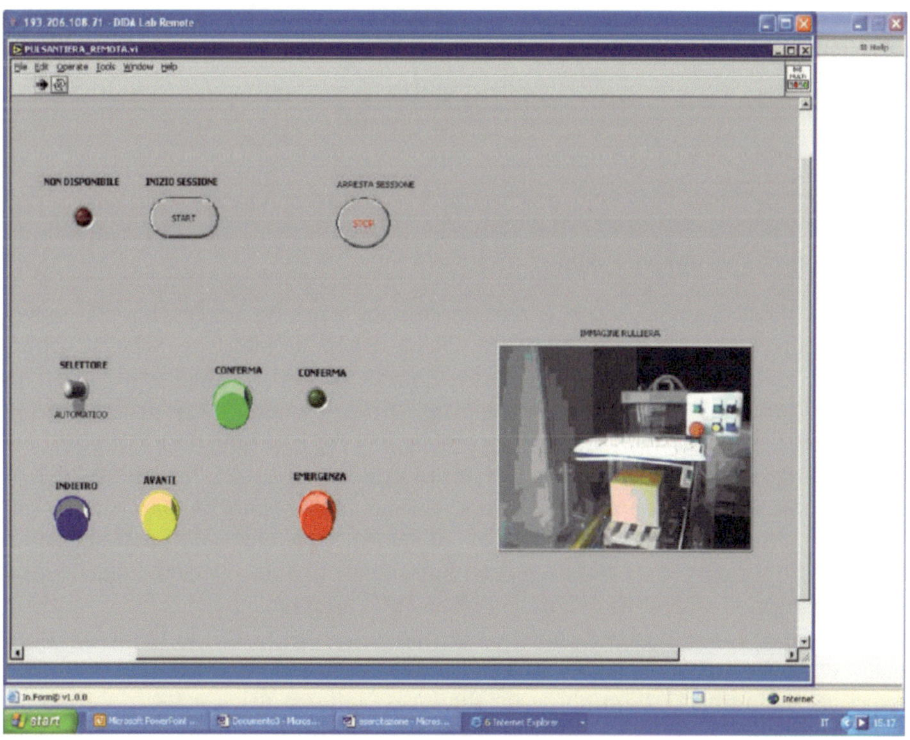

Fig. 2. Example of Experiment control.

- *Experiment creation* - this service allows the student to create remotely an experiment by interacting directly with specialized software executed on the servers used to control the measurement instruments. This feature enables the adoption of *Project-Based Learning* (PBL) pedagogy (Batatia et al., 2002; Blumenfeld et al., 1991), as didactic model. Under the supervision of the teacher, the students can develop a specific project producing, in an individual or collaborative manner, the VI to control a set of real instruments (see. Fig.3).

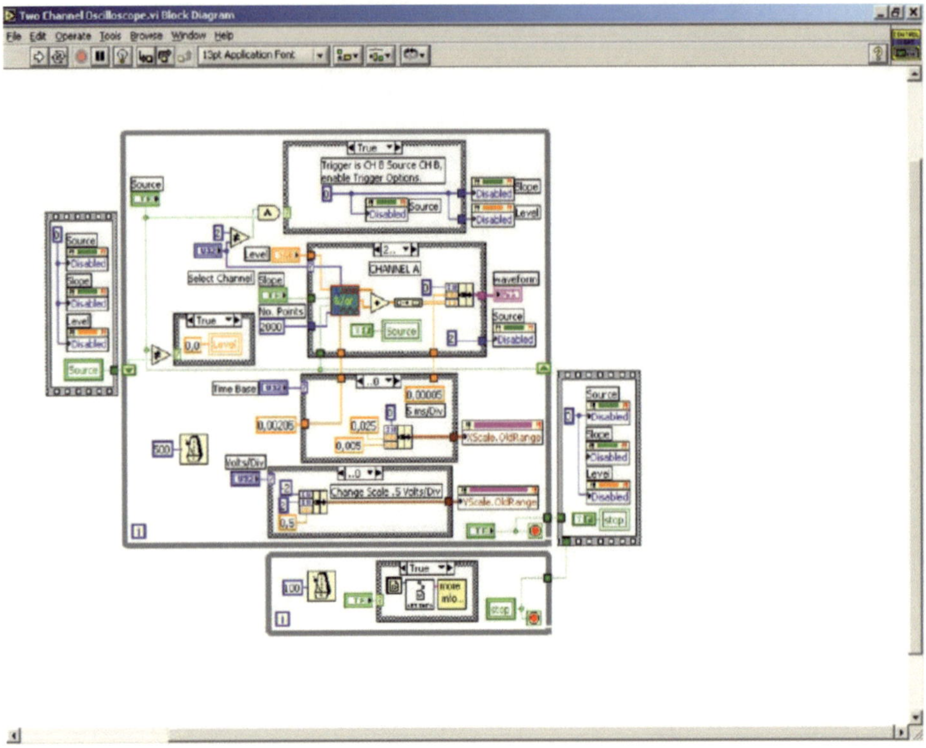

Fig. 3. Example of Experiment creation.

Fig. 4 shows what happens when a remote student working on his/her PC enters the LA.DI.RE. using the *thin-client model,* a client-server architecture where application execution and data management are performed on the server (*Terminal Server*). His/her PC interacts with a lightweight client (*Presentation Client*), usually a web browser which connects to the *Terminal Server* and is responsible only for handling user input and output, such as sending user input back to the server and receiving screen display updates over a network connection. Therefore, the client needs few resources and has a simple configuration, thus reducing support and maintenance costs. This solution also extends the class of possible learners to mobile users, owning a smart phone, a personal data assistant or a notebook equipped with a modem or a wireless LAN adapter.

A remote student can watch and control a device in the LA.DI.RE. in the following steps (Grimaldi et al., 2005, 2006; Rapuano & Zoino, 2006):

1. executes the authentication phase on the LMS platform using a login and password, interacting with the Web Server used by the LMS platform;
2. chooses a service (Experiment Visualization, Experiment Control, Experiment Creation);

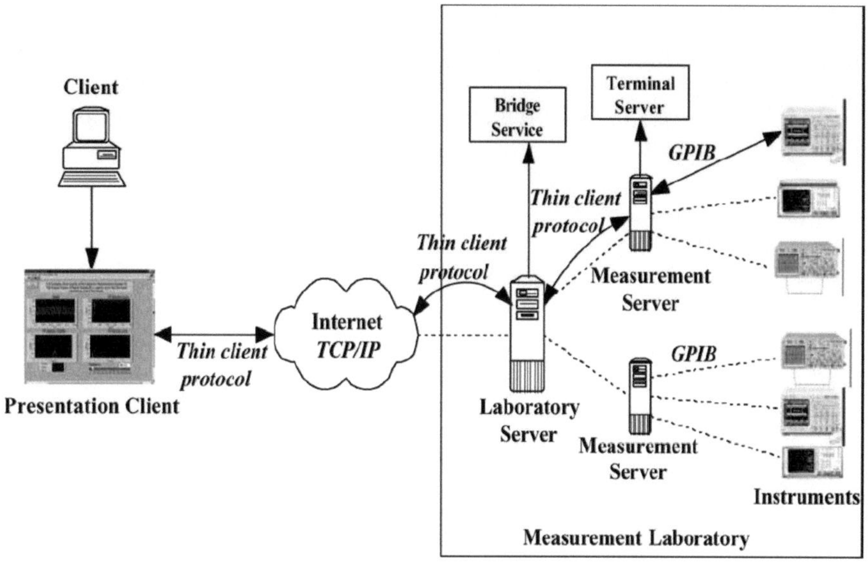

Fig. 4. Remote visualization interactions.

3. displays on his/her desktop the VI front panel on the Measurement Server which he/she is connected to.

If the chosen service is *Experiment Visualization*, the student is connected to the *Laboratory Server* where the teacher is performing the experiment. The *Bridge Service* of the *Laboratory Server* finds the *Measurement Server* that is currently used by the teacher, and allows the student to connect to the related *Terminal Server* in order to watch the experiment on his/her own computer. On the other side, if the chosen service is *Experiment Control* or *Experiment Creation*, the student chooses one of the available experiments and connects to the *Laboratory Server*, whose *Bridge Service* of the Laboratory Server finds the *Measurement Server* connected to the required measurement instruments. Thus, the student is allowed to connect to the related *Terminal Server* in order to view, manage or develop a new VI from his/her own computer.

Fig. 5. Course interface in Remote Didactic Laboratory.

The student interested in the FPGA course enters the system and is enabled to follow learning activities (Fig.5) and to get transparently the remote control of real Programmable Logic devices and display the results by a web cam sending real-time images to a VI. Details on how to manage real-time visualization of the measurement instrument during experiment sessions are given in the next subsection.

2.2 Software and hardware architectures of the LA.DI.RE.

The remote access to the distributed environment is enabled by a Web-based multi-tier distributed architecture, centred on the LMS that, managing the list of available instruments, schedules the user requests and redirects them to one of the partner laboratories, in which the selected instrument is currently available. The multi-tier architecture consists of the following three tiers:

1. *the presentation-tier*: it manages the experiment visualization on client-side. It is based on standard Web browsers, with no need of specific software components (no specific operating system is required). The only software component needed is the Java 2 Runtime Environment, which is used in order to employ the Java Applet technology for the experiment visualization and control on the client machine;
2. *the middle-tier*: it manages the system logic on server-side. It is composed of the following distributed server components (Fig. 6):
   - The LMS is executed on a central server of the overall distributed laboratory, called *Laboratory Portal*. The LMS interfaces to the users through a Web Server, that is hosted on the same machine;
   - A *Laboratory Server* (LS) is used to interface a real measurement laboratory with the rest of the distributed architecture. There is a LS for each measurement laboratory of the universities involved in the project. It delivers the access and the control to the laboratory measurement equipments through a service, called *Bridge Service.* Moreover, the LS is the only machine in a measurement laboratory directly accessible through the Internet, while the other server machines are not accessible and typically constitute a private local network. For this reason the LS can also be used for security purposes in order to monitor the accesses to the measurement laboratory and to protect it against malicious accesses;
   - A *Measurement Server* (MS) is a server located in a measurement laboratory that enables the interaction with one or more instruments. A MS is physically connected to a set of different electronic measurement instruments through an interface card. The GPIB interface has been used to connect the MS to the instruments. The used VIs are stored in a database of the MS, where the LabVIEW environment is installed. No adjustment is needed to include a VI in the virtual learning environment and, therefore, the wide number of existing VIs can be reused without requiring additive work;
3. *the storage-tier*: it performs the data management, related for example to the management of the user profiles and the distributed management of the data related to the available experiments at the different measurement laboratories. It is based on a series of geographically distributed databases, managed using the relational database management system (RDBMS).

To overcome the well known security weakness of Microsoft-based networks, each laboratory is protected by a Linux-based gateway machine that operates as firewall and Network Address Translation (NAT).

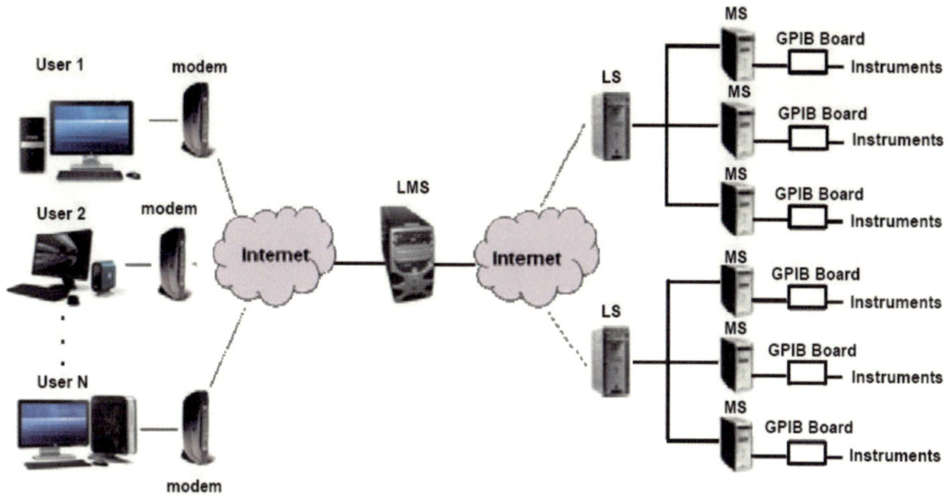

Fig. 6. The structure of the remote didactic laboratory.

The real-time visualization of the measurement instruments during each experiment session is managed by remote users by means of a video acquisition device connected to the MSs. As shown in (Ranaldo et al. 2007), a client-server architecture developed in Java and an Axis 207 IP camera with an integrated MPEG-4 encoder are used to remotely set the video capture parameters and acquire videos from each instrument of the measurement laboratory.
The video transmission relies on the Real-Time Protocol (RTP) instead of the Remote Desktop Protocol (RDP) used for remote access to the VIs. In fact, RDP is neither effective nor flexible for video transmission since it does not permit modification of parameters such as codec, video formats, and frame rate and involves a very high bandwidth occupation.
In more detail, the architecture presents the following software components:

1. *RTPProxy*: This component is the core of the system. In fact, it represents the LS interface interacting with the LMS to receive the authentication information. This component checks the authentication phase status and manages all user accesses;
2. *AppletClient*: This component is delivered to the student. It acquires connection permission from the LMS, sets up an encrypted connection with the RTPProxy module, allows the student setting up some camera parameters (codec compression factor, frame rate, frame sizes, bit rate) by means of the user interface, and enables MPEG-4 players;
3. *ManagerUsers*: This application controls the access permission, forwards the parameters to set up on the video device, estimates the available bit rate, and enables the forwarding permissions of the visualization request;
4. *TCPProxy*: This component sets the codec and camera parameters as they come from the ManagerUsers component;
5. *PortRedirector*: This application forwards the video stream to the clients and includes the BridgeUDP functions of the first architecture.

Then, the LS starts a direct communication with the client, delivering both the instrumentation access through the VI front panel and the video-stream transmission coming from the IP camera associated with the chosen experiment. In this case, the video stream has an independent part from the MS. No application runs on the MS. Before starting the experiment, the student can choose among different displaying options such as no visualization, photo displaying with different resolutions, visualization of 1 frame/s with different resolutions, visualization of 10 frames/s with different resolutions, and visualization of 25 frames/s with different resolutions. During the experiments, the student can observe the VI front panel and the instrument video in two floating windows, as shown in Fig.7.

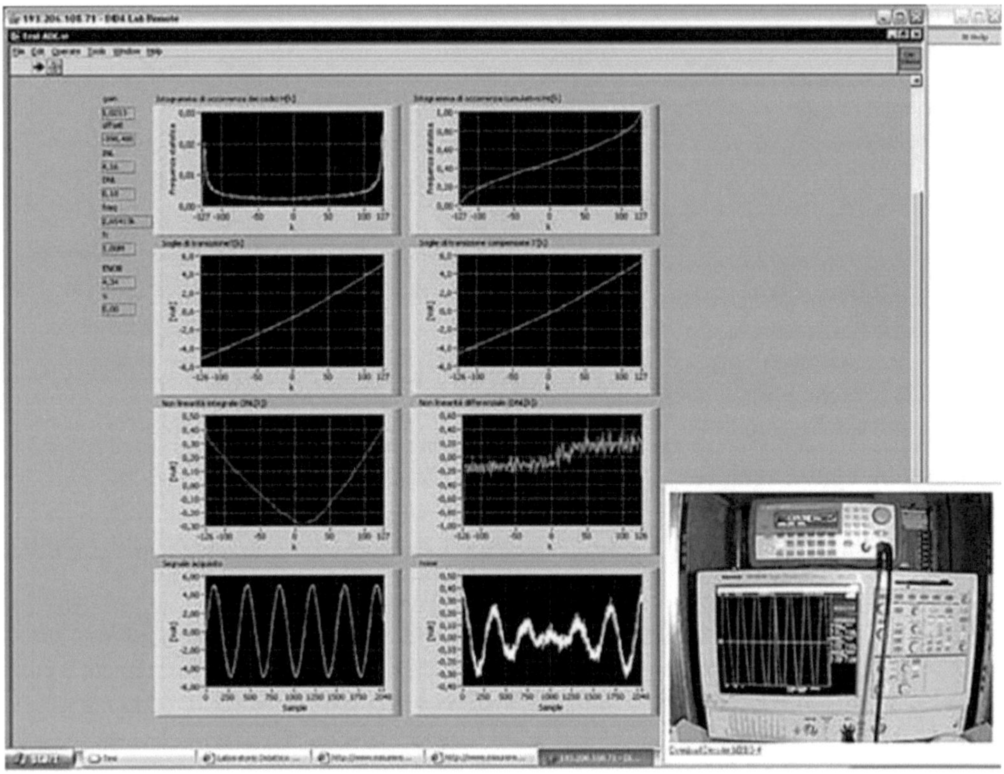

Fig. 7. Visualization and control of measurement instrumentation.

3. Structure of the *E-learning* FPGA course

Like in any other web-based course in engineering and science disciplines, typical teaching material could be given by:

i. lectures and seminars, sometimes interactive, provided by hardware or software producers, mainly directed to professionals that want to reduce the time to market for a new application;
ii. support to University courses, including slides of lectures and exercises;
iii. simulation of actual experiments to be executed either remotely or on student's PC;
iv. remotely accessible laboratories, where the learners can access real instrumentation using Internet.

In our course, theoretical lessons, computer-aided design (CAD) and laboratory practise are intended to provide tools for studying hardware design of digital circuits based on FPGA. The FPGA course interface of Fig. 5 is shown on the client PC to the student entering the home page, where he/she finds a menu of the available learning activities. Besides following theoretical lessons, he uses ALTERA Quartus II CAD to cope with design, synthesis and simulation of FPGA-based projects. Finally, he/she is acquainted with a programmable core integrated in an evaluation board UP1X produced by ALTERA. This choice was due to the easy-to-use and highly educational characteristics of the UP1X board. However, other manufacturers like Xilinx, Actel, Lattice Semiconductors etc., could be taken into consideration.

3.1 Theoretical course

The tutorial structure provides an introduction to hardware and software features of programmable logic devices. In particular, remote students entering the LA.DI.RE are enabled to access to the theoretical lessons providing following contents:

i. notions of FPGA architecture, analysis of hardware available characteristics (UP1X board);
ii. presentation of software development environment (Quartus II) and its tools for FPGA projects;
iii. definition of VHDL language and its properties.

As far as the FPGA architecture is concerned, the meaning and description of basic concepts and topologies such as logic gate density, configurable logic blocks, routing channels, look-up tables, switch box and connect box are given. Also, details of both the FPGA chips and the additional components on the UP1X demo board used in remote experiments, are presented.

Then, learners are introduced to ALTERA® Quartus II, a software environment used to design, develop and simulate projects based on the UP1X board. Fundamental concepts like hierarchical approach, design entry, floorplanning, technology-mapped netlist, logic synthesis, place-and-route process, and timing analysis are thoroughly explained.

Among the several design entry methods (*graphic editor, waveform editor, floorplan editor, text editor*), the text editor approach based on Hardware Description Language (HDL) is the most widely used, thanks to its powerfulness, flexibility and portability. Thus, a general introduction to definition of VHDL languages, their features as compared to other software languages (C, C++, System C) and use of the main VHDL commands are developed in the last section of theoretical lessons.

Afterwards, remote students are ready to interact with CAD design tools and FPGA-based applications available in the remote laboratory. Before doing this, however, they are encouraged to execute a test to estimate their achieved degree of competence.

3.2 Computer aided design and simulation of FPGAs

In this section remote students log on to the server from their client PC and via RDP and uses Quartus II to create their own experiments, edit their projects, and check programming errors. This software environment allows managing the design complexity using a hierarchical approach that enables one to shorten its design cycle and improve its design performance and utilization. The remote designers come across the steps of *design entry, synthesis and simulation*. Once the project has been developed (*design entry*) and no programming errors are found, a technology-mapped netlist is generated and, using a place-and-route process, is mapped into the actual ALTERA FPGA architecture (*synthesis*). Then, the map and the place-and-route results can be validated via timing analysis, waveform analysis, and other verification methodologies (*simulation*). Once the design and validation process is complete, a binary file generated is used to (re)configure the ALTERA FPGA devices.

3.3 Laboratory practice

A key part of the course is the laboratory experience, where the students are actively involved in learning the differences between simulations and experiments. To this scope,

FPGA devices are made remotely accessible and monitored by means of LabVIEW VIs and Java applets. By his/her client PC, a student can access from anywhere through Internet, manage the hardware device programmed for a specific application, modify the digital value at the input pins, and obtain the corresponding outputs via a front panel, a Graphic User Interface (GUI) formed by a control panel and a web-cam based LabVIEW VI.

3.3.1 FPGA board

Hardware benches used in remote experiments are UP1X boards, delivered by ALTERA, a leader in the production of programmable logic devices. These boards are equipped with two FPGA chips (Fig.8): the EPM7128SLC84-7 (from MAX7000S family), located on the left side, has a gate count of over 2.500 and EEPROM internal memory, and the EPF10K70RC240-4 (from FLEX 10K family), on the right side, a SRAM based FPGA device with over 70.000 gates (Hamblem & Furman, 2001).

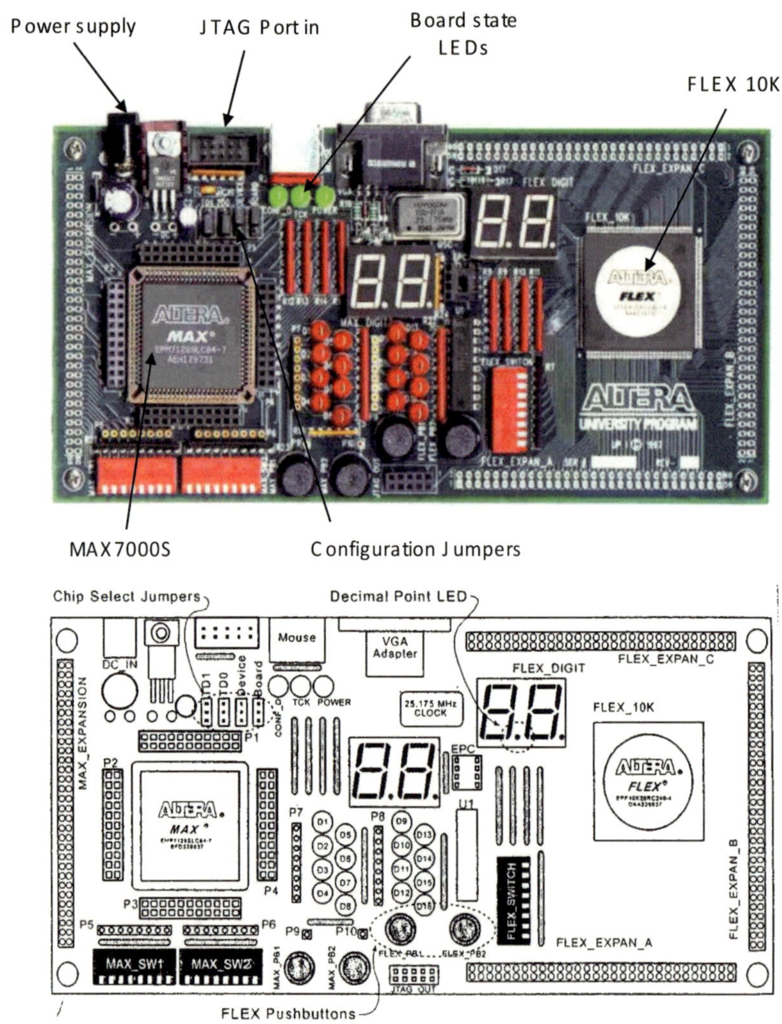

Fig. 8. ALTERA UP1X main board and board scheme.

The former component is used in remote experiments for its non-volatile memory. The UP1X board is also equipped with several additional components. The most important are:

1. a power input module, that receives either a regulated DC power supply between 7 and 9 V (DC_IN) or an unregulated supply (RAW Input), that is regulated on the board by a LM340T before feeding the internal circuitry;
2. a crystal oscillator, operating at 25 MHz, which provides a clock signal to both FPGA devices;
3. four chip select jumpers (TDI, TDO, DEVICE and BOARD), that are used to choose one of the following actions: program EPM7128SLC84-7 device only, program EPF10K70RC240-4 device only, program both FPGA devices, connect multiple boards together;
4. three green LEDs (POWER, TCK, CONF_D), which give to the designer information on board status. The POWER light is on when the supply voltage feeds the board, the TCK LED goes on during the board programming, the CONF_D LED switches on when FLEX and/or MAX devices have been programmed;
5. three switches (MAX_SW1, MAX_SW2, FLEX_SW), three pushbuttons (MAX_PB1, MAX_PB2, FLEX_PB), two digit display (MAX DIGIT and FLEX DIGIT) and sixteen red LEDs (D1-D16), which are all used to check the design results. In detail, the switches and pushbuttons settle the inputs of the FPGA devices, whereas the red LEDs switch on or off depending on the expected output results.

Either or both FPGA devices are programmed using a JTAG ByteBlaster cable attached to the MS printer port. Each step of the project on UP1X board has been supported by Quartus II.

The key part of the course is the laboratory experience, in which the students are actively involved in learning the differences between simulations and real experiments. To this scope, FPGA devices are made remotely accessible and monitored by means of VIs. Remote access is possible from anywhere through Internet, and interaction with hardware is based on the idea of using the parallel port of the MS physically connected to the FPGA device. The operation of setting the voltage of parallel port pins connected to I/O pins of the UP1X board is performed by VIs.

3.3.2 The FPGA-based experiments

Three different experiments of application control on FPGA have been carried out. For each experiment the same *Block Diagram* of the LabVIEW VI is used, setting the voltage of parallel port pins and managing the video stream coming from a web-cam. The web-cam is connected to the same MS and is used to show to the student the result of his/her remote commands.

The first example is a simple binary-to-decimal digit converter, whose VI front panel is shown in Fig. 9. The GUI is formed by five horizontal LEDs which represent, from left to right, the most significant bits that are converted into a decimal value. A remote user sets the LED values by a mouse click: a light coloured turned-on LED button means a programmed "1", a darker turned-off led button means "0". The binary sequence in Fig. 9 is "01011" and the corresponding decimal value "11" is shown on the on-board display, monitored by the web-cam.

The second and third experiments implemented for the remote laboratory are automation applications (Fig. 10): the former drives a two-wheel vehicle based on MAX7000S chip, the latter controls movements and actions of a robotic arm prototype (Lynxmotion Lynx5 Satellite Arm without electronics) (LINOXMOTION).

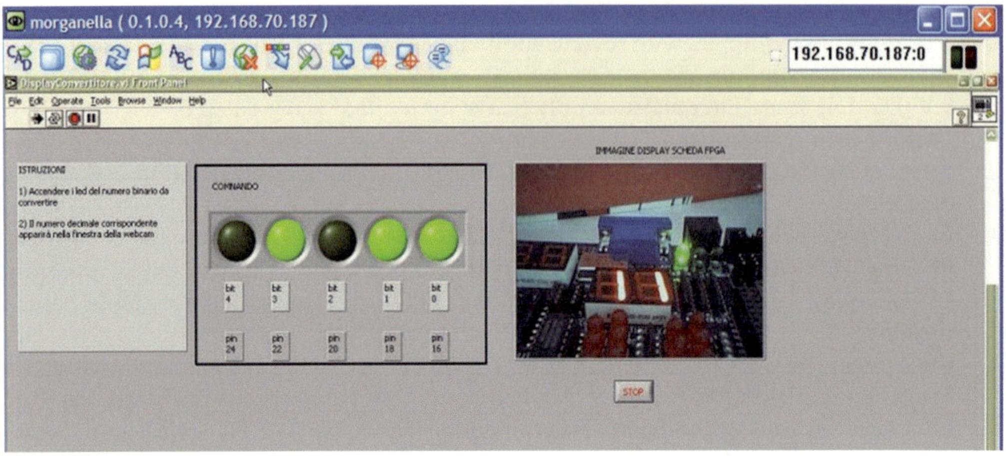

Fig. 9. Graphic user interface (GUI) of a binary-to-decimal digit converter.

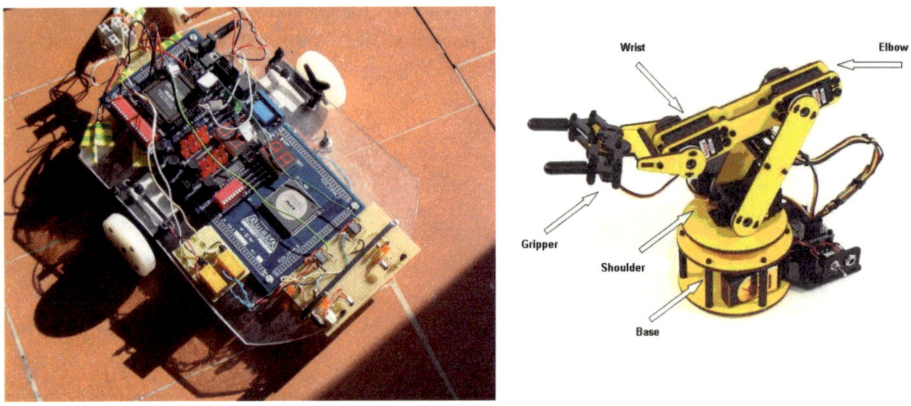

Fig. 10. Two-wheel FPGA-based vehicle (left) and robotic arm prototype (right).

The hardware realizing the two-wheel prototype consists of the UP1X board, two servos Futaba S3003, a 7.2 Volt battery and an infrared sensor. The control algorithm, written in VHDL for the MAX7000S FPGA, allows the remote students to drive the robot in all of the four perpendicular directions (ahead, behind, left and right). The VI control panel (Fig.11) is formed by six vertical LEDs which, when are on, operate as follows (from the top to the bottom):

1. supply voltage to the UP1X board is switched off. The default state (LED off) is UP1X board turned on;
2. supply voltage to the two servos Futaba S3003 is switched on. This LED is usually on, in order to let the vehicle wheels to move. Its main goal is to have distinguished supply voltages to the UP1X board and to the servos, so the MAX7000S can be reprogrammed when the vehicle is not moving;
3. Marcia in Avanti (i.e., ahead march) is selected;
4. Marcia in Dietro (behind march) is selected;
5. Rotazione Destra (right march) is selected;
6. Rotazione Sinistra (left march) is selected;

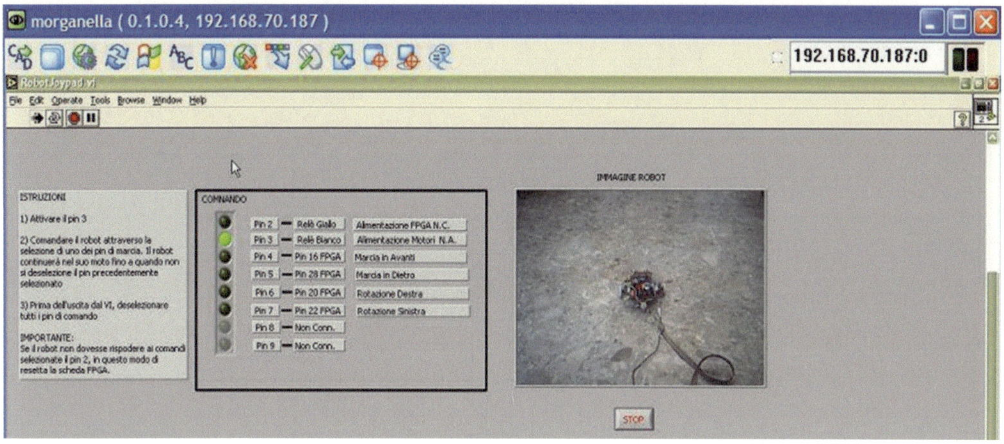

Fig. 11. VI front panel of the two-wheel vehicle.

When they select "Rotazione Sinistra" on the VI, Pin 7 turns on and the vehicle goes to the corresponding direction counter-clockwise by blocking the left wheel while the other starts to rotate back. The right direction movement is obtained in a similar way. The user commands on the VI operating on the LEDs from Pin 4 to Pin 7, which enable the movements in different directions, are mutually exclusive. To detect obstacles, the vehicle is equipped with infrared sensors that can be used to realize different experiments, in phase of development, by reconfiguring the FPGA board with new applications.

The circuit top-level design, that is synthesized to generate the gate-level circuit and to be mapped into the FPGA chip, is shown in Fig. 12.

The module **clk_div** reduces the clock of the FPGA device (25 MHz) to the operating frequency (1 kHz) of each of the modules **dietro** (i.e., behind march), **giradestra** (right march), **girasinistra** (left march) and **avanti** (ahead march) driving the pins 5, 6, 7 and 4 of the VI control panel, respectively.

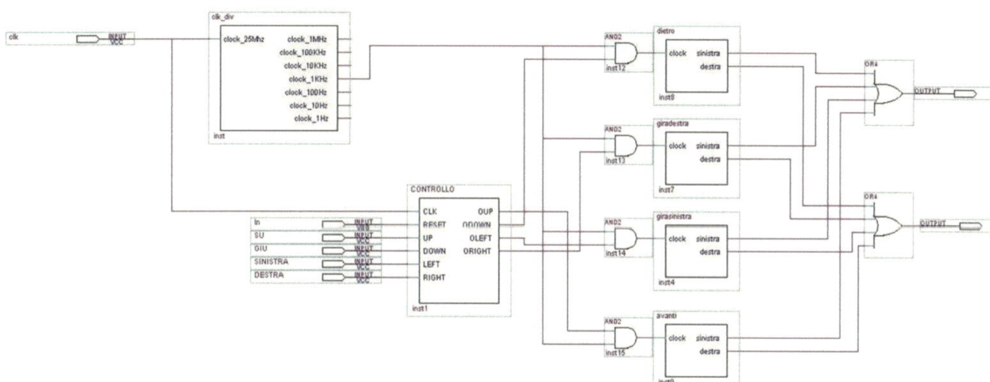

Fig. 12. Top level design of the two-wheel vehicle.

The module CONTROLLO (control) is a finite-state machine and rules the correct operation of the circuit. Its Moore finite-state machine representation is shown in Fig. 13.When two inputs are erroneously both set to 1, the circuit sets to the default steady-state (rest position).

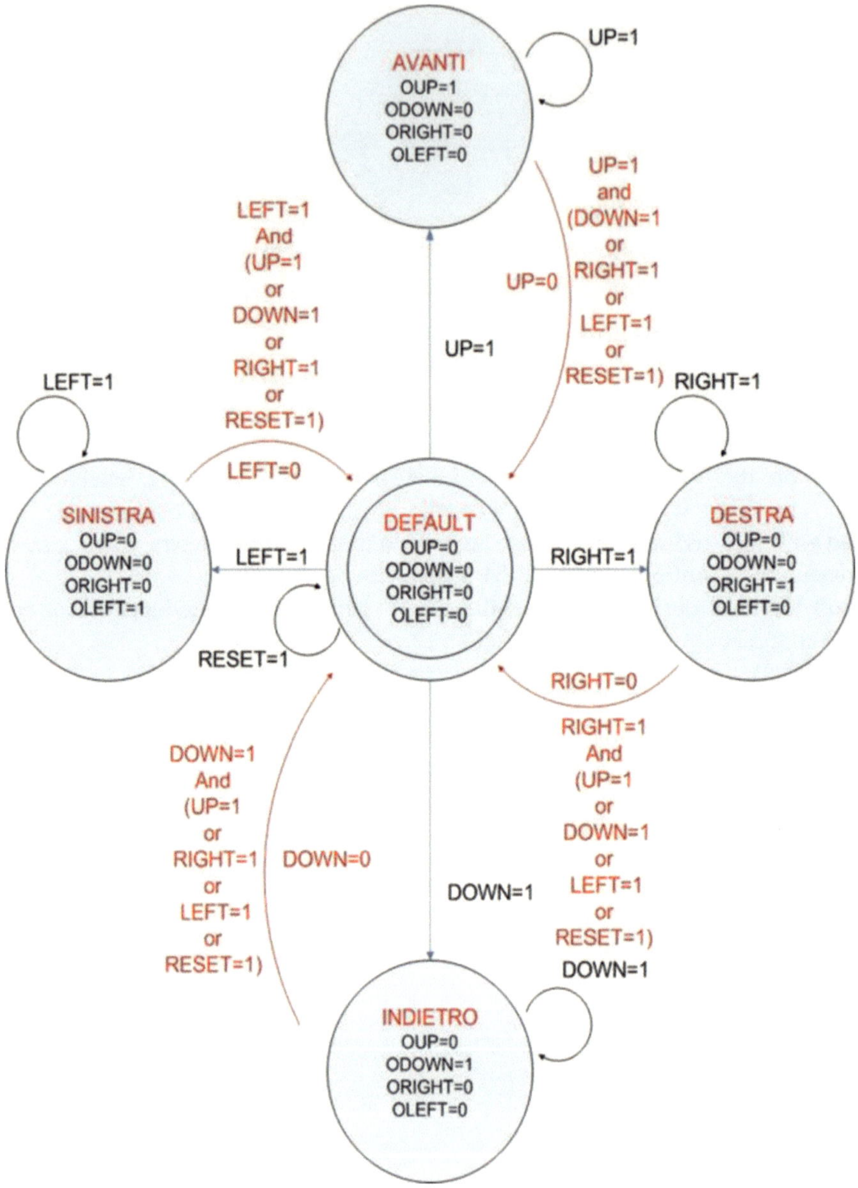

Fig. 13. Moore finite-state machine representation of the two-wheel vehicle.

The VI front panel of the robotic arm prototype is shown in Fig. 14.

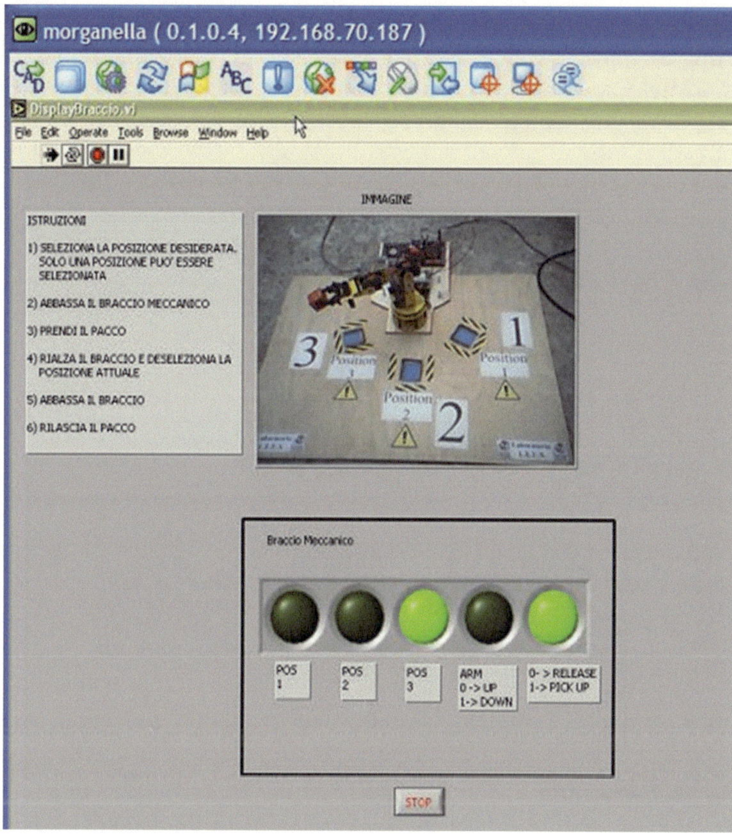

Fig. 14. VI front panel of the robotic arm prototype.

The VI control panel delivers commands for base rotation, shoulder, elbow and wrist motion, and for driving a functional gripper. The remote user can interact with this application moving the arm through different angular positions and driving it to take and to release objects. The five horizontal LEDs in the control panel, when are on, activate the following actions:

1. Set the robotic arm in position 1 (right);
2. Set the robotic arm in position 2 (middle);
3. Set the robotic arm in position 3 (left);
4. Put the robotic arm is lowered position. The default state (LED off) means robotic arm in raised position. For a safe operation, the robotic arm can move to a new position (right, middle or left) only when the arm is up;
5. Close the gripper and pick-up objects. For a safe operation, the robotic arm can pick-up and release objects only when the arm is steady in the lower position.

4. Extension for *M-learning* operations

In the previous sections we have dealt with the extension from a local to a remote *E-learning* designer of all the facilities available for the development of FPGA-based applications. As schematically resumed in Fig. 15 in the example of robotic arm prototype, this operation is done by inserting an Internet connection (no wireless) and a server system to the local path from the User to the Experiment. In this section we describe how to extend the design of FPGA-based application to remote *M-learning* user.

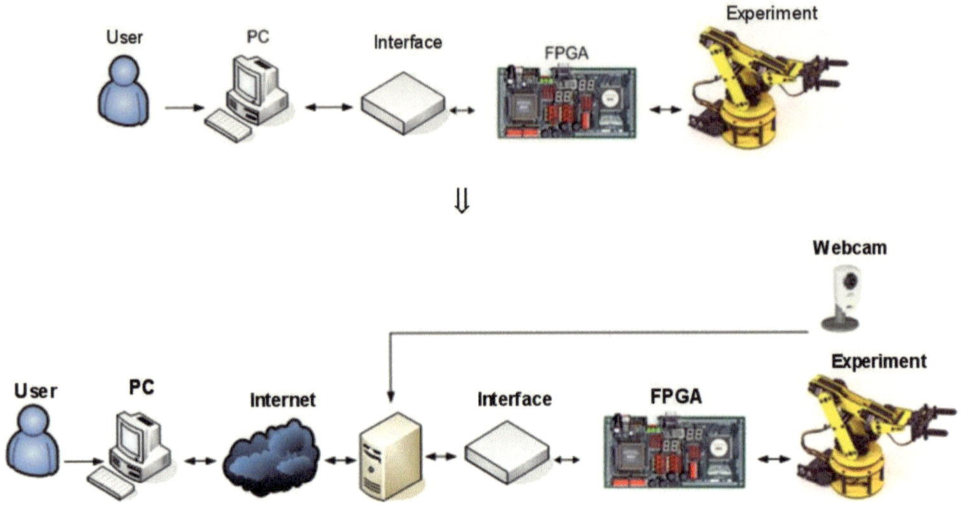

Fig. 15. Evolution from local to remote *E-learning* development of the robotic arm prototype.

4.1 M-learning vs. E-learning

M-learning has been around for longer than *E-learning*, with the paperback book and other portable resources, but technology is what shapes its usage today. Technology now allows one to bring in his/her pockets portable devices, such as and-held PCs and smartphones, and to access them wherever he/she finds it convenient. With the advent of broadband connections also working habits have changed and, hence, it is usual to see a manager outside his/her office that is working and using a Personal Digital Assistant (PDA) as mobile terminal connected to Internet.

As *E-learning* took learning away from the classroom or campus to the home PC, *M-learning* is taking learning away anytime and anywhere. Therefore, *E-learning* can be seen as an alternative to classroom learning, but *M-learning* is a complementary activity to both *E-learning* and traditional learning (Holzinger et al., 2005). It is gaining appeal among younger generations who have grown up using portable video game devices and wireless technology.

While the opportunities provided from the use of portable devices for M-learning are new, the challenges to overcome the limitations of the technical characteristics of the MDs are quite old. These challenges mean that adapting existing E-learning services and didactic contents to M-learning is not a trivial task.

Three different kinds of problems can affect MDs remote operations (Daponte et al., 2010):

- *Hardware* - Small displays, no touch screen and limited processor power are the main drawbacks. The reduced display size without any standard format requires an adaptive run-time environment and specific Graphical User Interfaces (GUIs); absence of touch screen in most smartphones (most PDAs have instead this feature) makes the navigation control harder; finally, due to the limited processor power, applications must be very "light," consuming memory as little as possible in order to reduce the response time of the applications running on the device;

- *Software* - Differently from traditional and laptop PCs, MDs have a wide variety of installed software from different producers and with different versions that are sources of huge interoperability problems for developers. Also depending upon the MD operating system (OS), the JavaTMPlatform, Micro Edition (Java ME) varies greatly in versions and in terms of built-in packages from device to device. The same problem exists concerning the browser capabilities of supporting JavaScript and other web-based languages;
- *Bandwidth* - As a wireless LAN is not always available to the potential user, the system should be able to work over UMTS, EDGE, or GPRS connections. In particular, GPRS has high latency and restricted bandwidth, which is a major drawback for applications or services requiring to be always connected, like those controlling the instrumentation in real time.

In order to extend the functionalities of the LA.DI.RE. to MDs and, thus, to deliver services in a BL environment, the primary target is to enhance the software platform to allow remote students to display, control, and create experiments from smartphones, PDAs, etc. This last aspect makes the major difference from the common *M-learning* systems.

4.2 Enhancement of LA.DI.RE. services for *M-learning* delivery

Due to the hardware, software and bandwidth limitations of MDs, *Synchronous virtual laboratory* is hard to be delivered to remote students. On the other side, the three asynchronous services (namely *Experiment visualization*, *Experiment control*, and *Experiment creation*) can be integrated in MDs operating as follows:

- *Experiment visualization* - as the thin client paradigm used for *E-learning* is born for the MDs, it is inherently suited also for *M-learning* applications. The presentation logic runs on the server, while the thin client has the only task of showing the GUI that often reproduces a window of the application running on the server. A system based on a modified ProperJavaRDP client is used to connect to a server delivering the experiment and running Windows terminal services. The client grabs the image of a VI front panel and, by means of XMLHTTPRequest, handles it dynamically to a "lightweight" web page that provides the front panel presentation on the MD screen. Since the image dimensions are very small on MDs, some cashing algorithms would be just consuming processor power of the sever disabling it to be highly *scalable*, while handheld devices would lose their limited resources on cashing and compression, with small benefit in bandwidth usage. Therefore, no caching has been adopted in the application;
- *Experiment control* - it is based on a Javascript, which "catches" mouse coordinates and key pressed from the device keyboard and transfers them to an intermediate web server, realized for such task, which passes the data through the ProperJavaRDP client to the RDP server. Web pages are also dynamically loaded with JavaScript reducing the start-up time of the experiments;
- *Experiment creation* - a traditional approach is based on the implementation of all the functionalities of the measurement instrumentation (MI) into the VIs (i.e., a complete mapping of the MI into the VI) and, hence, is too heavy for MD memory. As shown in (Grimaldi & Lamonaca, 2007), a feasible approach is given by splitting up the traditional

VI of the MI in several modules which contain only the functionalities required by the measurement procedure and are able to exchange data by using a virtual bus. In this case a remote user downloads only the modules employed in the measurement procedure and has therefore a reduced occupancy of his/her PDA memory.

4.3 Remote control of a FPGA-based traffic control in a railway station

The proposed experiment is an example of a FPGA-based traffic control system of a railway station. Depending on the inputs entered by the user, the control system generates signals that rule 4 railway switches (points) to a position corresponding to a shift of the train from one track to another. Moreover, traffic signals system governs rail traffic, so that the simultaneous presence of two or more trains is managed by the common rules of precedence in order to avoid possible collisions. A sketch of the station under test, consisting of 5 tracks, is shown in Fig. 16 (left).

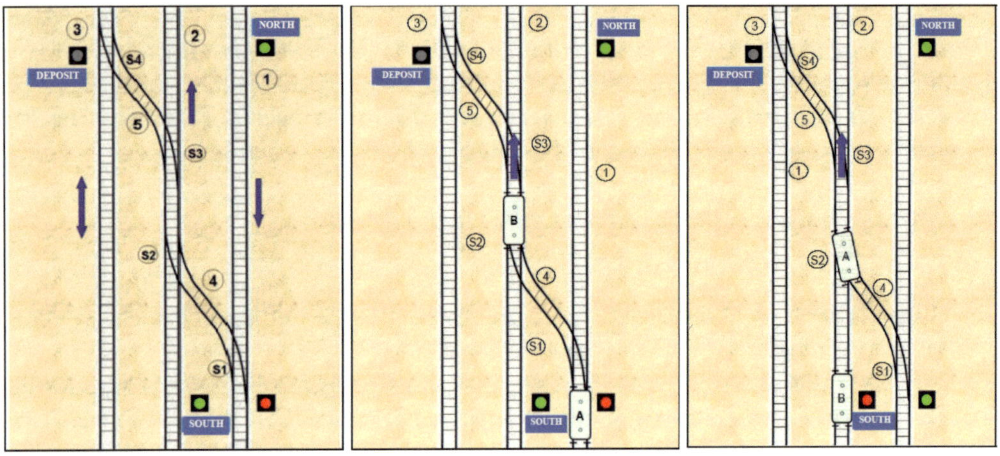

Fig. 16. Railway station outline (left) and traffic examples (middle, right).

The track marked as 1 is reserved for trains coming from North and going Southward, track 2 is for trains coming from South and moving Northward, while the track 3 is a "deposit" track that allows both the input and output trains. The tracks marked as 4 and 5 link the tracks 1-2 and 2-3, respectively. All points are marked with the following identification letters: S1, S2, S3 and S4 (see Figure 16, left).

Being a simple dynamic system that evolves with time depending on the user's input signals, it can be modelled as a finite state machine. The inputs are the incoming trains that lead the system to a specific state, which is recognized by the user by means output signals.

The main precedence rule is that each train that no need to change its track has precedence over a train that is about to change its track. As an example, in the case represented in Fig. 16 (middle) the train B (which does not change its track) has priority over train A, which has to go northward but it is still on track 1. In fact, before to change the S2 and S3 points, the train A must await the departure of train B. The main precedence rule is no more valid when the train B arrives as the train A is already on track 4, moving to track 2, as shown in Fig 16 (right). In this case, the point generates a red signal waiting to train B.

The set-up realized to remotely control the FPGA application described previously is shown in Fig. 17 and can be seen as the evolution to *M-learning* of the scheme of Fig. 15.

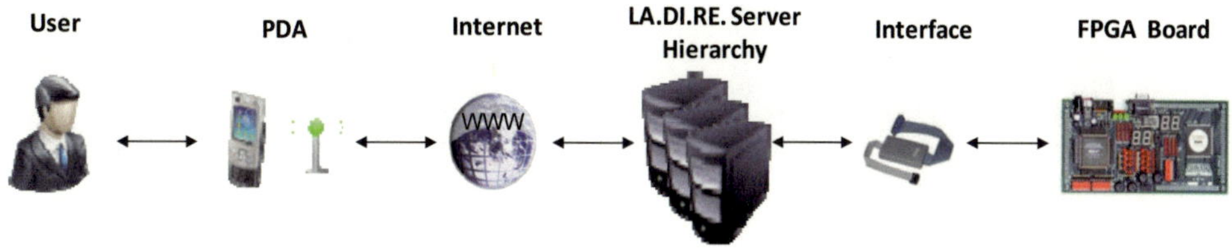

Fig. 17. *M-learning* configuration scheme.

The remote user executes the developed program on the FPGA board by connecting a common PDA to Internet. Then, after an authentication phase on the LMS, he/she is routed to the user interface of the program running on the FPGA board by means of a communication hardware interface.

The remote control of the FPGA application has been performed by a VI which contains only the functionalities required by the experiment. The VI processes data coming from Internet in bit strings form and routes them to the register of the parallel port connected to the FPGA board. As shown in Fig.18, a couple of text boxes were also considered in developing the VI, to account for local displaying of the input/output data flow between the FPGA and the network.

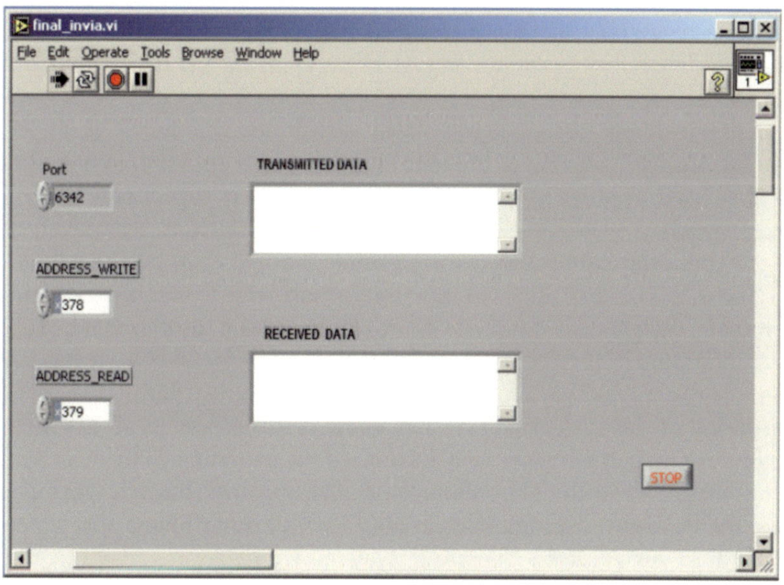

Fig. 18. VI front panel.

The PDA thin client works as follows:

1. when the application starts, a full screen image is displayed (Fig. 19 left), showing the application logo;
2. straight afterwards, an interactive graphical user interface representing the railway station, is shown (Fig. 19 tight). The remote user has a continuous monitoring of the trains position and can also manage the train station incoming traffic. The remote user can select the incoming traffic and its destination while the FPGA application routes the traffic automatically.

Fig. 19. Remote PDA front panels.

5. Conclusions and future work

In this chapter a new and complete web-based remote course on FPGA theory, computer aided design and laboratory practise using ALTERA Quartus II and UP1X evaluation board, has been presented. The course has been developed in the LA.DI.RE. "G. Savastano", an *E-learning* system which includes a geographically distributed laboratory. Using the *thin-client model*, a remote student can follow theoretical lessons, design and simulate, program and execute FPGA-based applications by using a client PC equipped only with an internet connection, a standard web browser and a Java Virtual Machine. Moreover, as a unique feature of the proposed web-based course, remote students can perform their laboratory practise having a full control and real-time interaction with FPGA, thus extending from a local to a remote designer all the facilities available for the development of FPGA-based applications. Extension of the LA.DI.RE. services to account for *M-learning* has been done by allowing remote experiment visualization, control and creation using a PDA. The current *M-learning* functions of the system still do not allow a full access to all the features of the LA.DI.RE.. For example, the remote visualization of the experiments by means of a webcam could not be integrated in the PDA thin client. The ongoing research work is devoted to fully replace the PC-based user interface in Fig.15 with a smartphone and tablet-based one to be executed in an Android operating system. By exploiting the inner multimedia characteristics of the Android-based applications the student can be provided with a real-time video displaying of the experiments. Moreover, the acceleration and position sensors on the modern smartphones could be used to provide a sensitive feedback channel to the LA.DI.RE. system.

6. References

Albu, M.; Holbert, K.; Heydt, G.; Grigorescu, S. & Trusca, V. (2004). Embedding remote experimentation in power engineering education, *IEEE Transanction on Power Systems*, vol.19, n.1, pp. 144-151

Attewell J. & Smith., C.S. (2004). Mobile learning and social inclusion: Focusing on learners and learning. *Learning with Mobile Device,*. Available from http://www.LSDA.org.uk

Arpaia, P.; Baccigalupi, A.; Cennamo, F. & Daponte, P. (1996). A distributed measurement laboratory on geographic network, *Proceeding of IMEKO 8th Int. Symp. on New Measurement and Calibration Methods of Electrical Quantities and Instruments,* Budapest, Hungary, pp. 294-297.

Arpaia, P.; Baccigalupi, A.; Cennamo, F. & Daponte, P. (2000). A measurement laboratory on geographic network for remote test experiments, *IEEE Transaction on Instrumentation and Measurements.*, vol. 49, n.5, pp. 992-997.

Bagnasco, A.; Chirico, M. & Scapolla, A. M. (2002). XML technologies to design didactical distributed measurement laboratories, *Proceedings of the 19th IEEE Instrumentation and Measurement Technology Conference,* USA, vol.1, pp. 651-655, Anchorage, Alaska, USA.

Bagnasco, A. & Scapolla, A.M., (2003). A grid of remote laboratory for teaching electronics. In *Proceedings of the 2nd International Work on e-Learn and Grid Technologies: A Fundamental Challenge for Europe,* Paris, France, http://ewic.bcs.org/conferences/2003/2ndlege/index.htm

Batatia, H.; Ayache, A. & Markkanen, H. (2002). Netpro: an innovative approach to network project based learning, *Proceedings of the International Conference on Computers in Education,* pp.382-386., Auckland, New Zealand.

Benetazzo, L.; Bertocco, M.;, Ferraris, F.; Ferrero, A.; Offelli, C.; Parvis, M. & Piuri, V. (2000) A Web based, distributed virtual educational laboratory. *IEEE Transactions on Instrumentation and Measuring,* vol. 49, n.2, pp.:349–356.

Benetazzo, L. & Bertocco, M. (2002). A distributed training laboratory. In *Proceedings of the Eden Annual Conference on Open and Distance Learning in Eurpe and Beyond,* pp. 409–414, Granada, Spain.

Blumenfeld, P.C.; Soloway, E.; Marx, R. W.; Krajcik, J. S.; Guzdial, M. & Palincsar, A.(1991): Motivating project based learning: Sustaining the doing, supporting the learning, *Educational Psychologist,* vol.26, n. 3-4, pp. 369-398

Bonk, C. J. & Graham, C. R. (2004). *Handbook of blended learning: Global Perspectives, local designs,* San Francisco: Pfeiffer Publishing

Borsic, M.; Cmuk, D.; Daponte, P.; De Capua, C.; Grimaldi, D.; Kilic, T.; Mutapˇci´c, T. & Riccio M. (2006). Italian-Croatian Remote Laboratory distributed on geographical network. In *Proceedings of the IEEE Softcom,* pp. 357–362, Split-Dubrovnik, Croatia.

Canfora, G.; Daponte, P.; & Rapuano, S. (2004). Remotely accessible laboratory for electronic measurement teaching, *Computer Standards and Interfaces,* vo1.26, no.6, pp.489-499.

Chirico, M.; Scapolla, A. M. & Bagnasco, A. (2005). A New and Open Model to Share Laboratories on the Internet, *IEEE Transaction on Instrumentation & Measurements,* vol. 54, n.. 3, pp. 1111-1117.

Cmuk, D.; Borsic, M. & Zoino, F. (2006). Remote versus Classical Laboratory in Electronic Measurements teaching - effectiveness testing. In *Proceedings of the IMEKO XVIII World Congress*, Rio de Janeiro.

Cooper, M. (2005). Remote laboratories in teaching and learning - issues impinging on widespread adoption in science and engineering education, *Internat. Journal of Online Engineering*, vol. 1, n. 1, available at *http://www.ijoe.org/ojs/*.

Daponte, P.; Grimaldi, D. & Marinov, M.(2002). Real-time measurement and control of an industrial system over a standard network: implementation of a prototype for educational purposes, I *IEEE Transaction on Instrumentation and Measurements*, vol. 51, n.5, pp. 962- 969.

Daponte, P.; De Capua, C. & Liccardo, A.(2004a). A technique for remote management of instrumentation based on web services, *Proceeding of IMEKO-TC4 13th Int. Symposium on Measurement for Research and Industry Applications*, pp. 687-692. Athens, Greece.

Daponte, P.; Graziani, A. &. Rapuano, S. (2004b). Final report on "Progetto preliminare di teleducazione", *Agenzia Spaziale Italiana*, available at http://progetto-teleducazione.cres.it

Daponte, P.; Grimaldi, D. & Rapuano, S. (2010). A Software Architecture for the m-Learning in Instrumentation and Measurement. In F. Davoli, S. Palazzo, and S. Zappatore, editors, *Remote Instrumentation and Virtual Laboratories*, pp. 443–455, Springer.

Donzellini, G. & Ponta, D. (2003). DEEDS: E-Learning Environment for Digital Design", *Proceedings of the 3rd European Symposium on Intelligent Technologies, Hybrid Systems and their implementation on Smart Adaptive Systems)*, pp. 370-376, Oulu, Finland.

EACEA, Education Audiovisual Culture Executive Agency, http://eacea.ec.europa.eu/static/en/elearning/index.htm, European Commission.

El-Medany, W. M (2008). FPGA Remote Laboratory for Hardware E-Learning Courses, *Proceedings of the IEEE Region 8 International Conference on Computational Technologies in Electrical and Electronics Engineering (Sibircon)*, pp. 106-109, Novosibirsk, Russia

Etxebarria, A.; Oleagordia, I. J. & Sanchez, M. (2001). An Educational Environment for VHDL Hardware Description Language using the WWW and Specific Workbench, *Proceedings of 31st Frontiers in Education Conference*, pp. T2C-1-7, Reno, USA.

Fujii, N. & Koike, N. (2005). A New Remote Laboratory for Hardware Experiments with Shared Resources and Service Management, *Proceedings of the 3rd International Conference on Information Technology and Applications,* vol. 2, pp. 153-158, Sydney, Australia, July 2005.

Grimaldi, D.; Rapuano, S. & Laopoulos T. (2005). Aspects of Traditional versus Virtual Laboratory for Education in Instrumentations and Measurement, *Proceedings of the 22nd IEEE Instrumentation and Measurement Technology Conference*, vol. 2, pp. 1233-1238, Ottawa, Canada, May 2005.

Grimaldi, D.; Rapuano, S. & Laopoulos T. (2006). Exploring the capability of web-based measurement systems for distance learning. In F. Davoli, S. Palazzo, and S.

Zappatore, editors, *Distributed Cooperative Laboratories: Networking, Instrumentation and Measurements*, pp. 373–393. Springer.

Grimaldi, D. & Lamonaca, F. (2007). Dynamic configuration of measurement procedures on PDA by using measurement application repository server, *Proceedings of IEEE International Workshop on Intelligent Data Acquisition and Advanced Computing Systems: Technology and Applications*, Dortmund, Germany

Hamblem, J.O. & Furman, M.D. (2001). Rapid Prototyping of Digital Systems: A tutorial Approach, 2nd Ed., *Kluwer Academic Publishers.*

Holzinger, A.; Nischelwitzer, A. & Meisenberger, M. (2005). *Lifelong-Learning Support by M-learning: Example Scenarios.* e-Learn magazine, http://www.elearnmag.org/ subpage.cfm?section=research\&article=6-1

Leiner, R. (2002). Tele-Experiments Via Internet - A New Approach For Distance Education, *Proceedings of the 11st Mediterranean Electrotechnical Conference,* pp. 538-541, Cairo, Egypt, May 2002.

LINOXMOTION - http://www.lynxmotion.com

Ong, S.S.; Hawryszkiewycz, I. (2003). Towards personalised and collaborative learning management systems, *Proceedings of the 31st IEEE Internatonal Conference on Advanced Learning Technologies*, pp. 340-341,Athens, Greece.

Persiano, G.V.; Rapuano, S.; Zoino, F.; Morganella, A.& Chiusolo, G. (2007). Distance learning in digital electronics: laboratory practice on FPGA, *Proceedings of the 22nd IEEE Instrumentation and Measurement Technology Conference*, pp. 1-6, Warsaw, Poland.

Persiano, G.V.; Rapuano, S & Villanacci, M. (2010). Mobile-learning on electronic instrumentation based on FPGA, *CDROM Proceedings of the 17th IMEKO TC-4*, Kosice, Slovakia.

Pellerin, D. & Thibault, S. (2005). Practical FPGA Programming in C, *Prentice Hall Modern Semiconductor Design Series.*

Quintans, C.; Valdes, M. D.; Moure, M. J.; Mandado, E. & Fernandez-Ferreira, L. (2005). Digital Electronics Learning System Based on FPGA Applications, *Proceedings of 35th Frontiers in Education Conference*, pp. S2G-7-12, Indianapolis, Indiana, USA.

Rapuano, S. & Zoino, F. (2006). A Learning Management System on Measurement Instrumentation, *IEEE Transaction on Instrumentation & Measurements*, vol. 55, n. 5, pp. 1757-1766.

Ranaldo, N.; Rapuano, S.; Riccio, M.& Zoino, F.(2007). Remote control and video capturing of electronic instrumentation for distance learning, *IEEE Transactions on Instrumentation and Measuring*, vol. 56, n. 4, pp. 1419–1428.

Sanchez Pastor, J.; Gonzalez, I.; Lopez J.; Gomez-Arribas, F. & Martinez, J. (2004). A Remote Laboratory for Debugging FPGA-Based Microprocessor Prototypes. *Proceedings of the 4th IEEE International Conference on Advanced Learning Technologies,* pp. 86-90, Joensuu, Finland.

Vossen, G. & Jaeschke, P. (2003). Learning objects as a uniform foundation for e-learning platforms," in *Proceedings of the 7th IDEAS*, pp. 278–287, Hong Kong, SAR.

Zuver, C. K.; Neely, C. E.& Lockwood J. W. (2003). Internet-based Tool for System-on-Chip Project Testing and Grading. *Proceedings of the 2003 International Conference on Microelectronic Systems Education*, pp. 119-120, Reno, USA

3

Promoting E-Learning in Distance Education Programs in an African Country

Kenneth Addah, Desmond Kpebu
and Olivia A. T. Frimpong Kwapong
University of Ghana,
Ghana

1. Introduction

The idea of widening access to education, promoting independent and lifelong learning and adopting alternative approaches to delivery of education is prominent in the goals of education in Ghana. To facilitate human resource development in the country and widen access to education at all levels, the educational policy of the country has emphasized the promotion of e-learning in its distance education programs. Supported with information and communication technology, thousands of people from remotest parts of countries have been able to access education through distance learning [1].

The traditional notion of education is the type of teaching and learning that occurs in personal contact between the teacher and the learner in the classroom setting. This is anchored in the reality that teaching and learning take place at same time and same place. With the introduction of new communication technology it has became clear that formal, informal or non-formal teaching and learning at the higher level could also be done via technology. The rapid development in learning theories and advancement in technology has made it possible to shift from institution-led learning to own-time self-learning at a distance using e-learning platforms. Thus from face-to-face teaching to self-paced-learning, which is moving towards flexibility and openness. This experience has progressed to the alternative delivery system known as e-learning. E-learning as in the sense of electronic delivery of education for students who are separated from their teachers both in time and space has existed and operated under different terms such as distance education, distance teaching and distance learning for over one hundred years in the more developed regions and for one or two generations in the developing regions. Since e-learning thrives on information and communication technology, the advancement in technology gives direction to e-learning provision in Ghana. Using secondary resources this chapter assesses the progress that has been made on the promotion of e-learning in tertiary distance education programs in Ghana. Though e-learning can support both on-campus and off-campus (distance learning) programs, the focus of this chapter is how e-learning is being utilized in distance higher education programs in Ghana. The first section discusses the e-learning concept in distance higher education, followed by an assessment of education in Ghana with special focus on distance learning. The final sections discusses on efforts at promoting e-learning in Ghana and the challenges thereof.

2. The E-learning concept in distance higher education

Traditionally, education in which teachers and learners are separated by time and distance has been referred to as distance education or distance learning. Distance education could be explained as planned learning that normally occurs in a place that is different from where the teaching takes place. It requires special techniques of course design, instruction and methods of communication by electronic and other technology. Distance education could be offered at the basic, secondary or higher level of education. It could also be for formal or non-formal educational programs. The term e-learning on the other hand is relatively new in the field of education. Much as it has its roots in relatively older fields such as correspondence course, distance education/teaching or distance learning, it is an educational practice that is gaining prominence in the world of education for the past 15 to 20 years. E-learning comprises all forms of electronically supported learning and teaching. It covers a wide set of applications and processes, such as web-based learning, computer-based learning, virtual classrooms, and digital collaboration. E-learning is essentially the computer and network-enabled transfer of skills and knowledge. In e-learning content is delivered via the internet, intranet/extranet, audio or video tape, satellite TV or CD-ROM. It can be self-paced or instructor-led and includes media in the form of text, image, animation, streaming video and audio [2].

The combination of distance education and e-learning can take different forms. There could be pure distance learning as in learners working alone either online or with print and video materials. There could also be partial distance where learners work independently but also regularly meeting with others who are studying the same curriculum. A third model which, is blended learning combines face-to-face tutorials with distance learning. Another model, which is not the focus of this chapter, could be classroom supplement where online learning is used to facilitate regular classroom work as in purely on-campus academic programs. In each of these models, electronic technologies provide additional resources and expanded opportunities for two-way communication between the learner and the instructor or educational agency [3]. The influence of electronic facilities on education at a distance has contributed to its description with terms such as open learning, technology-mediated learning, online learning and virtual campus all of which could be used inter-changeably to mean one thing – e-learning [4].

The growing demand for work and study have made most higher education institutions to utilize e-learning tools to support the interactivity in distance education programs. The use of e-learning tools for teaching and learning at a distance implies teacher-directed learning activities using computers, completing and submitting assignments electronically, participating in-group chats involving near-simultaneous written dialogue, and giving feedback electronically. In this process learners organize their learning independently which make them take over some of the roles of the instructor [5]. The use of e-learning tools in a teaching learning process facilitates a high level of interaction among learners, which help to overcome the isolation in distance learning. Because greater emphasis is placed on student interaction and reflection, e-learning has been found to be better than the purely print-based distance learning courses [6]. In addition to freeing current students to study at times and in places convenient for them, e-learning as part of distance education offers the potential of serving additional students who, for a variety of reasons, cannot or do not want to enroll in face-to-face classes or tutorials. Distance education, particularly via e-learning, can adapt to the scheduling needs of students and teachers. It can also address the specific learning needs of students. E-learning helps to remove distance constraints and promotes interpersonal communication dynamics. It is explained by [7] that in the use of the e-learning tools for teaching and learning, students process information electronically rather than through face-to-face contact with teachers and other students.

In the light of the various developments in communication technology and its relative impact on distance education. In [8] Bates has defined three generations of distance learning as follows:

- First generation learners studied alone, with limited contact from the educational provider as in correspondence study
- Second generation distance education provides learning resources in one or more media and support services usually in a face-to-face mode
- Third generation distance learning provides learning resources in one or more media and interaction among learners as well as between the tutor and learner via conferencing technologies (audio, video, computer), email or face-to-face meetings

These generational phases show how electronic facilities have changed the face of the delivery of education to enhance interactivity.

The application of e-learning has been evolving in parallel with the arrival of newer and intelligent technologies. With the increasing desire for education at all levels and the commitment to attain the EFA goals coupled with the flexibility and dynamism in e-learning, the philosophy is constantly emerging as the most convenient way of responding to the growing need of education. E-learning is breaking the barriers of space and time, it provides the population with truly equal opportunity and an efficient way to continue education and personal development, in line with the massive and effective access to higher education in the current society of knowledge. It also permits a new type of alliance between the university and business, the state and diverse organizations. E-learning is in use in many developed and developing countries, providing varied educational opportunities to meet the varied needs of learners.

E-learning presents tremendous educational opportunities for women as well. The potential of e-learning tools in facilitating interaction at a distance and creating artificial social presence makes it suitable for the learning styles of women who find it difficult to leave home for on-campus studies. Generally e-learning makes learning more productive and more individualized, gives instruction a more scientific base, makes it appropriate and more effective, more immediate and equalizes access to all educational resources provided one has the connectivity. The potential benefits of e-learning include cost-effectiveness, enhanced responsiveness to changing circumstances, consistency, timely content, accessibility, and more rapid feedback all of which go to suit women and make higher education accessible to them. Using connected communication tools both male and female students can decide about their studies, learning time, place and resources in a more convenient way. They can also work in more supportive environments, seek help from tutors and colleagues, and share their learning experiences and ideas in a cosmetic and productive fashion [9].

The discussions so far has shown the utility of e-learning tools in enhancing interactivity in distance learning programs for both men and women. In spite of the potential of e-learning tools there has been intellectual argument over its ability to promote social presence in a teaching learning process recognizing that in traditional classroom social presence enhances instructional delivery and the classroom experience. Social presence implies the connections between participants and the tutor to enhance student satisfaction, perceptions of learning, and retention. Various studies have however been undertaken to justify the possibility of creating a social presence in an e-learning platform. A richer, more engaging learning community can be formed in the online learning classroom through the creation of online communities to fulfill the human need for social interaction with peers and instructors in an online class. A study by [10] indicates that students agreed that seven of the nine functions provided by the web-based online course management system enhanced their learning in the following ways: private email (92.3%), calendaring (88.5%), course notes (88.5%), discussion forums (84.5%), online grades (84.5%), assignment descriptions (80.8%), and online quizzes (80.8%). Another study has also been observed by [11] that email and other Internet programs are effective tools for interaction as well as to make a bridge of communication between both tutors and learners. In their study most of the learners (94%) gave their opinions that email technologies supports the teachers or tutors to consult in a better way while almost 82 percent learners showed eagerness to communicate with teachers by email. These confirm the possibility of using e-learning tools to create social presence in a distance education program. With the technological advancement, the distance and isolation in the distance learning system has been overcome to a very large extent. An account of the sorts of engagements that go on in mobile telephony, Facebook and twitter for instance testify to the possibility of having a social presence in e-learning programs which can be harnessed to support distance education programs in a developing country such as Ghana.

2.1 Education in Ghana

Following independence, Ghana continued to search for a system of education that is relevant to the world of work, adequate for rural development and the modernization of its agriculture-based economy. The country has also been interested in a system of education that seeks to promote national and cultural identity and citizenship. The mission of the Ministry of Education is "to provide relevant education to all Ghanaians at all levels to enable them acquire skills that will assist them to develop their potential, be productive, facilitate poverty reduction and promote socio-economic growth and national development" [12].

It is estimated that Ghana has 12, 130 primary schools, 5,450 junior secondary schools, 503 senior secondary schools, 18 technical institutions, 38 training colleges, seven theological colleges, eight tutorial colleges, 10 polytechnics, six public and 13 private universities that serves a population of about 20 million. Total school enrolment is estimated at almost 2 million with a breakdown of 1.3 million primary; 107.600 secondary; 489,00 middle; 21,280 technical; 11,300 teacher training; and 5, 600 university [12]. There is increase in educational facilities but this does not match the growing population and their educational demands.

In the year 2004 the Government of Ghana set up an Education Review Committee to review the education policy of the country. This was in response to the demands of education in a fast changing world that is driven by science and technology [13] [14]. In connection with global trends and the potential of information technologies to facilitate teaching and learning and productivity in the world of work, the Committee had the responsibility to examine the use of information technology for distance learning at all levels of education in the country. The Committee recommended independent continuous lifelong learning through open and distance learning modes instead of a one-shot formal school experience. The focus of the policy of education in Ghana has made distance education and the use of e-learning facilities in education very critical then.

In addition to the policy provisions, the current state of education in the country coupled with limited space for the increasing enrolment makes it crucial to promote e-learning. There is the challenge of limited space and a mismatch between the qualified applicants and existing facilities. A high percentage of qualified applicants do not gain admission to existing universities to pursue further studies. Available statistics indicate that from 1996-2001, only about 32% on the average, of qualified applicants for admission into the universities, and about 54% of same for admission into the polytechnics, were actually admitted. The figures have not changed much over the period. For the 2005/2006 academic year, 55% of qualified applicants were admitted into all the public universities and 78% into the polytechnics. For the same period, statistics indicate that the male-female enrolment for both the universities and polytechnics has increased slightly meanwhile the gap is still very wide. In 2005/2006 academic year the male to female enrolment ratio was 65:35 for the universities and 70:30 for the polytechnics. This is far below the national norm of 50% males to 50% females. At the tertiary level about 5,000 undergraduates are enrolled in secular degree-granting programs in the existing nine private institutions [15].

2.2 Focus on distance learning

For decades the country was faced with a situation of turning away a large number of qualified applicants every year because of the limited space available for the enrolment of qualified applicants especially at the higher level of education. The Government of Ghana then planned to use distance learning to respond to the growing demands for higher education in the country and to decongest the campuses of the public universities. The government of Ghana has thus adopted distance learning as a viable complement to the conventional face-to-face education.

The mission of distance learning program in Ghana is to make quality education at all levels more accessible and relevant to meet the needs of Ghanaians in order to enhance their performance and improve the quality of their lives. Specifically governments of Ghana have sought to use distance learning to:

- provide opportunity for a large number of qualified applicants who do not get admission into the face-to-face programs as a result of limited facilities to have access to tertiary education
- create the opportunity for work and study
- increase access to and participation in education at all levels for all
- facilitate progression through the education system from basic to tertiary
- improve the capacity of Ghanaians to cope with the technological advancement and the knowledge society and be able to enhance their contribution to nation building
- increase equality and democratization of education
- provide cost-effective and affordable education
- serve as an avenue for financial resource mobilization for the public universities

Currently four of the public universities, University of Ghana (UG), University of Cape Coast (UCC), Kwame Nkrumah University of Science and Technology (KNUST), University of Education, Winneba (UEW) are offering higher education programs in a dual mode. The higher education distance learning program was first begun in UEW in the year 1996, followed by UCC in 2001, then KNUST in 2004 and finally UG in 2007. Before then, in collaboration with the Commonwealth of Learning, the University of Ghana, had been delivering a Diploma in Youth in Development Work since 2001. The programs are being patronized greatly by both males and females in the country, and characteristic of most distance learning institutions the percentage of female enrolment cannot compare to that of on-campus programs. For instance, statistics of the various institutions indicate that UEW, which began in 1998, has approximately 7000 students with 53 percent females and 46.5 percent males at its Level 300 for the 2006/7 school year; UCC which began in 2001 has over 18,000 students, 49.7 percent females and 50.2 males in the Dip. Ed. Courses [16].

All the four universities that have started distance learning (UG, KNUST, UCC, UEW) are now dual-mode institutions. As a practice for parity of esteem and standardization, the institutions use the same faculty, curriculum, course structure and content for both the on-campus and the distance learning students. The admission and examination process is similar for both sets of students. Similar matriculation and graduation programs are organized for both sets of students as well. Delivery mode at a distance has been predominantly print-based supported with regular face-to-face tutorials at the various learning centers. While some institutions conduct both mid-semester and end-semester assessments at their centers in the regions, others do it at a central point, usually the main campus of the university [17].

The review of the tertiary distance learning programs raises several issues of concern. It is exciting to know that the various programs are providing higher education opportunity for people who though qualify, might not have had the opportunity to pursue higher education. An institution such as IEDE has made conscious effort to enroll more women, which has contributed to increase female enrolment on the program. Available report also indicates that IEDE is making effort to use facilities such as radio to compliment delivery.

There are however challenges which have to be considered for a better equitable provision of higher education in the country. To date the print media continues to be the most medium used by the various institutions offering higher distance education programs. The distance learning programs are mainly print-based supported with occasional face-to-face where students meet their tutors at a center for discussions. Assignments are either hand delivered or mailed by post. Students meet at a designated center to write their end of semester examinations. In cases where course materials are not ready, lecturers either meet to lecture the students in the various centers or students join the on-campus lectures. Distance learning students also share the already over-stretched facilities such as library spaces with the on-campus students. Meanwhile the purpose is to use distance education to decongest the various campuses. Allowing distance learning students to share libraries, attend lectures and share other on-campus facilities will no doubt congest the system further. Much as these educational processes create opportunity for those who will otherwise not gain admission to pursue their life dream education, it presents enormous challenges to the institutions and most especially learners from remote parts of the country. Travelling to centers for tutorials or lectures will not only expose learners and students to the risks of highway robbery and accident but may not be cost effective for the institution and the student as well. Considering distance learning as a mode that meets women's lifestyle because they can conveniently work, keep their homes and study, excessive use of face-to-face interactions may not find them well. For some women, obtaining permission from their husbands could be more challenging than obtaining permission from the workplace [17]. A continuation of such practices may make the programs lose its distance learning philosophy and probably turn to be a face-to-face program instead. In this case learners may be forced to leave their jobs more often and those who may not afford to leave the workplace or cannot obtain permission may drop out of the program. These are challenges that most countries, especially those in the developed world, have used e-learning to overcome. An institution could compliment the instructional materials with basic electronic media such as e-learning resources such as CDs copies of the instructional materials and course websites for effective communication and interaction among tutors and students, administrators and students and among students. A unifying body and an effective collaboration between the various institutions could facilitate the sharing of both academic and information technology infrastructural resources for promoting e-learning as well.

Considering the strength in e-learning in promoting interactivity and making education accessible to all, the distance learning institutions in the country are pushing for the incorporation of e-learning tools in its distance education programs.

3. Promoting E-learning for distance learning in Ghana

For the past ten years, the country has made the effort to introduce ICTs into the education sector to facilitate e-learning. This is in recognition of the key role that e-learning can play in making the existing higher education distance learning programs accessible to a wider section of the population [13] [14]. In 2004 Parliament passed into law Ghana's Information and Communication Technology for Accelerated Development (ICT4AD) policy, which is currently at various stages of implementation. This policy represents the vision of Ghana in the information age. In view of the need to have a coordinated, focused and properly managed approach to the adoption and utilisation of information technologies and to maximise the use of e-learning tools, the education sector decided to draw up a comprehensive policy on information technologies. Generally the policy document seeks to provide a clear purpose and rationale for how information technologies will be effectively integrated into the education sector, including identifying opportunities, issues, challenges and strategies that will be employed. The mission of the Policy is to articulate the relevance, responsibility and effectiveness of utilizing information technologies in the education sector, with a view to addressing current sector challenges and equipping Ghanaian learners, students, teachers and communities in meeting the national and global demands of the 21st Century.

The fundamental objective of the policy is to ensure that the Ghanaian education sector provides adequate opportunities for Ghanaians to develop the necessary skills, regardless of the levels of education (formal and non-formal), to benefit fully from the information society. In view of this the overall policy goal is to enable graduates from Ghanaian educational institutions - formal and non-formal to confidently and creatively use e-learning tools and resources to develop requisite skills and knowledge needed to be active participants in the global knowledge economy by 2015. The ICT in Education Policy is based on the premise that there are several key elements that underpin the use of information technologies. These include teaching and learning; management and administration; communication; and access to information. Furthermore, it is recognized that these elements will be dependent on policy reforms, both within education sector as well as within other related sectors including communications, local government and rural development. The policy document focuses on seven thematic areas, which covers management, capacity building, infrastructure, information technologies in curriculum, content development, technical support for maintenance and monitoring. The policy document acknowledges that if effectively used, e-learning tools can among other things:

- Provide multiple avenues for professional development of both pre-service and in-service teachers, especially through distance education
- Facilitate improved teaching and learning processes
- Improve teacher knowledge, skills and attitudes and even inquiry
- Improve educational management processes
- Improve the consistency and quality of instruction both for formal and non-formal education
- Increase opportunities for more student centred pedagogical approaches
- Promote inclusive education by addressing inequalities in gender, language, disability
- Widen the traditional sources of information and knowledge
- Foster collaboration, creativity, higher order thinking skills
- Provide for flexibility of delivery
- Reach student populations outside traditional education systems

Concerning access to infrastructure, the expected impact on end-users (learners, teachers, managers and administrators) will very much depend on affordable and continuous access to hardware, software and connectivity. This in turn will be dependent on the availability of appropriate physical infrastructure including power sources such as electricity or solar.

The general policy efforts is directed at using ICTs to facilitate education and learning within the educational system and promote e-learning and e-education as well as lifelong learning within the population at large. Under the thematic area to use ICT for capacity building, the policy has an objective of using distance education and virtual learning systems to reduce cost and the number of teachers who leave the classroom for study leave. Strategies for achieving the objective includes postgraduate distance education program for faculty in ICT, building infrastructure to facilitate distance learning for teachers and setting up digital e-libraries to support distance learning programs. Similarly, in the third thematic area, which is on infrastructure, e-readiness and equitable access, the policy seeks to facilitate equitable access to ICTs for all schools and communities. Some of the strategies under this theme again seek to develop infrastructure to support distance education and put in systems that will help bridge the rural and urban divides.

The thematic area on content development seeks to develop appropriate content for open, distance and e-learning. The policy acknowledges that

- Digital content is critical to e-education because it can be easily and randomly accessed, adapted and manipulated, and is accessible from many locations
- Digital content is easier and less expensive to update and distribute
- Development of digital content will promote the use of indigenous culture in the education system
- Multimedia digital content can facilitate effective learning

As part of its strategy under this theme, the policy proposes to

- Institute and organize cost effective distance education program to cover all levels of education in the formal and informal sectors.
- Promote the development and utilization of a national educational portal / website which will provide links to help teachers, students and the public access educational information readily.

Much as one will question the extent to which some of these strategies have been implemented or will be implemented, it is good to know; at least that the country has set up these plans. This gives an indication that in response to international trends, the Government has the 'will' to utilise e-learning systems to support distance learning [13] [14]. A review of current trends of information technology infrastructure provision will give an idea of the extent of the implementation of the ICT4D Policy.

The Ministry of Communication has reported that the country is likely to exceed the telephone penetration target for universal Internet access by 2012 and the UN's Millennium Development Goal targets for 2015 for telephone lines, cellular subscribers, personal computers in use and Internet users [14]. In a 2007 World Bank Survey on ICT and Education in Africa, it was remarked in the Ghana country study that compared to other West African countries, Ghana is among the leaders in the use of ICTs. As one of the first African countries to liberalise its telecommunication sector, Ghana has made tremendous progress in ICT infrastructure deployment. Available records from the Ministry of Communications for the year 2007 indicate that telephone subscription has hit the eight million mark, giving a telephone density of nearly 40%. Fixed lines increased to 376,509 by the end of 2007, from 248,900 lines in 2001. During the same period mobile phone users rose from 215,000 in 2001 to 7.6 million, bringing the total for fixed and mobile subscribers up from 463,900 to 7,980,552 at the end of December 2007. Telephone penetration at the end of the period was 36.3%. Mobile phone services cover all of the 10 regions in the country, Internet subscription is estimated at 1.5 million users, while broadband subscribers number just over 13,000.

The first phase of the country's fiber-optic development is complete and this is expected to facilitate the deployment of ICT applications nationwide and the speedy implementation of the 20-year ICT4D policy [18].

The Internet services that are provided on mobile telephony can be used to supplement e-learning programs in the country. The mobile telephony operators have made a substantial inroad into the market over the last years with an estimated mobile subscriber base of 8 million as at the end of 2009. Mobile telephony now represents 63 percent of the total telecom market. Ghana has six licensed cellular/mobile operators which include Vodafone (formerly GT Onetouch), MTN, Tigo, Kasapa, Zain and Glo (Globacom). There are two fixed line operators which are Ghana Telecom (Vodafone) and Westel (now Zain). The rest of the market is represented by fixed line voice products (18%), data services such as Internet/broadband, leased lines and VPN (3%) and international traffic (16%).

One of the direct results of the ICT for Accelerated Development (ICT4AD) policy is the establishment of the Ghana Information and Communications Technology Directorate (GICTeD) as the operational arm of the Ministry of Communications for ICT policy implementation and coordination of governmental ICT initiatives. GICTeD is expected to identify and promote the development of innovative technologies, standards, guidelines, and practices, among government agencies within the national and local governments, and the private sector, to enable Ghana become a technology-driven, knowledge- and value-based economy. It is envisaged that GICTeD will help Ghanaians create a world-class online economy and society through its work, as well as developing, overseeing, and coordinating Government's ICT programs on electronic governance and commerce, online services with their associated infrastructure elements, and the Internet.

Reports from the country's ICT sector and higher education institutions indicate that the Ghanaian tertiary education sector is the most advanced in the deployment and use of ICTs in the country. All the country's major universities have their own separate ICT policy, which includes an ICT levy for students. This enables students to have access to 24-hour computer laboratories with broadband Internet connection. With funding support from the World Bank through Teaching and Learning Innovation Fund (TALIF), the Ghana Education Trust Fund (GETFund) and other funding agencies the National Council for Tertiary Education (NCTE) has been able to provide infrastructural and capacity building support to the distance learning programs in the public universities that are offering higher education distance learning programs. The various distance education institutions have been able to acquire basic facilities such as computers, internet connectivity, libraries, refurbishing of learning centers in the regions and other infrastructural and logistical support. Training support have over the years been received from both local and international institutions such as the NCTE, Ministry of Education Science and Sports, International Extension College of the United Kingdom and Simon Frazer University Distance Education Centre of Canada, British Overseas Development Administration (ODA), The Commonwealth of Learning in the areas of writing, formatting and editing of instructional materials, learners support services and general administration and management of distance learning programs. These supports have been very useful in building the local capacity/expertise for e-learning.

A broadband wireless Internet and voice telephony facility has been inaugurated on the campus of the Kwame Nkrumah University of Science and Technology (KNUST). Known as the KNUST E-Campus Network, the facility has the potential of transforming the mode of teaching and learning on campus, as it would provide members of the university community with in-room and on-campus wireless Internet and voice telephony. The project is the first phase of a comprehensive e-learning plan, which is aimed at integrating all educational institutions into the global ICT network with KNUST as the hub.

The University of Ghana and the Kwame Nkrumah University of Science and Technology have proposed to run a special regional university under a five-year Pan African tele-education project. With the support of the Indian Government and the African Union when completed, the project will provide open access broadband connectivity nationwide at affordable rates. Currently, within the African context, although the high-speed broadband access, vital to modern businesses, is now available in many capital cities and major towns, it comes at a high price.

It is anticipated that all these efforts will go to improve e-learning programs in the country.

4. Issues emerging and conclusion

There is evidence of some technological breakthroughs that will support e-learning for distance education. There are however persistent in country challenges which must be noted if the country can make good progress in the promotion of e-learning.

- Access to information technology facilities still remains highly inadequate and unevenly distributed throughout the country. There is an urban bias with rural communities lagging behind.
- The capacity of teachers and educators to manage e-learning programs still remains low. While some do not have the adequate skills, others are averse to using e-learning platforms
- There is inadequate collaboration between the various stakeholders and agencies to check duplication and efficient utilization of the few available e-learning resources
- There is insufficient equipment and slow Internet connectivity in most parts of the country

- There is also unreliable access to electricity
- Not all tertiary institutions in the country are equally endowed and there are instances where students are forced to patronize Internet services that are run by the private sectors such as cyber cafés on campuses

In addition to the challenges enumerated above, there are some gender specific challenges that affect women most. There is relatively high level of illiteracy, low levels of ownership of computers, telephone lines, radios, televisions, and access to the Internet affect among women [19]. Studies have shown that the manufacture of ICT systems is not gender friendly [20]. Computing remains a heavily male-dominated field. Only a few Internet content is available that meets the information needs of women in developing countries in a form they can use. Women have also not been fairly treated in terms of portrayal on the Internet. In some cases the Internet has been used for women's sexual exploitation and harassment. There is trafficking of women through the Internet, pornography, sexual harassment and use of Internet to perpetuate violence against women. In most parts of the country, women are not culturally permitted to share the same public space with men. They may thus be challenged in sharing e-learning facilities that may be installed in public places [16] [21] [22]. These and many other factors may not encourage women to use the Internet for more serious business such as e-learning. Subsequent studies could explore how both men and women are making use of the available ICT facilities for distance learning and the support they require.

E-learning has come to stay. Developing countries have no excuse for not utilizing it fully to support their distance learning programs. With conscious policy directives, basic e-learning resources could be fully utilized to supplement and improve the delivery of the existing distance learning programs.

5. References

[1] H. I. Touré. (2007). Current Situation in Africa. Available: http://www.itu.int/ITUD/connect/africa/2007/bgdmaterial/chap1-5.html

[2] A. L. Wong, "Cross-cultural delivery of e-learning programmes: Perspectives from Hong Kong", *Turkish Online Journal of Distance Education-TOJDE*, vol. 9, 2/1, 2008.

[3] S. Imel and E. Jacobson, "Distance education and e-learning: New options for adult basic and English language education", *Research Digest*, vol. 4, 2006.

[4] M. Kim, "Factors influencing the acceptance of e-learning courses for mainstream faculty in higher institutions", *International Journal of Instructional Technology and Distance Learning*, vol. 5(2), 2008.

[5] D. Annand, "Re-organizing universities for the information age", *The International Review of Research in Open and Distance Learning*, vol. 8(3), 2007.

[6] C. Latchem, A. Maru and K. Alluri. (2004), *Lifelong learning for farmers (L3Farmers) - A report and recommendations to the Commonwealth of learning on open and distance lifelong learning for smallholder farmers and agricultural communities.* Available: http://www.col.org/progServ/programmes/livelihoods/L3farmers/Pages/default.aspx

[7] D. Birch and M. D. Sankey. "Drivers for and obstacles to the development of interactive multimodal technology-mediated distance higher education courses". *International Journal of Education and Development using ICT*, vol. 4(1), 2008.

[8] COL (2004). *Distance education and open learning in Sub-Saharan Africa: Criteria and conditions for quality and critical success factors.* Available: http://www.col.org/SiteCollectionDocuments/04DEinSSA_CriteriaforQuality.pdf

[9] A. Albirini. (2008). *Wakunga ICT livelihood and education project.* Available: http://ijedict.dec.uwi.edu/viewarticle.php?id=360&layout=html.

[10] E.J. Schmieder. "Communication: The tool to interact with and control your online classroom environment". *International Journal of Instructional Technology and Distance Learning*, Vol. 5(3), 2008.

[11] K. M. R. Rahman, S. Anwar and S. M. Numan, (2008). *Enhancing distant learning through e-mail communication: A case of Bou.* Available: http://tojde.anadolu.edu.tr/tojde30/index.htm

[12] MOESS. (2009). *Educational statistics.* Available: http://www.moess.gov.gh/download.htm;http://www.moess.gov.gh/

[13] Ghana. (2004). *Republic of Ghana – National ICT Policy.* Available: http://www.ict.gov.gh/html/Landscape%20of%20ICT%20Human%20Resources %20&%20Expertise%20.htm

[14] Ghana. (2008). *General News: Ministry to encourage more women to venture into ICT.* Available: http://lcweb2.loc.gov/cgi-bin/query/r?frd/cstdy:@field(DOCID+gh0079).

[15] NCTE (2006). "Statistics on Tertiary Education in Ghana", Ministry of Education

[16] O. A. T. F. Kwapong, "Widening access to tertiary education for women in Ghana through distance education", *Turkish Online Journal of Distance Education-TOJDE*, vol. 8(4), pp. 65 - 79, 2007.

[17] O. A. T. F. Kwapong, *Education at doorsteps of women - Open and distance learning for empowerment of women.* Charleston, Booksurge Publishing. Chapters 1-9, pages 156, 2008.

[18] PCWorld. (2008). *Ghana likely to exceed targets for telephone penetration.* Available: http://www.pcworld.com/businesscenter/article/147145/ghana_likely_to_exceed_targets_for_telephone_penetration.html

[19] K. Kumar. (2008). *Education for a Digital World - Virtual design studios: Solving learning problems in developing countries.* Available: http://www.colfinder.org/materials/Education_for_a_Digital_World/Education_for_a_Digital_World_part1.pdf. *http://74.125.77.132/search?q=cache:uhWAY29iouAJ:www.colfinder.org/materials/Education_for_a_Digital_World/Education_for_a_Digital_World_part1.pdf+Kumar,+K.+Virtual+design+studios:+Solving+learning+problems+in+developing+countries.&cd=1&hl=en&ct=clnk&gl=gh#35*

[20] R. Siaciwena, (2000). *Case studies of non-formal education by distance and open learning.* Available: http://www.col.org/resources/publications/consultancies/Pages/2000-nonFormalEdu.aspx

[21] B. Abdon, R. Raab and S Ninomiya, "E-learning for international agriculture development: Dealing with challenges", *International Journal of Education and Development using ICT*, vol. 4(1), 2008.

[22] K. Alluri and R. Zackmann, (2008). *Technology-mediated open and distance education for agricultural education and improved livelihoods in Sub-Saharan Africa.* Available: http://www.col.org/resources/publications/consultancies/Pages/studyAfrica.aspx

4

Creating Life-Long Learning Scenarios in Virtual Worlds

Ayse Kok
University of Oxford,
UK

1. Introduction

Virtual worlds, such as Second Life, were considered an emerging technology surrounded by hype and growing educational expectations. These immersive world applications have the potential to support multimodal (using different senses) communications between learners; they set up the potential for problem – or challenge-based learning and offer the learner control through exploratory learning experiences (Saunders, 2007). In the recent Metaverse Roadmap Report 2007, Smart et al. (2007) envisage a powerful scenario over the next 20 years when:

> "[virtual worlds] may become primary tools (with video and text secondary) for learning many aspects of history, for acquiring new skills, for job assessment, and for many of our most cost-effective and productive forms of collaboration. (Smart et al., 2007: 7)"

However despite this, much needs to be understood about how to best convert these spaces for learning purposes such as seminars, simulations, modelling, learning activities, networked learning experiences, cybercampuses and streamed lectures (Prasolova-Førland et al., 2006). Otherwise, virtual worlds might be the next misused educational technology. Many educational technologists would agree that poor utilization of the features of a technology will enviably lead to complacency with that technology and probably lead to it being either being abandoned, or worse, massively underutilized (Rappe et. al, 2008). Derived from these statements, the purpose of this chapter is to describe the integration of metadata into Second Life to foster the growth of digital learning spaces.

In an effort to assist European practitioners (individuals as well as the existing communities) that work in the field of education and training educators and are genuinely interested in using Second Life within a Lifelong learning perspective the LLL3D (Life-long Learning in Three Dimensions) project team is promoting opportunities for teachers, trainers, researchers to discover, learn about and utilise different "learning scenarios" for virtual worlds. The learning scenario approach provides access to best practice case studies across formal, non-formal and informal levels and different sectoral activities. The LLL3D project is contributing to the establishment of a European research and practice area in Lifelong Learning, paying attention to the promotion of general awareness of the potential of MUVEs, dissemination and to increasing the acceptance of MUVEs (Multi-user Virtual Environments) as a highly promising cutting-edge technology for online learning. In the framework of the LLL3D project, the working group of different partners have created a set of services and tools in order to provide guidance to all practitioners who are interested in exploring the potential of Second Life for educational purposes, and learning how to use this environment. One of the essential aspects of the project was to integrate a metadata scheme into a grid that supplies researchers and practitioners with a system of existing and possible successful approaches to using MUVEs in learning and teaching. It is our desire that the examination of this project highlights the increasingly recognised importance of structured metadata for the development of learning scenarios and the transferability of this approach to other educational domains and eventually illustrate the possibilities, encourage you and spark ideas of your own.

After providing a general overview of case-based learning, this chapter proceeds with a metadata scheme that can be used for the integration of learning scenarios into MUVE s(Multi-user Virtual Envrionments) such as Second Life (SL). Although not all of the observations are positive on their own, pinning down the details of which educationally significant characteristics pertain to which entities in learning scenarios and which relationships are important is a crucial step in understanding what information is needed to create resource descriptions that meet educational requirements, and how to go about gathering that information.

2. Main definitions

A useful definition of metadata is that used by NISO (2004) "structured information that describes, explains, locates, or otherwise makes it easier to retrieve, use, or manage an information resource". This definition has two important parts. Firstly, it distinguishes metadata from unstructured textual descriptions of a resource. The structuring of metadata normally takes the form of elements with defined semantics to describe specified characteristics of a resource so that machine processing of the information can ocur without a need for computational semantic analysis techniques such as text mining. Secondly, the NISO definition stresses that metadata exists to facilitate a range of activities. Resource discovery is the most visible activity facilitated by metadata, and is the one that seems most closely associated with metadata by most people; however, appropriate management and use of resources are no less important.

Defining what we mean by learning scenarios is more difficult. However, we think that "anything used for teaching and learning" captures the essence of what we are interested in. At this stage, an example for a learning scenario would be “all learning settings that use collaborative learning for learning a language with adult learners only in-world”. This scenario would contain all the real cases that could be found in any MUVE and also those that are only imaginable. Our learning scenario grid consists of 4 dimensions (learning/teaching approaches, discipline/subject, target audience, type of interaction) with 20 sub-values. This grid should not be developed mainly by theoretical considerations but by empirical work, by collecting concrete examples of the classes of learning activities (e.g. an example/practice case for a face-to-face learning approach for language learning).

The following sections will focus on one of the main established metadata standard most relevant to learning scenarios, the IEEE LOM (Learning Object Metadata), and will briefly describe and reflect on its characteristics and applications. This paper will also outline the current work being undertaken on this schema. Finally we look at some of the future challenges facing the field of metadata for learning scenarious regardless of which specific standard one favours.

3. An overview of case-based learning

New standards and specification are more oriented towards describing learning scenarios than just contents. These specifications try to describe all the aspects and the elements more related to the learning process in itself, such as role playing, that is, the second level of description as aforementioned. It seems clear that all this this information needs to be stored in a higher semantic level. Although the metadata schemes may seem too complex for learning scenarios, their flexibility and multilevel description capabilities allow the specification of any learning process ranking from simple educational itineraries to complex processes including collaborative working capabilities. Nevertheless, these metadata schemes lack from a formal description for some of the definitions required for developing learning scenarios in virtual worlds.

Each case in the LLL3D is designed as one or more learning situations trying to reproduce real professional situations where students in one field need to apply practical knowledge for solving a problem, in a virtual world environment. This methodology, which tries to ensure a high quality of the learning process, takes into account all the learning activities that are designed with all the learning goals in mind, in the following structure:

Learning situations

Competences

Learning goals

Activities

Resources

This structure is also partially supported by a case study template with the description of the subject, which is human-readable, but non machine readable. Each case study template has been designed on the basis of the following premises:

- A sound formulation of competences and learning goals;
- Learning activities which are coherent with the competencies to be developed

Within the context of the LLL3D project, we define case-based learning (CBL) as an instructional strategy that uses case study as a resource and the case method as the learning scenario description where learners and instructor interact. The case study template is a descriptive document based on a real situation or event. The case tries to facilitate a balanced relationship between the multidimensional representation of the context, its participants and the the reality of the situation. A case can be used to generate different case studies from a subset of case patterns and a collection of learning resources, following an instructional design approach. Therefore, at the bottom level, we need formal representations for case-based learning scenarios, which involve all the elements in the learning process (learners, activities, competences, resources, etc.) (Barker et al, 2006). The goal is to provide a mechanism for scenario design for learning in virtual worlds according to learner preferences and already acquired competencies and learning goals given by teachers (Barker et al, 2006, Duval et al, 2002). It is necessary to adapt the particular needs of the virtual learning scenario to the specifications available where competencies are used to describe goals and outcomes of learning activities (Barker et al, 2006). In this sense, there is a lack of standards for describing competencies at a rich semantic level because major metadata schemes such as IEEE LOM are not enough to represent all these relationships identified previously.

4. IEEE Learning Object Metadata (LOM)

The IEEE LOM is (currently) an open and internationally recognized two-part standard for the description of "learning objects" and is composed of a conceptual data schema (IEEE, 2002) and an XML binding of that schema (IEEE, 2005). The definition of "learning object" used in the standard is "any entity digital or non-digital that may be used for learning, education, or training", which is comparable to the working definition used above. The LOM data schema specifies which characteristics of a learning object should be described and what vocabularies may be used for these descriptions; it also defines how this data model can be amended by additions or constraints.

The LOM conceptual data schema consists of a hierarchy of elements as shown in figure 1. The first level is composed of nine categories, each of which contains sub-elements; these subelements may be simple elements that contain data, or they may themselves be aggregate elements that contain further sub-elements.

The semantics of LOM elements are determined by their context: they are affected by the parent or container element in the hierarchy and sometimes by other elements in the same container. For example the various description elements (1.4, 5.10, 6.3, 7.2.2, 8.3 and 9.3) each derive their meaning from their parent element: e.g. 5.10, education.description describes educational characteristics of the resource; 6.3 rights.description relates to the terms and conditions of use of the resource, and so on. In addition, description element 9.3 also derives some of its meaning from the value of element 9.1 purpose in the same instance of the classification category element. The data schema also specifies the value space and datatype for each of the simple data elements. The value space defines the restrictions, if any, on the data that can be entered for that element.

For some elements the value space allows any string of Unicode characters to be entered; for other elements entries must be drawn from a declared list (i.e. a controlled vocabulary) or must be in a specified format (e.g. date and language codes). Some element datatypes simply allow a single string of characters to be entered; others comprise two parts as described below:

LangString datatype: where the data entered is likely to be text that would be read directly by a human the data is of a type defined by the LOM as a LangString. LangString items comprise two parts: one providing a language code and the second the Unicode text in the language specified by the code. The same information may be conveyed in multiple languages by repetition of data within an element as several LangStrings.

Vocabulary datatype: where the LOM data schema requires an element to be described by a controlled vocabulary the element will be of the vocabulary datatype. Such elements are composed of Source-Value pairs; the source should contain the name of the list of terms being used and the value should contain the chosen term.

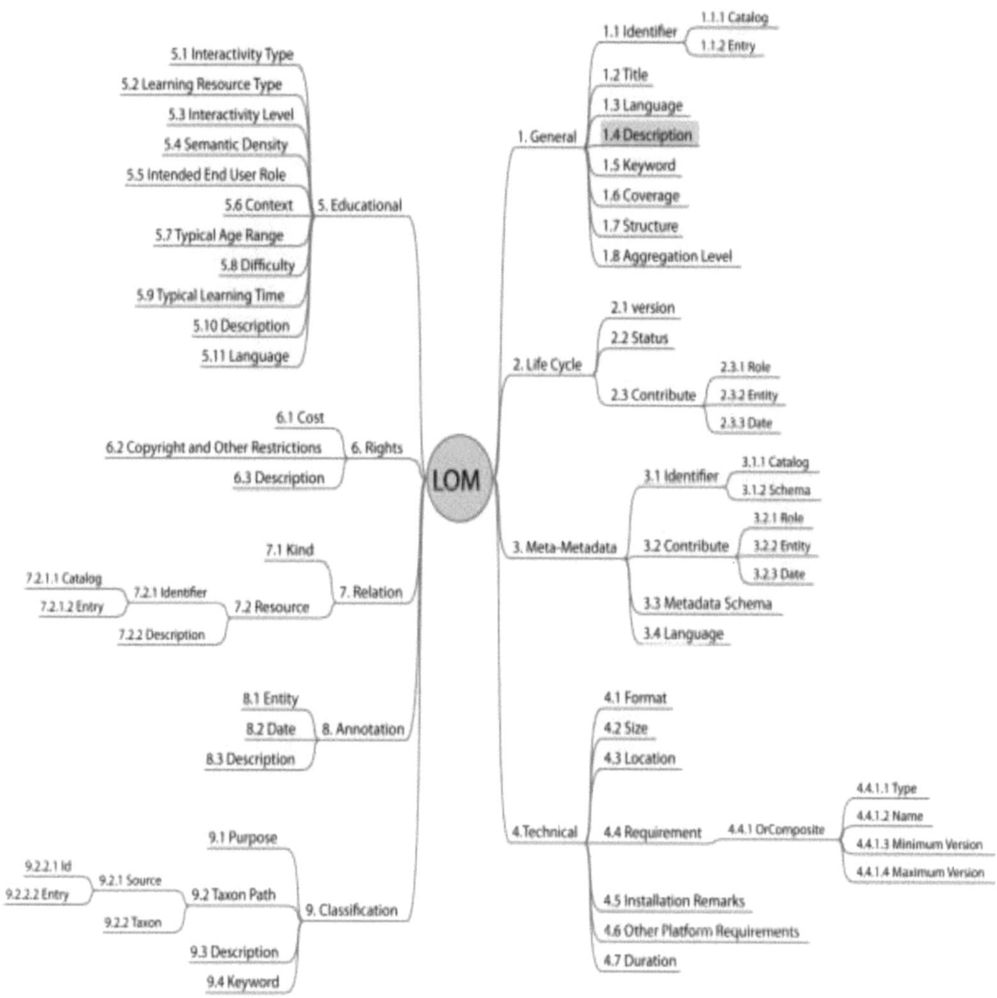

Fig. 1. A schematic representation of the hierarchy of elements in the LOM data model.

DateTime and Duration datatypes: these datatypes allow a date or period of time to be given in a machine-readable format (the value space is based on the ISO 8601:2000 standard; an example of a correctly formatted date is 2003-11-22); a human-readable description may be provided instead of or in addition to the formatted date (e.g. "late 20th century").

While implementing the LOM for the development of our learning scenarios we did not select all the elements in the conceptual data schema. The creation of of our own customized metadata schemes based on LOM allowed us to specify which elements and vocabularies we will be using mostly. While we discarded some elements from the LOM we also supplemented some of the LOM vocabularies with values that are appropriate to the teaching and learning community that we wish to support.

The LOM has been widely implemented by repositories and other learning resource providers, partly as a result of its status as an international standard, and partly through its association with other influential specifications, such as those produced by the IMS Global Learning and by ADL (SCORM)(no date). Examples of repositories and initiatives that have adopted the LOM are the JORUM (no date), a JISC funded repository of teaching and learning materials for UK Further and Higher Education; the European Ariadne foundation (Ariadne, no date); various European SchoolNet projects (European SchoolNet, no date); the Global Learning Objects Brokered Exchange (GLOBE, no date) federation; and many more.

5. The LLL3D metadata scheme

While the influence of the LOM has been considerable in terms of the development of our learning scenarios as it has formed the basis for resource, problematic issues have been noted. To begin with, the LOM conceptual data schema (the stated aim of which is to "ensure that bindings of learning object metadata (LOM) have a high degree of semantic interoperability" IEEE, 2002, section 1.2) is not based on an abstract model shared with other metadata schema. Essentially it is impossible to import elements from other metadata schema, such as Dublin Core or schema developed to support specific resource types such as images or specific features about these learning scenarios such as rights management or preservation. This is especially problematic since it is necessary for the LOM to accommodate general and non-educational characteristics (e.g. technical, rights, accessibility, etc) within the standard data schema rather than importing solutions from other domains.

We believe that IEEE LOM is mostly suitable in general for defining complex learning processes; nevertheless personalization capabilities are clearly insufficient for describing the complex requirements of ach learning scenario. Although LOM can be used for describing the learning scenarios, the description of the elements is not a simple process. Seven main levels of description can be identified. Each learning scenario is described using the following categories (See Appendix A):

General: This category identifies the general information that describes this case as a whole. It poinst towards features such as description, target audience, key words and source materials about the case study.

Life Cycle: This category describes the history and current state of the case and includes information about the status and date of the case study.

Meta-Metadata: This category describes the metadata record itself rather than the case that this record describes. This category describes how the metadata instance can be identified, how, when and with what references. This category is needed to ensure reutilization of learning resources in different contexts. The LOM standard defines a structure for interoperable descriptions of learning scenarios. Metadata for a learning scenario describes relevant characteristics of such scenarios to which applies, pursuing reusability.

Educational: This category describes the key educational or pedagogic characteristics of this case. It describes the different interaction levels and types between users.

Rights: This category describes the intellectual property rights and conditions of use for this case.

Classification: This category describes where this case falls within a particular classification system.

Other: This section provides the information required for a case to be completed. Any extension to include a more comprehensive description of terms is included in the 'other' category.

While LOM supplies the required information that can allow to build up a learning scenario, this extended version that we built up for the LLL3D project offers richer structures and takes into account other important features of a case study such as interests, success, failures and reflections. Furthermore, the inclusion of the category such as 'Other' into our model for educational metadata highlights the importance of some types of metadata that have, perhaps, been regarded as secondary metadata in the past, but which increasingly appear to be of primary importance to education. Indeed, it seems to follow from the working definition of learning materials as "anything used for teaching and learning" that the defining educational characteristics pertain not to the material itself but to the use of that material. We think that the relevant metadata schemas are those describing also the success and failure elements of a particular learning scenario.

We believe that such an extended metadata scheme does not only make a scenario easier to read and use, but also is able to incorporate new services and functionalities when required. For instance, Web 2.0 tools and other collaborative tools can be embedded within the learning scenarios (See Appendix A).

6. Future challenges

As Barker (2008) claimed, metadata requirements for educational resource types and purposes are not well understood and are less well articulated. Pinning down the details of which educationally significant characteristics pertain to which entities in learning scenarios and which relationships are important is a crucial step in understanding what information is needed to create resource descriptions that meet educational requirements, and how to go about gathering that information. For example, information about how a resource is used in a particular scenario,such as what course is it used for and the subject and educational level of that course, may be gathered by course management systems such as VLEs or MLEs, but this information is rarely, if ever, passed back to the system that manages the resource descriptions, i.e. the repository or catalogue.

The rationale for the latter example is that the quality of the search can be enhanced by aggregating the contents of several repositories; hence the service offered, can be enhanced by aggregating information about usage from several systems. As well as being distributed across many systems it is highly likely that the metadata will be heterogeneous: different systems will record different metadata and make it available in different formats. The concepts of the semantic web may be useful in dealing with such distributed heterogeneous metadata but this has yet to have much impact in practice, particularly in the educational domain.

Another observation made during the LLL3D project on metadata requirements for virtual world learning scenarios is that when precise metadata requirements are not well articulated for a particular scenario it is often common practice to provide descriptions in the form of free text. The original rationale for creating structured metadata was to record resource descriptions that were machine readable without some form of computational semantic analysis of free text. Key to this requirement is the assumption that a computer will be taking action on the basis of information conveyed in a resource description (for example selecting an appropriate resource for a given scenario) rather than a human taking this action. However, it is quite possible that in many cases it may be sufficient to find a description of the right thing (in terms of an entity or relationship in a scenario) and to present this in human readable form to the user who can then take action. This reduces the role of metadata to the well-understood role of supporting resource discovery, i.e. allowing the user to find the human readable description.

Also, we think that highly relevant to situations when precise metadata requirements are not widely agreed are approaches such as (social) tagging and folksonomies. These allow users, or groups of users, to apply descriptive keywords to resources without worrying about the details of the precise relationship between the concept expressed by the keyword and the resource. The users also do not necessarily have to agree with others about what term should be used to express the concept,though many of the systems that implement tagging approaches also include mechanisms for identifying commonly used tags for each resource, which can be useful in identifying any emerging consensus about which terms are appropriate.

7. Closing observations

Virtual worlds are becoming true learning scenarios for both blended and pure virtual distance education. Any learning scenario pertaining to virtual worlds should ensire a proper development for each learner, taking into account possible learning activities along with their success and failure aspects. As activities rather than content are crucial for interactive learning in virtual worlds, traditional metadata specifications need to be rethought in order to incorporate this vision.

In many ways the IEEE LOM standard appears to be based on a coherent record describing all aspects of a "learning scenario" and its use, complying with a single standard. We envisaged the description of any characteristics in the learning scenarios related to virtual worlds that was not already included in the LOM conceptual data schema as being achieved by extending that schema. By adopting an approach of "mixing and matching" metadata schema we can move away from this single schema approach and towards one where metadata from different schema can be mixed if they are based on a unifying abstract model.

8. Appendix A – Sample metadata scheme for a virtual world learning scenario

Must (x) Can (o)	Field Name	Description	Datatype	Value
X	**Identifier**	A globally unique label that identifies this case	CharacterString (smallest permitted maximum: 500 char)	5-14-2008-11-KCL
General This category identifies the general information that describes this case as a whole.				
X	**Title**	Name given to this case	LangString (smallest permitted maximum: 1000 char)	Wikitecture
X	**Language**	The primary human language or languages used within this case to communicate to the intended user	CharacterString (smallest permitted maximum: 100 char)	"en-GB"
X	**Description**	A textual description of what the case is about	LangString (smallest permitted maximum: 2000 char)	"Improving Architecture and City Planning by Harnessing the Ideas behind Mass Collaboration, Social Networking, Wikis, Folksonomies, Open Source, Prosumers, Networked Intelligence, Crowd Sourcing, Crowd Wisdom, Smart Mobs, Peer Production, Lightweight Collaboration, Emergent Intelligence, Social Production, Self-Organized Communities, Collective Genius, Loose Networks of Peers, Collaborative Infrastructures, Open platforms, Wiki Workplace, Open Innovation, Horizontal Networks, Collective Intelligence, Global Innovation Networks, Swarm Intelligence, Decentralized Collaboration, Participatory Culture, Web 2.0...and the like."
X	**Keyword**	A keyword or phrase describing the topic of this case	LangString (smallest permitted maximum: 1000 char)	MUVEs, architecture, design, collaboration, wiki, 3D, prototyping
O	**Structure**	Underlying organizational structure of the learning objects involved in this case	atomic: an object that is indivisible (in this context). collection: a set of objects with no specified relationship between them. networked: a set of objects with relationships that are unspecified. hierarchical: a set of objects whose relationships can be represented by a tree structure. linear: a set of objects that are fully ordered. Example: A set of objects that are connected by "previous" and "next" relationships.	Networked

Must (x) Can (o)	Field Name	Description	Datatype	Value
X	**Entity**	The identification of and information about entities (i.e., people, organizations) contributing to this case	CharacterString (smallest permitted maximum: 1000 char)	This project is primarily run by Beyond Distance Research Alliance in Leicester University and is connected to other MUVE projects through the JISC-Emerge U&I programme.
X	**Contact person**	Who? Or organisation?	LangString (smallest permitted maximum: 1000 char)	Scott Chase Email: s.c.chase@strath.ac.uk Phone: +44 141 548 3007 Skype: ScottChase SL: Scooter Gaudio
O	**Contact links**	Others associated to project?	Text	Ryan Schultz and Jon Brouchoud
X	**Target group**	Sector |	Multiple choice from fixed list	☒ HE ☐ CE ☐ AE ☐ VT ☐ IGL
X	**Aggregation level**	The functional granularity of this case	Multiple choice from fixed list	☐ Individual ☐ Session ☐ Course ☒ Institutional
X	**Source materials**	Supporting documents and resources	Text	Studio wikitecture blog: http://studiowikitecture.wordpress.com/ Related site: http://www.virtualsuburbia.com/
Life Cycle This category describes the history and current state of the case.				
X	**Status**	The completion status or condition of this case	Text	Ongoing
X	**Contribute**	Those entities (i.e., people, organizations) that have contributed to the state of this case	Text	Leicester University Beyond Distance Research Alliance School of Archeology & Ancient History London South Bank University
O	**Date**	The start date	DateTime	2008-01-18
Meta-Metadata This category describes the metadata record itself rather than the case that this record describes. This category describes how the metadata instance can be identified, how, when and with what references.				
X	**Metadata Schema**	The name and version of the authoritative specification used to create this metadata instance.	CharacterString (smallest permitted maximum: 30 char)	"LOMv2.0"

Must (x) Can (o)	Field Name	Description	Datatype	Value
X	**Language**	Language of this metadata instance. This is the default language for al LangString values in this metadata instance.	CharacterString (smallest permitted maximum: 100 char)	"en"
X	**Format**	Technical datatypes of all the components of this case	CharacterString (smallest permitted maximum: 500 char)	"video/mpeg", "application/x-toolbook", "text/html"
Educational This category describes the key educational or pedagogic characteristics of this case.				
X	**Interactivity type**	Predominant mode of learning supported by this case. "Active" learning (e.g., learning by doing) is supported by content that directly induces productive action by the learner. An active learning case prompts the learner for semantically meaningful input or for some other kind of productive action or decision. Active documents include simulations, questionnaires, and exercises. "Expositive' learning (e.g., passive learning) occurs when the learner's job mainly consists of absorbing the content exposed to him (generally through text, images or sound). A case displays information but does not prompt the learner for any semantically meaningful input. Expositive documents include essays, video clips, all kinds of graphical material, and hypertext documents. When a case blends the active and expositive interactivity types, then its interactivity type is "mixed".	Text	· simulation (manipulates, controls or enters data or parameters); · hypertext document (reads, navigates); · video (views, rewinds, starts, stops); · audio material (listens, rewinds, starts, stops).
X	**Interactivity level**	The degree of interactivity characterizing this case	Multiple choice from fixed list	☐ very low ☐ low ☐ medium ☒ high ☐ very high
X	**Intended end user role**	Principal users for which this case was designed	Multiple choice from fixed list	☐ Teacher ☐ Author ☒ Learner ☐ Manager
X	**Context**	The principal environment within which case is intended to take place	Text	Higher education

Must (x) Can (o)	Field Name	Description	Datatype	Value
X	**Typical age range**	Age of the typical intended user This data element shall refer to developmental age, if that would be different from chronological age.	LongString (smallest permitted maximum: 1000 char)	20-27
X	**Difficulty**	How hard it is to work with or through this case for the typical intended target audience?	Multiple choice from fixed list	☐ very easy ☐ easy ☒ medium ☐ difficult ☐ very difficult
Rights This category describes the intellectual property rights and conditions of use for this case.				
O	**Copyrights & other restrictions**	Whether copyright or other restrictions apply to this case	Multiple choice from fixed list	☒ Yes ☐ No
Classification This category describes where this case falls within a particular classification system.				
O	**Purpose**	The purpose of classifying this case	Multiple choice from fixed list	☒ Discipline ☐ Idea ☐ Prerequisite ☒ Educational objective ☐ Accessibility ☐ Restrictions ☐ Skill level ☒ Competency
O	**Taxon**	A particular term within a taxonomy. A taxon is a node that has a defined label or term.	CharacterString (smallest permitted maximum: 500 char)	{["12",("en","Architecture")], ["23",("en","Design")], ["34",("en","Collaboration")], ["45",("en","SL-tivities")]}
Other This section provides the information required for a case to be completed.				
X	**Mode**	SL/RL/VL/Blended	Text	Blended
X	**Interest**	Reasons we are interested	Text	"This is a rich case study for looking at collaborative design and how students have been working together inside Second Life."
O	**Successes**	What worked?	Text	
O	**Failures**	What did not?	Text	
O	**Reflections**	What were lessons learn?	Text	
X	**Tools**	Which tools and services have been used?	Text	Project blog: SL Project wiki: SL

9. References

Ariadne Foundation (no date). ARIADNE. Available from <http://www.ariadne-eu.org/> (Accessed January, 15, 2011).

Barker, P. Campbell, L. M., Roberts, A. & Smythe, C. (2006) IMS Meta-data Best Practice Guide for IEEE 1484.12.1-2002 Standard for Learning Object Available from <http://www.imsproject.org/metadata/mdv1p3/imsmd_bestv1p3.html> (Accessed January, 15, 2011).

Barker, P. (2008). Learning Material Application Profile Scoping Study - final report. Tech Rep. Available from <http://www.icbl.hw.ac.uk/lmap/lmapreport.d3.pdf> (Accessed January, 15, 2011).

DCMI (no date). DC-Education application profile. Available from <http://dublincore.org/educationwiki/DC_2dEducation_20Application_20Profile> (Accessed January, 15, 2011).

European SchoolNet (no date) European Schoolnet. Available from http://www.eun.org/ (Accessed January, 15, 2011). (Accessed January, 16, 2011).

GLOBE (no date). Global Learning Objects Brokered Exchange (GLOBE). Available from <http://www.globe-info.org/> (Accessed January, 15, 2011).

Godby, C. J. (2004). What do application profiles reveal about the learning object metadata standard? Ariadne, (41). Available from http://www.ariadne.ac.uk/issue41/godby/ (Accessed January, 16, 2011).

IEEE (2002). 1484.12.1—2002, Standard for Learning Object Metadata. The Institute of Electrical and Electronics Engineers, Inc.

IEEE (2005). 1484.12.3—2005, Standard for eXtensible Markup Language (XML) Binding for Learning Object Metadata data model. The Institute of Electrical and Electronics Engineers, Inc.

IMS (no date, a.) Learning Object Discover and Exchange Project Group Available from <http://www.imsproject.org/lode.html> (Accessed January, 17, 2011).

JORUM (no date). JORUM. Available from <http://www.jorum.ac.uk/> (Accessed January, 15, 2011).

Library of Congress (2007). SRU version 1.2 specifications. Available from <http://www.loc.gov/standards/sru/specs/> (Accessed January, 13, 2011).

Nilsson, M. (2008). Harmonization of metadata standards. Tech. rep. PROLEARN Consortium. Available from <http://ariadne.cs.kuleuven.be/lomi/images/5/52/D4.7-prolearn.pdf (Accessed January, 13, 2011).

NISO (2004). Understanding Metadata. [Online]. Available from: <http://www.niso.org/publications/press/UnderstandingMetadata.pdf> (Accessed January, 13, 2011).

Prasolova-Førland, E, Sourin, A. & Sourina, O. (2006) Cybercampuses: design issues and future directions. Visual Computing, 22(12): 1015–1028.

Rappa, N., Yip, D. & Baey, S. (2008) The role of teacher, student and ICT in enhancing student engagement in muve. *British Journal of Educational Technology*, [Online]. Available from: <http://www3.interscience.wiley.com/journal/117984068/home> (Accessed January, 10, 2011).

Saunders, R.L. (2007) The genesis of a virtual world revisited. International Journal of Web-Based Communities, 3(3): 271–282.

Smart, J., Cascio, J. & Paffendorf, J. (2007) *Metaverse Roadmap 2007: Pathways to the 3D Web. A Cross-industry Public Foresight Project*. [Online]. Available from: <www.metaverseroadmap.org> (Accessed January, 10, 2011).

5

E-Learning Practices Revised: A Compiling Analysis on 38 Countries

Carlos Machado[1] and Ugur Demiray[2]
[1]SOCO - IRMO, VUB (Vrije Universiteit Brussel), Pleinlaan, Brussels,
Faculty of Educational Sciences, Anadolu University, Eskisehir,
[1]Belgium
[2]Turkey

1. Introduction

"New technology makes access possible to a vast range of digital resources. The environment makes some activities possible and constraints others but it does not change the fundamental processes of human learning"

(David Boud, 2001:15)

At the dawn of the 21st century, with the pressure on governments of many developing countries to expand the use of Information Communication Technologies (ICTs) by international business and civic organizations like the World Bank, and as result to reduce the "digital divide", Higher Education Institutions (HEIs) are confronted with the unrelenting difficulty to put into place learning technologies (aka e-learning) in spite of limited funding possibilities and risks posed to educational quality. One can observe the existence of a strong technological and economic push for HEIs to adopt e-learning strategies in many regions of the globe. This is driven, partly, by the requirement of industry for lifelong learning and the influence of a process of global change. Simultaneously, there is a localised attempt to raise awareness among HEIs of the pedagogical issues that underpin good teaching and learning practice, stimulated by the creation of accreditation programs and related topics. These significant drivers of change are often experienced by these HEIs as discordant if not harassing mandates.

Understanding the *momentum* behind the rising focus on educational technologies requires some understanding of the national governments' view of globalization and the assumptions that have been made regarding the relationship between globalization, new technologies, knowledge and development. From a global perspective, now it is a time when authorities start realizing the need to develop effective strategies and anticipate the rising chorus of demands posed by a knowledge-based world, and to take steps which will ease the pressures for access while upholding the national interest of achieving a good quality higher education and responsible stewardship of local and global resources. HEIs in the current paradigm can be regarded as a knowledge server providing knowledge services - that is creating, preserving, transmitting or applying knowledge - in whatever forms is needed by contemporary society (Duderstadt, 1999: 6). Furthermore, built upon government and market pressures, the correlation between education and quality of learning, the shift from teacher-centered to student-centered learning, the move towards lifelong, asynchronous, interactive and collaborative forms of learning, HEIs in developing countries need to be more ready than ever so as to enter this "age of knowledge" imbued by a "culture of learning".

It can be argued that "globalization" has been consolidated by the extraordinary intrusion of new technologies, especially the Internet. Herein, e-Learning has developed greatly as the method of first choice for distance education and we are seeing a convergence between distance and conventional face-to-face education -due to moves by conventional education providers. Governments and corporations look at universities and colleges for innovative uses of new information technologies in teaching and administration, while also expecting that educational institutions will make their students sufficiently technology-literate to participate in a global economy. Policymakers, international organizations, higher education institutions and researchers in the field of education agree that ICT have the potential to stimulate international collaboration, to create flexible learning paths and to open the borders of the university. Most Western countries as well as other nations are increasingly embracing e-learning in education and training, both within their classrooms and in distance education. Arguably the most important consequence of new digital applications for higher education is that they make major innovation in education possible.

Given this background, the present chapter offers an overview of the current state of e-learning in HE from 38 country-based case-studies around the world (Demiray et al., 2010). Due to its relative extension, the original study was distributed in two volumes. The first volume consisted of the country cases of Armenia, Algeria, Belarus, Bulgaria, Egypt, Estonia, Finland, Greece, Jordan, Hungary, Iraq, Iran, Israel, Kazakhstan, Kyrgyzstan, Latvia, Lebanon and Lithuania, and in the second volume the case studies of Macedonia, Moldova, Morocco Norway, Oman, Palestine, Poland, Romania, Russia, Saudi Arabia, Serbia, Slovakia, Slovenia, Sweden, Syria, Tajikistan, Tunisia, Turkey, Ukraine, United Arab Emirates and Uzbekistan were reviewed making an extensive use of eLearning with their general education system and especially in their distance education applications and methods and media.

Herein, this contribution departs from the social dimension of education embedded in the so-called globalization process while providing statistics on the rates of technological penetration in the above-mentioned revised countries. Thereafter, our study continues towards the technological dimension of education considering not only e-learning and mobile or m-learning in isolation but also blended or mixed-mode learning, both in classroom environments and in distance education. To sum up, and based on these 38 case studies, this chapter outlines different clusters in e-learning develoment and it concludes with an indication about where we are heading on a worldwide basis.

2. Globalization and e-learning: *The social dim*ension of education in a knowledge-based society

"There is no greater context for educational change than that of globalization, nor no grander way of conceptualizing what educational change is about"

(Hargreaves, 1998: 322)

In response to the need for education reform in most of the so-called "developing" countries, local governments have called for the reform of education to meet the needs of a twenty-first century which is affected by a globalisation process and knowledge-based requirements. As governments, supra-organisations and civil society devote increasing attention to ways in which globalization can be an efficient tool for more equitable international relations, we come naturally to the question of how HEIs can, with different levels of development, turn the information technology revolution into an instrument that alleviates the digital illiteracy while embracing what Castells (1996) defined as the "network society".

In most countries around the world, a new social and economic paradigm has restructured the traditional dimensions of time and space within which we live, work and interact. The industrial revolution of the 19th century and the scientific revolution of the 20th century have prepared the necessary conditions for the rise of what we now today as a knowledge-based economy and society. This concept is directly intertwined with the appearance of the information society. This is a metaphor that has been used as a reaction to the evolution of globalisation in the international context, enhanced by the development of ICTs and the social and technological changes produced by these new technologies. These changes have influenced social theorists in understanding contemporary times very much in terms of the information society, rather than postmodern (Lyotard, 1984) or risk societies (Beck, 1992).

Over the last decades, from policy-makers such as Al Gore to sociologists like Anthony Giddens or management scientists like Peter Drucker, the claim has been made that we are living in an age in which society is organised around information and knowledge (Sampler, 1998). It is argued that information has been the starting point of new industrial and production processes (Castells, 1996:60-65). The shift to the informational age has been sustained by accelerated technological innovations during the second half of the twentieth century, mostly in the areas of computing systems and telecommunications. Manufacturing organizations, for example, have adopted an information-based strategy that incorporates information technology (IT) to maintain and deliver information required for knowing what, when, and how to make economical products. Correspondingly, information-based processes, placed within the larger context of the "new economy", are better understood as a development of the "informational age", global in reach, sustained by social and financial networks, and enabled by ICTs. Information then is viewed as a resource to improve commercial and industrial competitiveness and productivity: using information within and between organisations to improve systems and processes, management techniques and foster innovation (Moore, 1998). Ultimately the objective has been to shift from labour-intensive to knowledge-intensive operations (Grantham & Tsekouras, 2004).

The exchange of knowledge and information between societies —primarily through trade, the displacement of persons and later the transmission of written information— has played a major role in the process of producing, with fewer inputs, more goods and services of better quality (Sagasti, 2001). It is generally accepted that advantages in technological competences lead to a better performance in innovation, international competitiveness and trade (Archibugi and Michie, 1998) and many pieces of evidence that attest the importance of technological change as a source of economic growth (Rosenberg, 1972; Freeman & Soete, 1997; Brian Arthur, 2009). The accent herein is on the emergence of the "new economy" and its effects in terms of growth, trade and investment across all the sectors making use of the new ICTs. While information has been considered an important source for the advancement of humanity and of individuals, the difference today is that information is now viewed as a basic raw material and consumed at an enormous scale in socio-economic processes, and thus having important competitive value.

Already in 2001 McConnell International established a map based on the impact and innovation of all sustainable programs, reforms, and policies leading to an increase of connectivity, e-leadership, information security, human capital, and e-business climate. Their studies showed which countries were moving towards a knowledge-based society with actions that have the potential to make a real difference in their ability to participate in the digital economy. Today's country leaders in impact and innovation are the places where business opportunities are more likely to develop in the short-term.

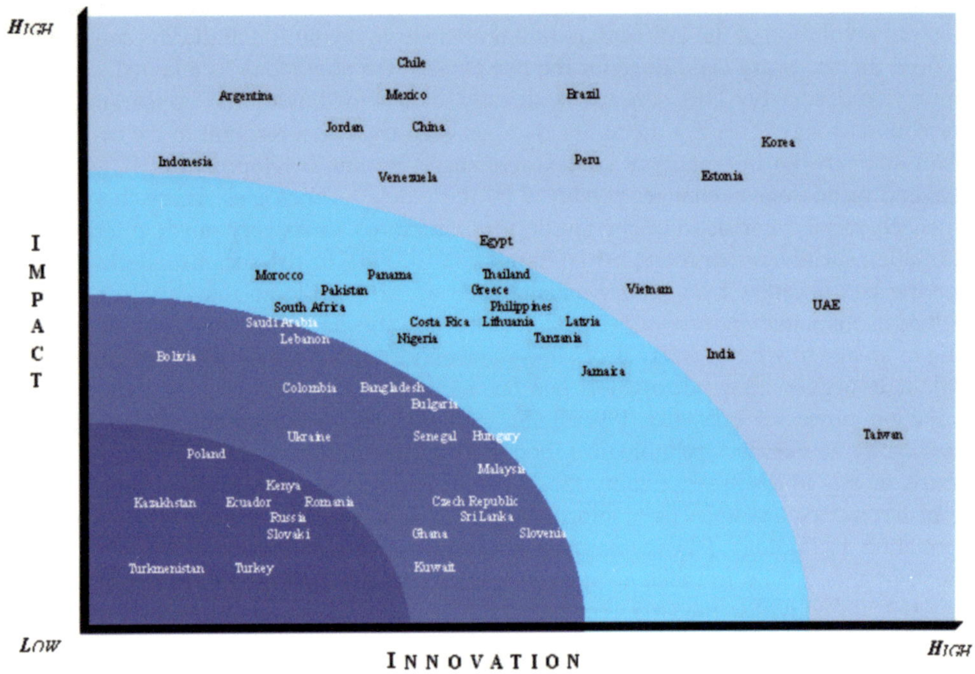

Source: McConnell Intl, 2001

Fig. 1. Impact and innovation in developing countries.

With the growth of the World Wide Web (WWW) and the explosion of the Internet into popular culture, many lecturers and academic departments have started to exploit the potential of these technologies and sophisticated network infrastructures are provided to enhance teaching and learning. The Internet standards allow anyone to access web-based content - at any time, from any location. Increasing numbers of teaching staff are beginning to put their lecture notes and reading lists on the web for students to browse and they are starting to communicate with students via e-mail. Some HEIs facilitate the publication of course outlines on departmental websites. Many international donors are providing the tools - and financial means - to support university libraries that have web-interfaces for searching, checking availability and reserving books. These simple innovations are only the beginning and it is not surprising that sooner or later they will acquire state-of-the-art technology (e.g. conferencing software used in to create online discussion groups amongst students) that enhances the learning process. Thus, the emergence of ICTs is coupled with innovation in education and new forms of teaching and learning in the sense that helps these countries to make the transition from teaching-centered to student-centered models of education. The role of technology in education is ingrained in literature (e.g. Masood, 2004; Roblyer, 2005; Musawi, 2011).

The philosophy of eLearning focuses on the individual learner although it recognizes that most learning is social. In the past training has organized itself much for the convenience and needs of instructors, institutions, and bureaucracies. Now eLearning is the convergence learning and networks, the Internet. New university systems are being developed to new global needs (Utsumi-Varis-Knight-Method-Pelton, 2001). The experience and critical function of the traditional universities is central in the efforts to create new eLearning environments. There are an increasing number of university networks of this kind all over the world, and the use of computers in the learning process, access to the Internet by students as a vehicle for self-directed learning, educational broadcasting and video-conferencing are all being stepped by (Dias, 1998: 370). Dias also reminds that higher education has to aim at quality and that internal and external evaluation methods should be more generally applied, thereby enabling it to be accountable to society. Higher education institutions are expected to train citizens capable of thinking clearly and critically, analyzing problems, making choices and shouldering their responsibilities. Thus the ethical role of universities is becoming every day more prominent.

Higher education cannot, however, be visualized any longer in purely national or regional terms. Future graduates have to be in a position to take up the complex challenges of globalization and rise to the opportunities of the international labor market. The equitable transfer of knowledge and the mobility of students, teachers and researchers, and with also the mobility of learning environments with the eLearning applications are crucial to the future of peace in the world. History shows that revolutionary changes do not take off without widespread adoption of common standards. For electricity, this was the standardization of voltage and plugs; for railways, the standard gauge of the tracks; and for the Internet, the common standards of TCP/IP, HTTP, and HTML. Common standards for metadata, learning objects, and learning architecture are mandatory for similar success of the knowledge economy. The work to create such standards for learning objects and related standards has been going on around the world for the past few years (http://www.learnativity.com/standards/htm retrieved on, 10 July 2009).

Learning technology standards are critical because they will help us to answer the following issue clusters:

- How will we mix and match content from multiple sources?
- How do we develop interchangeable content that can be reused, assembled, and disassembled quickly and easily?
- How do we ensure that we are not trapped by a vendor´s proprietary learning technology?
- How do we ensure that our learning technology investments are wise and risk adverse?

Whether it is the creation of content libraries, or learning management systems, accredited standards will reduce the risk of making large investments in learning technologies because systems will be able to work together like never before. Accredited standards assure that the investment in time and intellectual capital can move from one system to the next.

Our study on 38 case studies contains massive and impressive evidence of the progress of global e-learning. The emerging of life-long learning and new professional and vocational competencies as well as the globalization of society and the rise of a knowledge-based economy have raised expectations upon higher education institutions and related services to the society. Governments and corporations look to universities and colleges for innovative uses of new information technologies in teaching and administration, while also expecting that educational institutions will make their students sufficiently technology-literate to participate in a global economy. The vision of the new global learning emphasizes more than before the role of market forces in shaping the institution, the need to respond to users´ needs, and the need to deliver knowledge continuously through distance learning and lifelong learning. However, the vast majority of universities are as well as the public and private organizations they work with are unprepared to reorganize themselves to address these new demands. Government support, programs of international organizations and initiatives of private companies are the channels through which e-learning is promoted in the country.

Countries	Government support	Programs of international organizations	Initiatives of private companies	Internet penetration rate in 2007 (%)
Algeria	+	+	+	9.5
Armenia	+	–	–	6.0
Belarus	+	–	–	29.0
Bulgaria	+	+	+	33.6
Egypt, Arab Rep.	+	+	–	14.8
Estonia	+	+	+	66.2
Finland	+	+	+	80.7
Greece	+	+	+	35.6
Hungary	+	+	+	53.2
Iran, Islamic Rep.	–	–	+	18.3
Iraq	+	+	–	0.9
Israel	+	+	+	46.5
Jordan	–	+	+	20.9
Kazakhstan	+	+	-	4.0
Kyrgyz Republic	+	+	+	14.3
Latvia	–	+	+	59.0
Lebanon	+	+	+	18.7
Lithuania	+	+	+	49.6
Macedonia	–	+	–	36.3
Moldova	–	–	–	20.5
Morocco	+	+	+	21.1
Norway	+	+	+	87.1
Oman	+	+	+	16.7
Palestine	+	+	+	14.8
Poland	+	+	+	48.6

Countries	Government support	Programs of international organizations	Initiatives of private companies	Internet penetration rate in 2007 (%)
Romania	+	+	+	28.2
Russian Federation	+	+	+	24.6
Saudi Arabia	+	–	+	26.3
Serbia	+	+	+	44.2
Slovak Republic	+	+	+	61.8
Slovenia	+	+	+	56.5
Sweden	+	+	+	82.1
Syrian Arab Republic	+	+	–	17.3
Tajikistan	+	+	–	7.2
Tunisia	+	+	–	16.8
Turkey	+	+	+	28.6
Ukraine	+	+	–	13.8
United Arab Emirates	+	+	+	51.8
Uzbekistan	+	+	–	7.5

Table 1. How and why ICT is working its way into learning in the various countries, its potential, and how its integration and broader use may be promoted.

A true revolution in e-learning requires high-speed access and high internet penetration rates to the World Wide Web, and the flexibility to offer a variety of media. The new services are profoundly changing the professional research and educational work when it is possible to retrieve and save articles and other materials, search all kinds of information from images and animation to texts, and receive e-mail alerts and have access to sources not conceivable before. The development of communication and information technologies makes it possible for distance teaching institutions to strengthen their position in the educational landscape. They also pave the way for lifelong education for all and at the same time are spreading the traditional universities, more and more of which use distance teaching methods in their activities, thereby making the distinction between the two types of institutions virtually meaningless. Therefore, the basic question for universities is - and has always been - what kind of people we want to have as our leaders-capable of taking responsibility of the future, environment and development.

The penetration rate on the graph underneath shows the potential of the country to further develop e-learning activities.

Other studies (Gong et al., 2007; Lee-Kelly and James, 2005) suggest that the increase in the internet penetration rate is also influenced by non-income factors such as culture and the attitude of the government towards new technologies.

Regarding the cultural and legal environment of the countriess analysed figure 3 shows another three components of the overall readiness index. The category of Social and Cultural environment, with 15% weight in the overall score, is the average of educational level, internet literacy, innovation growth and entrepreneurship skills. In other words, it demonstrates the readiness level and ability of the local population to meet the requirement

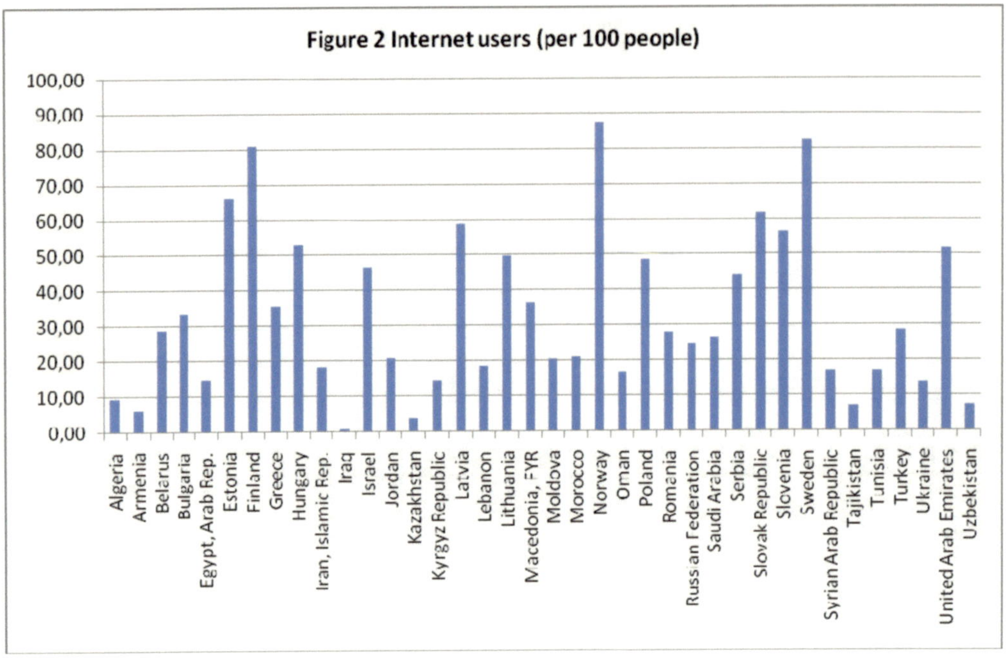

Fig. 2. Internet penetration and usage rates (internet users) among 38 countries in study of Demiray et al. Data available for 2007.

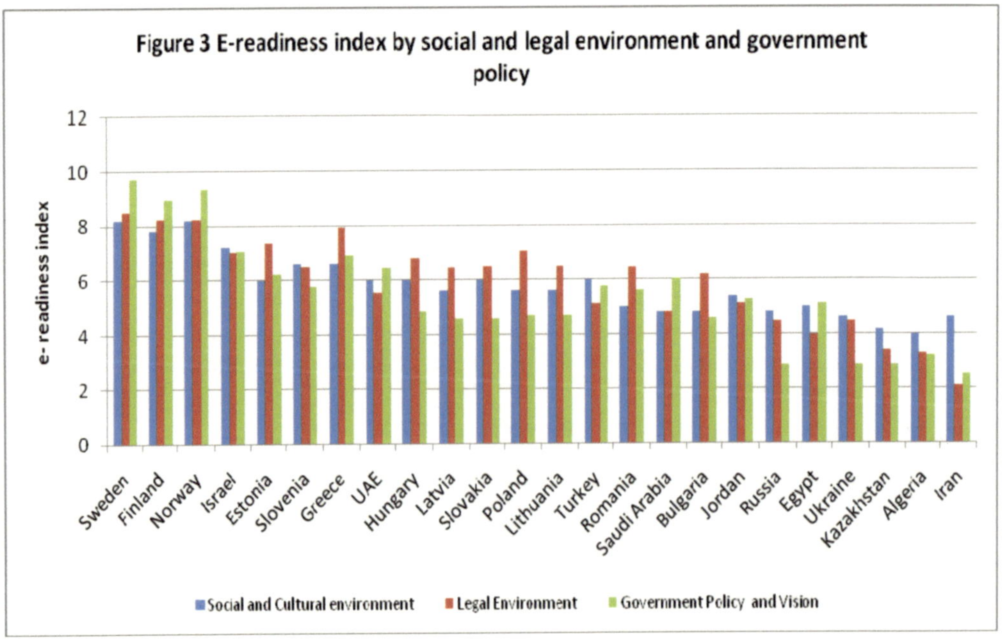

Fig. 3.

of to the new IT environment. Legal Environment category, which accounts for 10% of the overall score, shows the degree of censorship and the coverage for internet laws. Government Policy and Vision (15%) shows the level of commitment of the local governments to enhance the supply of e-government services.

Here the examples of Iran and Egypt can demonstrate different attitude to e-development in the countries with similar social and cultural background. Both countries have a similar level of IT literacy of the population given by social and cultural environment variable. While these countries are Islamic nations, their government visions of e–development differ significantly. For example, the government policy and legal environment in Egypt are more conducive for the development of e-technologies and e-learning than in Iran. The importance of the government policy regarding e-development can also be seen in the example of the front-runners such as Sweden, Finland and Norway. They all have significantly higher scores of the government policy and vision compared to other countries. Integrated efforts from leaders in academic, educational, and technological fields get the most out of institutional and national, regional or local government coordination and support. This could take forms of committees to share ideas, exchange experiences, set plans and strategies, and make decisions on using technology for academic and administrative purposes.

UNeGovDD (The United Nations E-Government Development Database) provides two fundamental measures of internet development across the nations. The first index is E-Participation index. It captures the willingness of citizens to use internet services to communicate with the public agencies and the sum of the state programs aimed at promoting the participation of people in the governance activities. High e-participation index implies that citizens are actively participating in the public and social areas through IT resources. In particular, e-participation assesses the level of access of the citizens to e-information, the development of e-consultation services and growth of the number of participants. The second is E-Government index. It is the weighted average of three indices: Human Capital index, Online Services index and Infrastructure index. Human capital index measures the overall literacy rate, which includes adult literacy rate and the combined primary, secondary and gross enrolment ratio. Online Services index shows the level of the online transactions and communications that people engage in. Infrastructure index comprises the ratios such as the internet penetration rate, the number of computers per 1000 persons, etc.

Figure 4 demonstrates that the availability of facilities do not always ensure the high participation ratio of citizens. For example, Estonia and Finland have similar e-government indices: 0.76 and 0.75 respectively (Table 8). However, the participation ratio in Estonia is 0.73 against only 0.27 in Finland. The participation of citizens is determined by their political activeness and the e-government facilities serve to increase the efficiency of participation.

It can be argued that the development of e-learning is related to a country's progression from survival values to those of self-actualisation - in terms of Maslow's hierarchy of needs. This parallels the shift from early-industrial society to the post-industrial society, and is clearly partly related to economic development. Nations need a critical level of economic and social development before they can afford to integrate new technologies in daily life, but it is also true that leaders need to be motivated to build the infrastructure needed for e-learning. The following table presents the most common constraints observed in the 38 countries of our study.

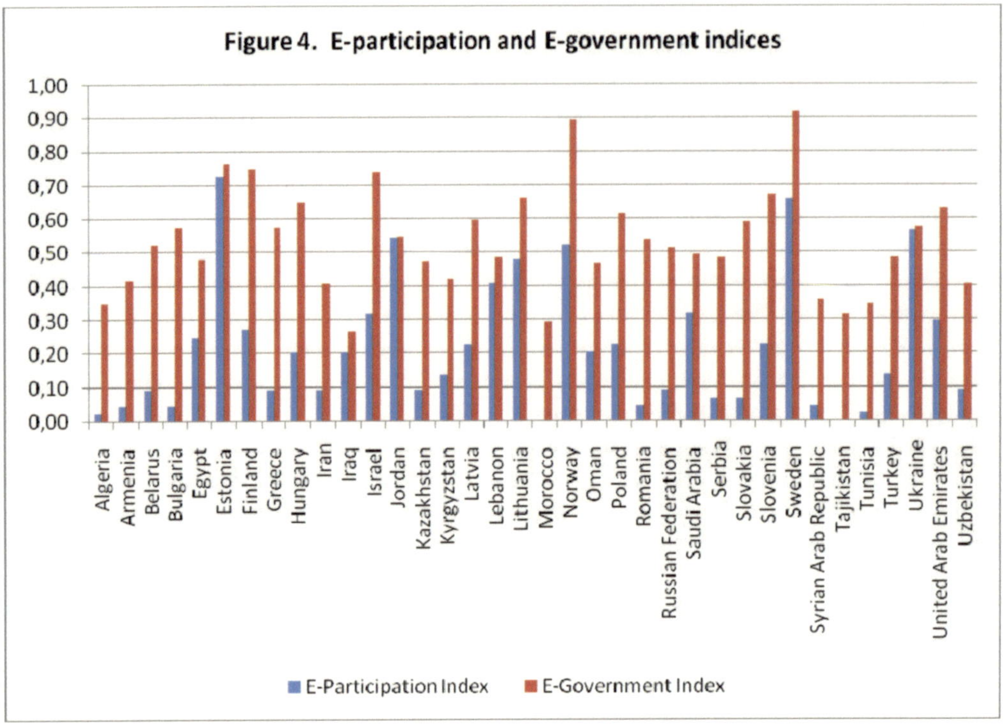

Source: UNeGovDD (2008)

Fig. 4.

Constraints on e-learning development	Countries
High costs	Algeria, Iran, Kazakhstan, Moldova, Morocco, Serbia, Slovak Republic, Tunisia, Ukraine
Weak state support, lack of investment, outdated technologies, an insignificant implication on the education system	Armenia, Belarus, Hungary, Iran, Kyrgyz Republic, Lebanon, Macedonia, Moldova, Serbia, Slovak Republic, Syrian Arab Republic, Tajikistan, Ukraine, Uzbekistan
Lack of adequate training for teachers	Algeria, Armenia, Bulgaria, Egypt, Hungary, Jordan, Kazakhstan, Kyrgyz Republic, Latvia, Lebanon, Macedonia, Moldova, Serbia, Syrian Arab Republic, Tajikistan, Tunisia, Uzbekistan
Strict state control over IT sector	Belarus, Syrian Arab Republic
Poor reputation of e-learning amongst prospective employers	All countries, except for Estonia, Finland, Israel, Lithuania, Norway, Poland, Romania, Sweden
Lack of the quality assurance in e-learning institutions	All countries, except for Estonia, Finland, Israel, Lithuania, Norway, Poland, Romania, Sweden
Lack of adequate government legislation	All countries, except for Estonia, Finland, Israel, Lithuania, Norway, Poland, Romania, Sweden

Table 2. Constrains on e-learning development.

Another factor to be considered in the development of e-learning in particular and ICT in general is related to intercultural competence. With the steep rise of multiculturalism, there is an increasing need for people to be able to deal effectively and competently with the diversity of race, culture and ethnicity. In general terms, one's ability to deal effectively and appropriately with diversity is referred to as intercultural competence - also defined as multicultural competence or cross-cultural competence. Traditionally speaking intercultural competence or competence in general is often divided into three main components:

- Knowledge: also known as cognitive factors
- Motivation: also known as attitude
- Skills: also known as competence in social relations and communication behavior

Becoming inter-culturally competent demands a wide range of culture-general knowledge from peoples' behavioral repertoires and people are also required to apply that knowledge to the culture that they interact with. People also have to be emotionally and skillfully responsive with various ranges of choices in order to act competently depending on the limitations of any given situation. They also have to have extensive intercultural interaction experiences and have the know-how of adjusting to different patterns of thinking and behaving. There is a process of internationalization of curriculum in universities that should lead to develop inter-cultural skills.

It is evident that the common global challenges are leading to an intensified regional and international cooperation also in the field of skills. Good example of this is the growing emphasis on skills and competencies in the common policy of the European Union. Another example is the intensified global cooperation within the framework of skills competitions. International skills competitions offer an excellent tool for the analysis of the common future needs of industry and societies all over the world, for the determination of the key skills needed in different trades, for cooperation between skills and working life and for improving the quality of for skills by transferring good practices and new innovations and by giving a possibility to international benchmarking.

There are other majors' threats for development of working-life skills that are not bound to any continent or historical tradition but globally equip students with skills that enable them to build up their own future and life in global and multicultural environment. Some educational institutes are already expanding out of the geographical orders to global actors on the field when utilizing e-learning and possibilities of ICT. Learning community and tutors may be distributed in various countries and cultures. The trend is also towards examinations and qualifications of skills that are internationally recognized.

3. Education and new technologies: Where 38 countries stand today

Today's learning and education technology is developing with overwhelmingly speed. It is also changing the way faculty teaches and students learn. It becomes a critical complement to the educational experience, opening more opportunities for the learner than can be encompassed by physical campuses. Just recently eLearning technology applications are changing its structure by integrating new discussion technologies such as mLearning, IPTV (tLearning) and uLearning. Consequently, Yang & Yuen (2010) indicate that learning is dramatically and continuously influenced by information and communication technology (ICT). There is no doubt that ICTs keeps bringing excitement in to learning and communication. Multimedia on the internet, telecommunications, wireless applications, mobile devices, social network software, Web 2.0 etc are radically redefining the way people obtain information and the way to learn (Yang & Yuen 2010, xxiv).

E-Learning has developed greatly as the method of first choice for distance education and we are seeing a convergence between distance and conventional face-to-face education -due to moves by conventional education providers. Conventional universities and schools throughout the world are pro-actively adopting distance learning technologies not only to reach the unreached providing wider openness and access but notably as augmentation for their current on-campus students. The use of computers in education can be classified into four types; -computer-assisted instruction (CAI), computer-managed instruction (CMI), computer-based multimedia (CBM), and computer-mediated communication (CMC). The fourth CMC involves computer-to-computer transactions including email, is sometimes referred to as online learning, and is commonly referred to as 'e-learning' (Kawachi, 2005; Kawachi 2008a).

Under e-learning, educational interactivity can be among the institution(s), tutor(s), and student(s), for both academic purposes as storage, delivery and retrieval of content, and non-academic purposes as administration and counseling support. Library resources support services are the most common CMI use of computers. Asynchronous emailing appears to be the most common CMC use. In highly developed centers of excellence such as in Hong Kong, Japan, or Korea, synchronous text-chat is common, and this occasionally becomes multimedia with the addition of digital graphics and even video transmissions along with plain text. In rural developing countries, computers have widely entered into classrooms in the past few years, though as recently as two years ago, for example in India, schools were despondent with their computers in the room and no educational interactivity taking place.

One reason why more educationally effective use cannot be made of these computers in the classrooms is the lack of regional infrastructure- such as no internet provision and inadequate or unreliable connectivity (regarding telephonic transmission rate or very low

Extent and nature of e-learning and blended learning provision	Countries
All educational institutions provide e-learning and blended learning facilities	Estonia, Finland, Lithuania, Norway, Oman, Poland, Romania, Saudi Arabia, Sweden
e-learning and blended learning are limited to a few universities (private or public)	Algeria, Armenia, Bulgaria, Egypt, Greece, Hungary, Iran, Iraq, Israel, Jordan, Kazakhstan, Kyrgyz Republic, Latvia, Lebanon, Macedonia, Moldova, Morocco, Palestine, Russia, Serbia, Slovak Republic, Slovenia, Syrian Arab Republic, Tunisia, Turkey, Ukraine, United Arab Emirates
There are no distance learning practices	Belarus, Tajikistan, Uzbekistan
Pure form of e-learning is available *	Estonia, Finland, Lithuania, Norway, Palestine, Poland, Romania, Saudi Arabia, Sweden

*- there is no requirement to attend classes, but students may be required to take the final exam face to face.

Table 3. The extent and nature of e-learning and blended learning provision.

bandwidth) -preventing the use of multimedia and e-learning. These difficulties in connectivity and infrastructure- seen in many of the countries reviewed in this book - could be circumvented by the use of CD-hybrids.

E-Learning is generally taken to mean learning that has utilized electronic means of information and knowledge management in a wide sense, and social constructivist learning through computer-mediated communications in a virtual space in a narrow sense. E-learning is a relatively new term, and derives from the development of alliances and consortia consisting of corporate businesses and education providers emerging at around 1995 (Jegede, 2001, p.75). This development has occurred through the internet and has brought internationalization through sharing of knowledge. It has also brought globalization and different cultures into juxtaposition, and into superimposition. Now conventional face-to-face institutions are opting to utilize e-learning and open learning values in the classroom.

The developed chart below, show us the latest trends of technology. Herein, education institutions are likely to adopt their education or material producing strategies according to newest technologies indicated in chart 1 underneath.

Policymakers, international organizations, higher education institutions and researchers in the field of education agree that ICTs have the potential to stimulate international collaboration, to create flexible learning paths and to open the borders of the university. Throughout the last decade, numerous initiatives have been set up to experiment with the establishment of ICT-enhanced activities, under various frameworks and to varying degrees of success. The higher education area is a very complex world with a diverse list of providers; these include traditional universities, distance education providers, public and private institutions, associations and consortia. (Schreurs, 2010:7). Through an extensive study of 38 countries all over the world (mainly from Europe, Russia and former soviet republics, Middle East and North Africa) we could perceive the different levels of development and key factors for the success or failure of elearning and other technologies for education.

On top of the scale we could find three Nordic countries – Finland, Norway and Sweden. Although Sir John Daniel (in Demiray 2010: lii) notes that 'the vast majority of universities, as well as the public and private organizations they work with are unprepared to reorganize themselves to address these new demands', this observation certainly does not apply to the three countries above mentioned. For the middle group of countries, in which we include Bulgaria, Egypt, Greece, Jordan, Kuwait, Latvia, Lebanon, Macedonia, Poland, Romania, Russia, Serbia, Slovakia, Slovenia, Ukraine and the United Arab Emirates, the example of Serbia will serve to illustrate a point for contention. If among the 38 countries studied, the three Nordic countries are the state-of-the-art for eLearning, Serbia must qualify as the member of the class making the most rapid progress. Indeed, Serbia's situation points up the obvious correlation between eLearning development and economic growth. After a difficult period of turbulence following the break-up of former Yugoslavia and the Balkan wars of the 1990s, Serbia is now the fastest growing economy in its region and has the most rapid growth in Internet use (25% annually since 2000) in Europe.

Figure 5 demonstrate that there is an upward trend in the link between growth and internet penetration rates (both usage rates and fixed broadband). The statistical calculations show that as income increases by $1000, the share of internet users increases nearly by 2 % and the share of fixed broadband connections by 1 %. Subsequently, the internet penetration rates are higher in the high-income countries. Norway, Finland, Sweden are the front-runners in

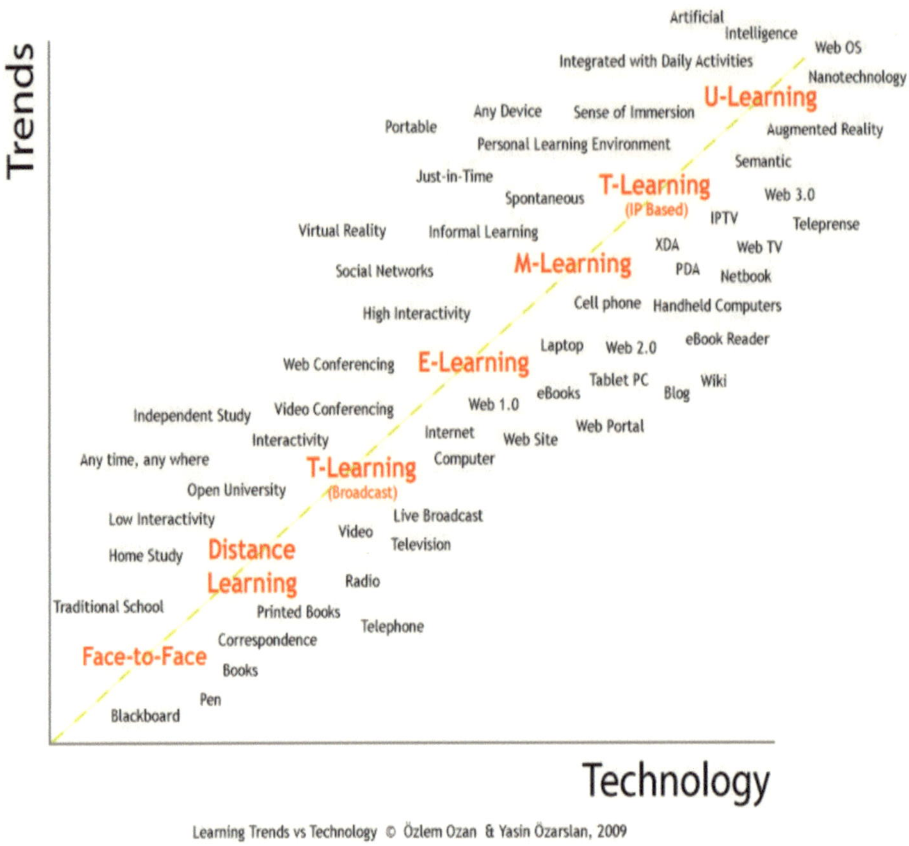

Source: Yamamoto, G. T., Ozan, O & Demiray, U. (2010).

Fig. 5.

our sample, followed by the Central and Eastern European nations. However, income level is not the only determinant of the internet development. For example, the United Arab Emirates, while having income level similar to the countries in the Western Europe, nevertheless, has achieved a moderate success in the internet growth.

Not only Western countries but also non-Western nations are increasingly embracing e-learning in education and training, both within their classrooms and in distance education. E-transformation has been much slower in the education systems of the Eastern Europe, Nordic, Turkic, Middle East, Arab and North African countries. It is therefore considered timely to conduct an inquiry into the ways and extent of e-learning in these countries, the factors driving and constraining such developments, and how progress might be further encouraged. Searching the literature, it is possible to find reports, accounts, research findings and conference presentations on e-learning in these countries but many of these are in languages other than English.

As with the case of the Nordic countries, Serbia sees the development of eLearning in the perspectives of lifelong learning and the empowerment all citizens, although neither perspective seems as deeply embedded in national policies as in Finland. Serbia has, however, articulated policies for integrating ICT into research and development as well as into open and distance learning. On the other hand, it has not been as proactive as Finland in creating new virtual networked initiatives, leaving it to institutions to expand eLearning within government policy. Unfortunately, satisfying the associated procedural requirements can be quite cumbersome, with the result that prestigious academic units such as the Faculty of Economics at the University of Belgrade appear to be more successful at navigating through their courses than newer start-ups. Even if a sound policy framework is in place, there is a need for real government support in making Serbia a knowledge society, contributing with different measures to a widespread pace of Internet penetration through all layers of society.

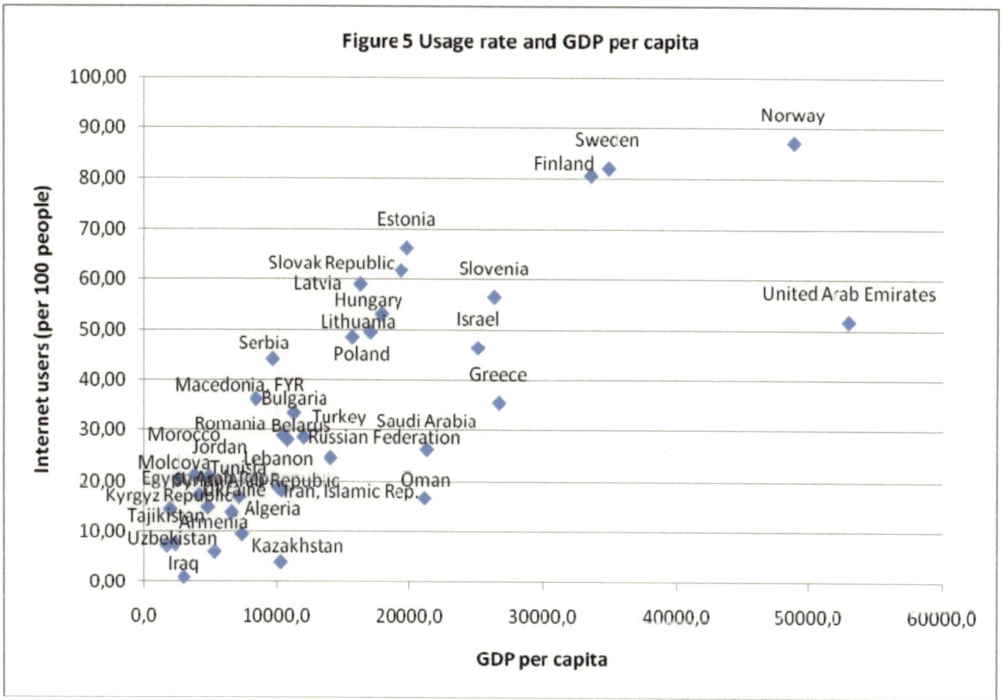

Fig. 6.

It is hard to be as optimistic about the last group of countries reviewed in our study in which we have placed Algeria, Belarus, Iran, Iraq, Kazakhstan, Kyrgyzstan, Moldova, Morocco, Oman, Saudi Arabia, Syria, Tajikistan, Tunisia and Uzbekistan. Taking Tajikistan as an extreme example of countries where the use of ICTs in general and of eLearning in particular, remains more in the domain of aspiration than reality at the present time. Although the government of Tajikistan has made various declarations of intention about ICTs in education, most of the measures to implement them have been *ad hoc*, 'chaotic and unsustainable'. Tajikistan suffers from a direct lack of capacity in all areas. It was the poorest of the republics of the former Soviet Union and had the least developed telecommunications infrastructure.

Since the five-year civil war that followed the break-up of the Soviet Union ended in 1998, economic growth has been rapid, but from a very low base. Individual telephone ownership is only 38 per 1,000 and not more than 1% of the populations are Internet users. The authors of the Tajikistan review suggest that eLearning will only develop with the help of international donors, but even for that to happen the country will need major reforms. There is very little capacity in government, even if there were the will, to plan and implement these reforms and endemic corruption discourages local initiatives. The need for Distance education is understood, but so far this consists mostly of cross-border programmes from Russia that contribute nothing to local institutional capacity building.

The illustrations that were given of the state of eLearning in these three exemplar countries demonstrate two points. First, the state of development of education varies greatly even between neighboring countries. Second, looking at education systems through the development of eLearning, as our study does, is a powerful way of assessing their readiness for change and development - in short their fitness for purpose in a global 21st century.

4. Future steps in e-learning practices in the World

Hitherto, our study on 38 countries examined how and why ICT is working its way into learning in the various countries, its potential, and how its integration and broader use may be promoted. It took into account factors that could constraint e-learning development, government initiatives that promote ICT literacy and the use of e-learning in education and training, extent and nature of e-learning and blended learning provision, some of the cultural and pedagogical implications of e-learning and policy-making and organizational dimensions of e-learning.

A useful instrument to analyse the level of technological development of every country is the e-readiness index which was originated by the intent to provide a unified framework to evaluate breadth and depth of the so-called 'digital divide' between more and less developed or developing countries. Chart 2 shows that Western European region has the advanced scores across all e-readiness indexes. Central and Eastern Europe has a better performance than North Africa and Middle East and Central Asia. North Africa and Middle East have more progress with the online services, participation and infrastructure indices compared to the countries of the Central Asia. On the other hand, the Central Asia region has a higher score of human capital, which measures the educational background but a very low score in terms of infrastructure, e-government and e-participation.

Many countries including most reviewed generally hold onto an apprentice model and experiential learning through a cooperative process. Even with e-learning technology, the apprentice model is still employed. Internationalization through e-learning has brought the two processes of collaborative learning and cooperative learning into the same forum. In many of these countries, the social economics has meant a student who is busy e-learning is more isolated from his or her surrounding culture, than a student for example in London where the surroundings may be all high technology, conducive, motivating, encouraging and accepting of a person engaging e-learning. In rural developing countries, it is easy to imagine that the student is not only physically alone but psychologically and emotionally as well -without social infrastructure supporting e-learning. Thus, computers and multimedia are not simply instruments for the student but provide a total environment for learning.

E-Learning offers many opportunities for individuals and institutions all over the world. The reader is referred to Kawachi (2005) for comparative review of e-learning in Bangladesh, (mainland) China, Hong Kong (China), India, Indonesia, Iran, Japan, Korea, Malaysia, Pakistan, the Philippines, Singapore, Sri Lanka, Thailand, and Vietnam. Individuals can access to education they need almost anytime and anywhere they are ready to. Institutions are able to provide more cost-effective training to their employees. E-learning context is very important. It is common to find educators who perceive e-learning as internet-only education that encourages a static and content-focused series of text pages on screen. Others envisage the shallow and random online messages that are typical of a social real-time chat session, and wonder how that type of communication could add any value to academic discourse. Some may have experienced e-learning done poorly, and extrapolate their experience into a negative impression of all e-learning.

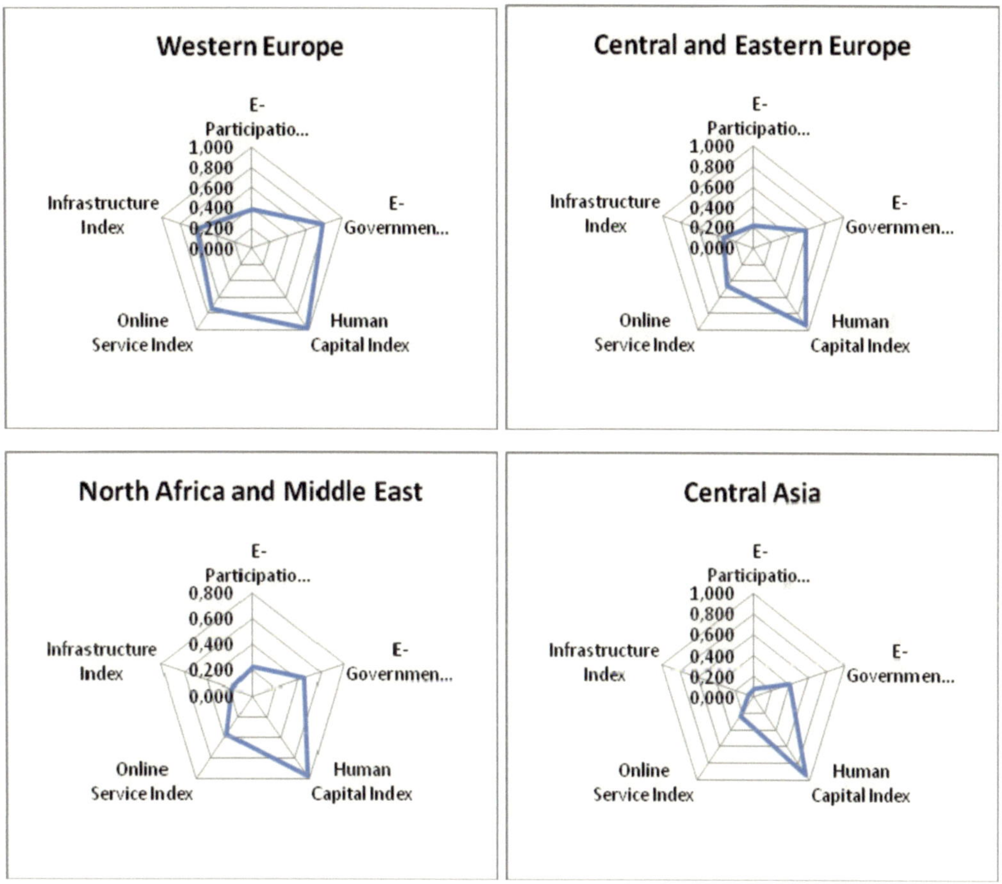

Chart 2. Regional average of the participation index, e-government index and its components.

The invention of the World Wide Web in the early 1990s introduced the ability Access resources from anywhere in the world through Universal Resource Locators (URLs). But the Web was a step backwards in terms of animation and interactivity because of the slowness of computers, modems and the network at the time it was introduced. It is only now that the capabilities of networked computers are catching up to the level necessary to produce the quality of e-learning that was possible using CD-ROMs. (Woodill, 2007, p. 9)

The new learning landscape is a multichannel learning environment that can be seen as a "complex adaptive system". For the most part, this environment is "self organizing" and because of that it is difficult to exactly predict how it is all going to turn out in the next decades. But, there is no question that a major shift is taking place -a turn from instructor centric curricula towards learner centric searching for relevant resources of learning as need. The shift is from instructor controlled classroom learning and instructor controlled e-learning to a mix of approaches that includes instructor control when appropriate (for specific certifications, for example) along with many different channels of resources and requirements from which learners can choose and explore. Emerging e-learning will not be simply mixed with "face-to-face" learning to form blended learning. Rather, all learning will be multichannel learning. The "e" in e-learning will gradually disappear, as electronic support for learning by any means becomes invisible and taken-for-granted (Norman, 1999, quoted from Woodill, p. 16).

As general conclusion, e-learning continues to evolve with new delivery methods -to PDA or mobile phone (called mLearning) and via blogs, wikis, podcasts, and easier-to-use tools both in developed and the so-called developing countries to a higher or lesser extent. There is also a trend seen in the transition from training to learning that leverages the power of the Internet to go beyond eLearning through knowledge management, competency management, and performance support and to HR processes like performance management, talent management, succession planning, and hiring. Web 2.0 (and e-learning 2.0) technologies are driven by collaboration. This is the next phase of eLearning in the world (Clarey, 2007: 29).

5. References

Archibugi, D. & Michie, J. (eds.) (1998) *Trade, Growth and Technical Change*, Cambridge: Cambridge University Press.

Brian Arthur, W. (2009), *The Nature of Technology: What it is and How it Evolves*, London: Penguin Books.

Beck, U. (1992) *Risk Society: Towards a New Modernity*. London: Sage.

Boud, D. (2001). 'Introduction: Making the Move to Peer Learning'. In Boud, D., Cohen, Ruth & Sampson, Jane (Ed.). Peer Learning in Higher Education: Learning From & With Each Other. London: Kogan Page Ltd, 1–17.

Castells, M. (1996) *The Rise of the Network Society*, Blackwell Publishers.

Clarey, J. (2007).*E-Learning 101: An Introduction to E-Learning, Learning Tools, and Technologies*, April 2007, Brandon Hall Research, USA.

Demiray, U.& et.al. (2010). *Cases on Challenges Facing E-Learning and National Development: Institutional Studies and Practices Volume I and Volume II*, with co-editors. Anadolu University Publications 2163/75, ISBN 978-975-06-0844, Eskisehir Turkey, available from http://www.midasebook.com

Dias, M. A. R. (1998). Higher Education: Vision and Action for the coming century. Prospects, Vol. XXVIII, No 3, September 1998.

Duderdstadt, J.J. (1999) 'Can Colleges and Universities Survive in the Information Age? In Katz, R. N. & Associates, *Dancing with the Devil: Information Technology and the New Competition in Higher Education*, San Francisco: Jossey Bass Publishers, pp. 1-25.

European eLearning Summit, May 10-11, 2001. Workshop Papers.

Freeman, C. and L. Soete (1997), *The Economics of Industrial Innovation*. 3rd Edition, London and Washington: Pinter.

Gong, W., Li, W.Z., Stump, R.L. (2007) "Global internet use and access: cultural considerations", Asia Pacific Journal of Marketing and Logistics, Vol. 19 Iss: 1, pp.57 - 74

Grantham, A. & Tsekouras, G. (2004) Information society: wireless ICTs' transformative potential. *Futures*, 36, pp. 359–377.

Hargreaves, A. (1996) Revising voice. *Education Researcher*, 25(1) pp. 12-19.

http://www.learnativity.com/standards/htm retrieved on, 10 July 2009

Jegede, O. (2001). 'Hong Kong', In Jegede, O., & Shive, G. (Eds.) *Open and Distance Education in the Asia Pacific Region*. Open University of Hong Kong Press, Hong Kong. pp. 44-79.

Kawachi, P. (2005). Computers, multimedia and e-learning. In U.V. Reddi & S. Mishra (Eds.), *Educational media in Asia*, (pp. 97-122). Vancouver: Commonwealth of Learning. Retrieved January 4, 2010, from http://www.col.org/colweb/site/pid/3329

Kawachi, P. (2008a). Empirical validation of a multimedia construct for learning. In Mahbubur Rahman Syed (Ed.), *Multimedia technologies: Concepts, methodologies, tools, and applications* (3 Volumes), (Volume 3 Section 5, Chapter 11, pp. 1156–1173). Hershey, PA: Information Science Reference/IGI Global.

Lee-Kelley, L. & James, T. (2005) E-Government and Social Exclusion: An Empirical Study in *Advanced Topics in Electronic Commerce,* Vol 1, pp 222-239. Idea group publishing.

Lyotard, J.F. (1984) *The postmodern condition a report on knowledge*. Translation from the French by Geoff Bennington and Brian Massumi. Foreword by Fredric Jameson. Manchester: Manchester University Press.

Masood, M. (2004). A ten year analysis: Trends in traditional educational technology literature. *The Malaysian Online Journal of In-structional Technology, 1. Available online at* http://pppjj.usm.my/mojit/articles/pdf/1204/A%20Ten%20Year%20Analysis.pdf

McConnell Intl. (2001) *Ready? Net. Go!* Partnerships Leading the Global Economy. Retrieved Nov. 22, 2010 from website: http://www.mcconnellinternational.com

Moore, N. (1998) 'Confucius or capitalism: policies for a information society', in Loader, B.D. (Ed.), *Cyberspace Divide: Equality, Agency and Policy in the Information Society*, London: Routledge, pp. 150–160.

Musawi, A. (2011) Redifining Technology role on education, *Creative Education,* 2(2) pp.130-135.

Roblyer, M. D. (2005). Educational technology research that makes a difference: Series introduction. *Contemporary Issues in Technology and Teacher Education, 5,* pp.192-201.

Rosenberg, N. (1972). *Technology and American economic growth.* NY: Harper & Row.

Sagasti, A. (2001) *The knowledge explosion and the digital divide*. Human Development Reports. UNDP. Retrieved Nov. 16, 2004, from: http://hdr.undp.org/publications/papers.cfm

Sampler, J. (1998) Redefining industry structure for the information age, *Strategic Management Journal*, 19, pp.343–355.

Schreurs, B. (Ed.) (2010). *Re.ViCa Online Handbook The Rise Of Large-Scale E-Learning Initiatives Worldwide,* EuroPACE ivzw, ISBN number: 9789081148030, retrieved on 2.01.2010, available from http://www.virtualcampuses.eu/index.php/Re.ViCa_Handbook

UNeGovDD. (2008). *UN E-Government Development Database.* Retrieved from http://www2.unpan.org/egovkb/index.aspx

Utsumi, T, Varis, T., Knight, P., Method, F. & Pelton, J (2001). Using broadband to close the digital divide. *Intermedia*, April 2001, Vol. 29, No 2.

Woodill, G. (2007). Emerging E-Learning Content: New Approaches to Delivering Engaging Online Learning Experiences, in *New Approaches to Delivering Engaging Online Training,* Brandon Hall Research, and 2nd edition May, 2007. USA.

Yamamoto, G. T., Ozan, O & Demiray, U. (2010). Drugstore For Learners: Learning Vitamins D-E-M-T-U Learning, accepted for presentation at the *Future-Learning 2010 International Conference,* May 10-14, 2010 Istanbul-Turkey.

Yang, H. H. & Yuen, Chi-Yin S. (2010). *Handbook of Research on Practices and Outcomes in E-Learning: Issues and trends,* Information Science Refererence-IGI Global, Hersey-New York, USA.

6

E-Learning in Higher and Adult Education

Nicoleta Gudanescu
Nicolae Titulescu University Bucharest
Romania

1. Introduction

This work is emphasizing the advantages and the limits of using the electronic tools for education at all levels, specially higher education systems and education for adults.
A few of the advantages are:

- The modernization of the educational process;
- A better communication between the professors/instructors and students/educable adults;
- A raising participation of the students/adults in educational programs, university courses or training sessions;
- The innovation in educational programs;
- Facilitates the educational act.

The limits at least in some of the countries like Romania are:

- The missing of the face to face contact between professors and students;
- Difficulties in the computer utilization by the older professors/instructors or students;
- The evaluation process is more stressing for the students, because the grades and qualifications are generated by the computer;
- Difficulties in publishing the courses (platform contents) because of the lack in author's rights legislation.

The context in which the electronic tools for education are used differs from higher education to education for adults as well as from university to university, from education provider to another, from country to country etc. In any case we can say that the system is useful and helps to modernize (innovate) and facilitate the educational process.
E - learning Innovations offers a core group of professional development courses designed to help anyone achieve professional advancement and personal enrichment. The programs are founded on an extensive experience and understanding of technology-based learning environments. They focus on the most current industry practices for various learning environments and best approaches for multiple learning styles. They ensure that the students get the information and skills needed to achieve more in teaching practice and to confidently enter the distance or online classroom.
E - learning Innovation's training is rigorous yet practical, and courses are taught by highly qualified faculty. They are offered online allowing you to work at your own pace and at your convenience. They blend the best of self-directed experiences, instructor-led sessions, and individual mentoring. Through the courses, you have the opportunity to work with peers across the nation and even around the world.

Certification is offered through a combination of selected courses or individual. Courses can be customized to an organization's specific needs and requirements.
E - learning Innovations is committed to your professional success. Benefits of our training include:

- A flexible and progressive online learning format
- A collaborative and blended learning environment
- Immediate, practical application
- Individual mentoring and coaching
- Certification through a combination of selected courses
- Can be tailored to specific technologies or environments

These course options are:

- Teaching Online
- Managing Distance Learning
- E - learning Course Builder
- Computer Application Skills Competencies

The latest E-learning Innovations such as mobile learning (MLearning - Tremblay, 2010) or web based collaborative open environments (Lewin, 2011) makes the education more competitive but also saves resources now and in the future.
The objectives of this chapter are: to explain the contribution of modern technologies and electronic systems to educational processes, the concept of technology based learning, to introduce the electronic tools for education, to present good practice examples in implementing E-learning systems in higher education and corporate environment in Romania and not for the last the new electronic learning systems.
The motivation of this work is to present the opportunities offered by this type of learning for the people and for the society also taking into consideration the global economic crisis that affects all the sectors, the education being one of the most affected. As a result in the future we will have less prepared generation due to the lack of resources. In the mean time introducing the computers and ITC in educational processes facilitates them and makes the educational system modern and efficient.
For reaching the objective the author used the personal anterior results of the own work in the educational field together with the international theoretical and practical achievements in the E-learning domain.
The results of the work is presenting the ways to do computer assisted education for students and adults, giving the good practice examples, presenting new electronic learning systems the advantages and limits and to try to emphasize that these days E-learning is one of the efficient way to reach education, no matter the age of the educable ones.
Considering the scope and the results of this work we can conclude that the E-learning is the best way to achieve education these days, when the resources are limited by the global economic decline, because is more cheaper for the people (students and adults) and for the educational institutions (a small number of teachers involved and one time buying the new technology).

2. Contribution of modern technologies and electronic systems to educational processes

In present we live in technology era, technology has become an important component our lives and we cannot develop diverse activities without it. Every day appears new gadgets or software that makes lives easier and improves the technology and software that already exists. Making lives easier is not, however, the only role technology plays in our lives.

Technology is playing an increasing role in education. As technology advances, it is used for the benefit of students and people of all ages in the learning processes.

Technology used in the classroom helps students to learn easier the materials presented in different courses. For example, since some people are visual learners, projection screens linked to computers can allow students to see their notes instead of simply listening to a teacher deliver a course without any technical mean.

In the same direction software can be used to supplement class curriculum, to improve the educative process by adding practical aspects to the course. Also, the programs provide study questions, activities, and even tests and quizzes for a class that can help students continue learning outside the classroom.

Technology has also become part of many curriculums, even for other courses out of computer and technology classes. Students use computers to create presentations and use the Internet in order to research topics for papers and essays, to get tests and materials for learning.

Students also learn how to use the technology available to them in any type of courses but especially in computer classes. This ensures that after graduation they will be able to use the information technology in their work, which may put them ahead of someone who didn't have access to a particular technology or software in their school.

The information technology advances yearly, so the students have better access to educational opportunities. When something new and "better" appears, the "older" technology becomes more affordable, allowing it to be used in educational processes, even when schools are on a tight budget. In the same way the professional preparation for adults can be assisted by the computer and it have to be in the cases of the courses that requires that.

Advantages to having technology in Education

Here are some of the advantages that technology helps provide for the educated ones today:

i. **Student Achievement**. Technology has been proven to help students achieve in reading, writing, and arithmetic. Each year teachers are instructed in order to use the information technology in educational processes. Technology gives educators one more tool to help them reach good results with the students.

ii. **Professional Requirements**. The beneficiaries of the technology in the education system are not only the students, it also benefits the educators. There are so many opportunities for teachers to learn and acquire new skills over the internet, keep up with credentials and in return help them improve their teaching abilities.

iii. **Meeting Special Needs**. Assistive technology for special needed students, and student with disabilities have been able to achieve in areas and ways that would not have been possible. Technology creates individualized learning environments for this kind of students and really can play a major role in special needs ones.

iv. **Continuing Education**. Technology has also made it possible for those who didn't finish college or high school to get back in education (education for adults) without having to even leave the comfort of their own home. And technology has made it possible for continued education (so called lifelong learning); those wanting to reach a little higher and gain more knowledge in something new or old. Technology brings the learning right to the students or educated ones; wherever they may be.

v. **Workforce skills**. And not for the last, technology has served students/people well because it has provided them with the skill and knowledge they need to enter the workforce.

It is becoming increasingly difficult for teachers to reach every child/student in the classroom. Class sizes keep getting larger, but teachers remain still one of the lowest paid salary jobs in Romania. Yet the need is still there to teach and prepare the children/students for the future; the need to prepare them for the "real" world. And the real world today is a world full of technology. So if we don't provide technology in our education system then when will students have a chance to get familiar with it? How will they train themselves for the "real" world? So, what exactly is the role of technology in education? Technology is making it possible for teachers to reach more to the students, allowing students the time they need to learn, accumulate, succeed, and providing our future workforce with competent, knowledgeable employees.

3. Technology based learning. Main concepts

Technology based learning is the way of learning using the electronic technology such as internet, intranet, audio and video conferencing, webcasts etc. We have also the concepts of ***computer based learning*** and ***on line learning*** that means the learning using the computer, respective the internet and modern technology. From these concepts derived the synonymous of Technology based learning - the **e-learning** concept, largely spread at all the levels of educational process in our days.

From other point of view ***Educational technology (learning technology)*** is the way of learning using and managing the appropriate technological processes and resources in order to develop human capabilities.

Considering the *Handbook of Human Performance Technology(J.A.Pershing, 2006)*, the word technology for the sister fields of Educational and Human Performance Technology means "applied science." In other words, any valid and reliable process or procedure that is derived from basic research using the "scientific method" is considered a "technology." The word technology, comes from the Greek "Techne" which means craft or art. Another word "technique", with the same origin, also may be used when considering the field Educational technology. So, Educational technology may be extended to include the techniques of the educator and educators often named Educational Technologists.

The Technology based learning process development

If we have to talk about the Technology based learning making a comparison between the beginning of the decade and present, the situation is as follows:

Old economy	Knowledge Based Economy
Four years degree	Forty-years degree
Training and Cost Center	Training as Competitive Advantage
Learner mobility	Content mobility
Distance education	Distributed learning
Correspondence & Video	High tech Multimedia Centers
Generic programs	Tailored programs
Geographic centers	Brand Name Universities and Celebrity Professors
Isolated	Virtual Learning Commities

Table 1. Education in knowledge economy. Source: N.Gudanescu, Using modern technology for improving learning process at different educational levels, Procedia Social and Behavioral Sciences

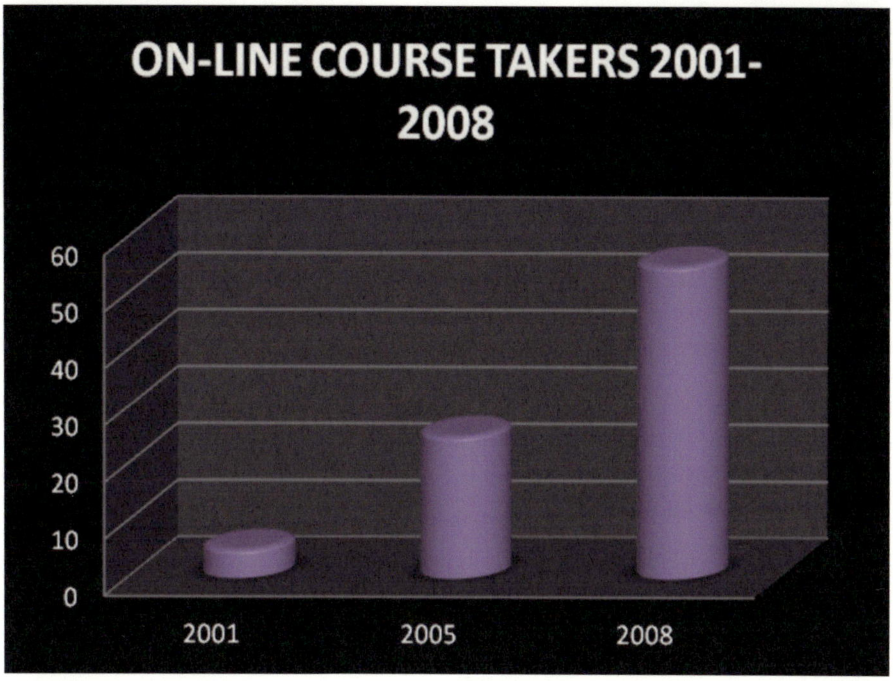

Fig. 1. On-line course takers - educational & training. Source: Institute for the quantitative Study of Society, 2008

Following the evolution of the technology introduction in educational processes at all the levels, we can observe a fast increase of the number of persons interested of this type of learning. The time saved and also the efficiency of using technology for educational purposes recommends it as the newest trend in the knowledge based economy and society. Making a parallel between education in old economy and in knowledge based economy.

"Educational technology" represents the using of modern technology in educational processes, in order to improve teaching and learning.

Educational technology is also known as „learning technology" or „instructional technology"

Educational technology can be used at all levels of education from children's education, to high school, university level and education for adults and specialization.

Educational technologies includes web-sites, electronic platforms, educational software, educational electronic materials, interactive blackboards and videoconference systems for distance learning.

E-learning comprises all forms of electronically supported learning and teaching. The information and communication systems, whether networked learning or not, serve as specific media to implement the learning process. The term will still most likely be utilized to reference out-of-classroom and in-classroom educational experiences via technology, even as advances continue in regard to devices and curriculum.

E-learning is essentially the computer and network-enabled transfer of skills and knowledge. E-learning applications and processes include Web-based learning, computer-based learning, virtual education opportunities and digital collaboration. Content is delivered via the Internet, intranet/internet, audio or video tape, satellite TV and CD-ROM.

Abbreviations like CBT (*Computer-Based Training*), IBT (*Internet-Based Training*) or WBT (*Web-Based Training*) have been used in time as synonyms to e-learning. Today one can still find these terms being used, along with variations of e-learning such as e-learning, E-learning, and E-learning. This system is largely used today, that's why it has to be reglemented by establishing rules and principles of functioning.

E-learning principles:

i. E-learning is a way of doing education that can be applied within varying education models (face to face or distance education)

This principle means that this is not a distinctive educational system in itself, but helps to provide a good educational act implementing various models recorded above.

ii. E-learning is a unique form of education that combines face to face and distance education.

In this kind of system the role of the instructor changes, the person became the form of transmitting the educational information but thorough the electronic instruments. The concepts and theoretical principles remains the same, only the information is delivered in another form. We can name this form of learning a mixed- mode which is seconded by a high technology component, the E-learning platform and the computers, and not for the last, the web environment. The E-learning system distinguish between face to face preparation and distance learning. Of course in both kind of teaching the technology is useful and improved the way of learning.

iii. The importance of how is technology used in the educational process and the technical level of a course.

The modalities to implement the E-learning methods have to be in accordance with the pedagogies.

Weller [1] presents as pedagogies the following methods: Constructivism, Resource based learning, Collaborative learning, Problem based learning, Narrative based teaching and Situated learning. The ideea is that the technology can be applied in any pedagogic method used for the educational process, but the way of using is established by the educator as author of the course and the guide for the students or whatever the category of the educated persons.

iv. The E-learning means the implementation of innovative educational methods.

This kind of systems offer to the educators the opportunities to innovate in educational process, to use new methods of learning and to bring the technology beside the theoretical and practical information, which is spread among the students. Obviously the system can present some weaknesses (for example – the small number of hours spent face to face) but as a whole education + technology is a innovative system of learning and accumulating knowledge.

v. E-learning can be used in two ways; the presentation of educational content, and the facilitation of educational processes.

E-learning includes digital materials storage and distribution (presentation) and on line communication, simulative interactivity, multimedia, and access tracking processes - each of them can be considered as innovative ways of learning.

In other words E-learning can both make information available and play a part in students' self-construction of knowledge.

[1] Weller,M. (2002). *Delivering learning on the Net*, UK: Kogan Page

vi. E-learning uses a standard model of courses accepted by the educational authorities from each country.

Each country has regulations regarding the educational system, respectively the predefined standards for educational levels (high school or university) and for the form of studies (full time or reduced time). The format of the e-courses is different from country to country, from specialization to specialization, form level to level.

vii. E-learning offers new opportunities of education for the users

For many students today is better to use alternative methods for education. Why? It is very simple, they are in almost cases very busy working for getting the money necessary to pay the courses and the time for them is precious. Using the computer technology for learning it shortens the time, the student stays home or go to a educational center for few hours a day and studies, in order to complete their knowledge.

Another two categories of users when is came to talk about the technology and education are knowledge students and knowledge workers. These two type of educable ones are representative for knowledge based economy and society in which we live today.

Knowledge students are the students that use technology in most of the learning processes.

Knowledge workers are the workers that are prepared/specialized using the technology and in their work they are using the information technology or more than others.

Living in knowledge based society the students as well as the workers have to adapt to the conditions dictated by the new society in which the technology and the knowledge are the leaders.

4. Electronic tools for education

In this section we will present a few of the many electronic tools used to deliver in modern conditions the education and specialization among students, respectively adults in the training sessions. Representative for the purpose of this work are Learning Management Systems (known as LMS), Integrated Learning Systems, On-line forums, and not for the last Web Conferences.

a. Learning Management Systems

A learning management system (LMS) is a software application or Web-based technology used to plan, implement, and assess a specific learning process. Typically, a learning management system provides an instructor with a way to create and deliver content, monitor student participation, and assess student performance. A learning management system may also provide students with the ability to use interactive features such as threaded discussions, video conferencing, and discussion forums. The Advanced Distance Learning group, sponsored by the United States Department of Defense, has created a set of specifications called Shareable Content Object Reference Model (SCORM) to encourage the standardization of learning management systems. Shareable Content Object Reference Model (SCORM) is an XML-based framework used to define and access information about learning objects so they can be easily shared among different learning management systems (LMSs). SCORM was developed in response to a United States Department of Defense initiative to promote standardization in e-learning.

In another definition a Learning Management System (commonly abbreviated as LMS) is a software application for the administration, documentation, tracking, and reporting of training programs, classroom and online events, e-learning programs, and training content. As described in (Ellis 2009) a robust LMS should be able to do the following:

- centralize and automate administration of documents, students and other useful information
- use self-service and self-guided services
- assemble and deliver learning content rapidly
- consolidate training initiatives on a scalable web-based platform
- support portability and standards
- personalize content and enable knowledge reuse.

LMSs systems have been created for managing training and educational records, to software for distributing courses over the Internet with features for online collaboration. In adult preparation or HR activities, corporate training use LMSs to automate record-keeping and employee registration. Computer based learning and training as well as collaborative learning are the future for the busy people/students from these days.

Some LMSs are Web-based to facilitate access to learning content and administration from distance. LMSs are used generally by universities (educational institutions) to enhance and support classroom teaching and offering courses to a larger population of learners across the country or continent but can be used very frequently for adult preparation and specialization at the work-place or in organized training sessions. For the employees some LMS providers include as module "HR performance management systems", which encompass employee progress, competency management, skills-analysis, succession planning for career, and multi-rater assessments. For the commercial market, some Learning and Performance Management Systems include recruitment and reward functionality.

i. LMS Characteristics

The virtual learning environment used by universities and colleges allow professors/tutors/instructors to manage their courses and exchange information with students for a course that in most cases will last several weeks and will meet several times during those weeks. In the corporate environment setting a course may be much shorter, easier to present as content and completed in a single instructor-led event or online session.The characteristics shared by both types of LMSs for universities and for education for adults and instruction are:

- Manage users, roles, courses, instructors, facilities, and generate reports for any person or activity.
- Generate Courses calendar
- Offers learning path
- Student messaging and notifications
- Assessment and testing handling before and after following the course
- Generates automatic tests choosing different ways to combine the questions
- Display scores and transcripts
- Grading of coursework and roster processing, including wait listing
- Web-based or blended course delivery

Specific to corporate training the characteristics include:

- Auto enrollment (enrolling Students/Employees in courses when required according to predefined criteria, such as job title or work location)
- Manager enrollment and approval
- Integration with performance tracking and management systems in the company
- Planning tools in order to identify skill gaps at departmental and individual level

- Curriculum, required and elective training requirements at an individual and organizational level
- Grouping students according to demographic units (geographic region, product line, business size or type, business units etc.)
- Assign corporate and partner employees to more than one job title at more than one demographic unit

ii. LMS Technical aspects and Learning Content Management System

Most of the LMSs are web-based in order to ensure the wide use of the interested ones. These are built using a variety of development platforms, like Java/J2EE, Microsoft .NET or PHP.

The main technical characteristics in order to have a good platform for E-learning are:

- High availability: the LMS must be robust enough to serve the diverse needs of thousands of learners, administrators, content builders and teachers/instructors simultaneously.
- Scalability: the infrastructure should be able to expand to meet future growth, both in terms of the volume of instruction and the size of the student body.
- Usability: to support a host of automated and personalized services, such as self-paced and role-specific learning, the access, delivery and presentation of material must be easy-to-use and highly intuitive.
- Interoperability: to support content from different sources and multiple vendors' hardware/software solutions, the LMS should be based on open industry standards for Web deployments and support the major learning standards.
- Stability: the LMS infrastructure can reliably and effectively manage a large enterprise implementation running.
- Security: As with any outward-facing collaborative solution, the LMS can selectively limit and control access to online content, resources and back-end functions, both internally and externally, for its diverse user community

The soft platform is not so important for the end users, they are interested in the facilities offered by the platform, easy access, courses posted, forums, tests, case studies etc. The information posted on the platforms is known as learning content.

A learning content management system (LCMS) is a related technology to the learning management system that it is focused on the development, management and publishing of the content that will typically be delivered thorough an LMS. An LCMS is a multi-user environment where developers may create, store, use, manage, and deliver digital learning content from a central object repository. In the university environment as well as in the corporate environment the content is made by courses, case studies and practical materials of study, tests and recapitulative questions sets, training modules etc. The learning materials (learning objects) are not only written materials, but graphics, audio and video materials for courses and training support. The materials are posted by the teachers, trainers and platform administrators but also by the students on share section.

iii. Learning management industry

In the relatively new Learning Management Systems market, commercial vendors for corporate and education applications range from new entrants to those that entered the market in the nineties. In addition to commercial packages, many open source solutions are available.

According (Bersin et al. 2009), LMSs represent an $860 million market, made up of more than 60 different providers. The six largest LMS product companies constitute approximately 50% of the market. In addition to the remaining smaller LMS product vendors, training outsourcing firms, enterprise resource planning vendors, and consulting firms all compete for part of the learning management market. Approximately 40 percent of U.S. training organizations reported that they have an LMS installed, a figure that has not changed significantly over the past two years. From the universities in the world 80% have a LMS installed and organize distance courses.

b. Integrated Learning Systems

Integrated Learning Systems (abbreviated as ILS) are hardware and software solutions designed to deliver instructional content. The effective delivery of that content is measured, monitored, and maintained with an array of assessment and management tools that may also be part of that system.

Integrated learning systems are generally associated with educational/academic environments, but are also deployed within corporate environment, for example, as a way to introduce employees to new, mission critical systems and software applications and to provide them training and specialization in different fields.

Comparing with static online help or even animated tutorials, Integrated Learning Systems are highly interactive and designed to provide feedback as to progress and grasp of the subject matter at hand. Built-in tools further allow professors or executive management or instructors/trainers to monitor and measure a student's progress.

Integrated Learning Systems are packages of networked hardware and software used for education. Such systems provide instructional content as well as assessment and management tools. Conventionally, instruction is organized around specific objectives and the software embodies a mastery learning approach to instruction. Integrated Learning Systems feature programmed instruction for teacher and student. Their purpose is to direct and coach the student through the learning experience. By the early 1990s, about 20 percent of American elementary schools had installed integrated learning systems as a primary component of their overall curriculum (Becker & Hativa, 1994). Integrated learning systems also have been developed for use in high school, college, and adult populations preparation (Bunderson and Faust, 1976).

Typically, integrated learning systems are part of a comprehensive educational system that a school purchases to integrate within its overall curriculum. The curricular goals for literacy may include teaching children skills in language-arts mechanics and phonics instruction. Yet integrated learning systems differ from off-the-shelf, drill-and-practice programs. In an integrated learning system program, each student studies at his or her level, because an adaptive testing algorithm places every student at a level appropriate for the instructional process. In a number of off-the-shelf, drill-and-practice programs, no adaptive testing occurs, and the student works at whatever "level" of the program he or she chooses.

More appropriately then, Integrated Learning Systems may be understood, not as "drill-and-practice" programs but as "testing and practice" programs (Osin, 1996; Osin and Lesgold, 1996). Students work individually and at their own pace through a series of exercises that are designed to give them practice in a targeted skill. This work may appear to resemble activities that students do in off-the-shelf, drill-and-practice programs; however, two critical distinctions exist. First, integrated learning systems are more extensive in their scope of instruction. In other words, they present many more exercises, and the exercises follow scope-and-sequence patterns of instruction found in traditional textbooks. Second, integrated learning systems regulate students' progress. They track students' progress in completing the exercises.

Recent research indicates that students who participate in learning activities using Integrated Learning Systems spend more time actively engaged in the learning tasks than their counterparts who are engaged in the same offline learning tasks in traditionally structured classrooms (Worthen, VanDusen, Sailor, 1994). Interestingly, when pairs of students work cooperatively to complete exercises in an integrated learning system, they outperform their counterparts who use the system on an individual basis.

To conclude, Integrated Learning Systems require a significant commitment of implementation expense, time, and effort. Researchers remain divided on their long-term value. Although these systems have been shown to teach a breadth of procedural skills (such as language arts mechanics), it is not clear that they teach depth of content or foster complex thinking skills required in debate or composition. So the Integrated Learning Systems (ILS) are computer-based systems for the delivery of curriculum material, via an individualized program of study. They are relatively new in Europe, although they have existed in North America for around 30 years. Advances in computer technology mean that these systems now offer teachers a powerful set of tools to assist in the development of basic numeracy and literacy. Pupils/students using these systems have been shown to perform significantly better than equivalent control groups. Being instructional systems can be successfully used for the adults also that are in the process of learning a trade.

What is an ILS? If we want to present it schematically.

An ILS is made up of two components, Computer Aided Instruction (CAI) modules (often called courseware) and a Management System.

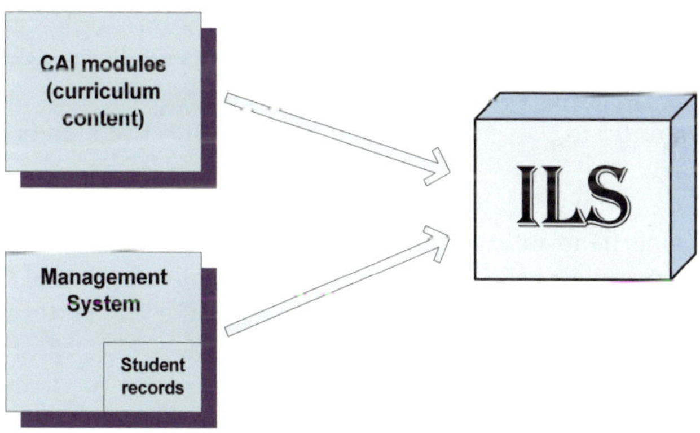

Fig. 2.The scheme of an Integrated learning system

The CAI modules present the teaching material in a similar way to existing educational software. The Management System keeps records of the students' performance and, in some cases depending on the software, moves them through the levels of difficulty as appropriate. It also allows the teachers to set up (configure) all the different course options, to suit their own teaching styles and the needs of their students.

Learning with an ILS

The key features of an ILS are as follows:

- Each student/person has an individualized learning program. If they perform well, they can make rapid progress onto higher levels of difficulty. If they experience problems, they are given more practice and may also be given additional tutorials and support questions on the various skills needed to deal with a particular topic.

- Teachers have access to a lot of data for monitoring students' progress. This will highlight stdents who are experiencing difficulty and who are in need of additional support. This data is gathered automatically and can be printed out in a series of different reports.
- Stdents performance is constantly monitored by the Management System.
- Students get immediate feedback after every question. This can raise motivation and accelerate learning.

The Benefits of an ILS

The benefits that can be achieved through the use of an ILS can be:

- Significant learning gains in mathematics
- Significant learning gains in English or any other language that uses the ILS
- Improved motivation and attitude to work
- Improved performance in all curriculum areas because of the first three benefits

c. On-line forums

An Internet, On-line forum, or message board, is an online discussion site where people can hold conversations in the form of posted messages. They differ from chat rooms in that messages are at least temporarily archived. Also, depending on the access level of a user or the forum set-up, a posted message might need to be approved by a moderator before it becomes visible. Forums have a specific set of jargon associated with them; For example a single conversation is called a "thread."

A forum is hierarchical or tree-like in structure: a forum can contain a number of sub forums, each of which may have several topics. Within a forum's topic, each new discussion started is called a thread, and can be replied to by as many people as wish to. Depending on the forum's settings, users can be anonymous or have to register with the forum and then subsequently log in order to post messages. On most forums, users do not have to log in to read existing messages.

How can we use forums for education? Very simple, the talkers share their own knowledge with others, by giving them information or advices, also specialists in different domains present on the forums can give the interested ones the right data. But, in the majority of the cases when we talk about electronic educational systems, the on-line forums are integrated in LMS or ILS. These forums are administrated by the teachers and platforms administrators that manage the entire system. In the case of the teachers as moderators they have to respond to the students' questions and guide them in the way of learning the most important things for their future.

How to manage on-line forums? Every day, millions of users log on to their favorite online forums, communities and social spaces and interact with others to get advice and discuss everything from the latest news and trends to their hobbies and professions to whatever else strikes their fancy. Administrators have to lead these communities, deal with difficult users, manage staff members and make tough decisions. Legal constraints, spammers and technical issues can turn the excitement of running an on-line community into chaos.

The steps to create an on-line forum are:

- Creating an organizational structure
- Designing and launching the community
- Deciding on user options like private messaging
- Promoting and attracting members
- Utilizing technology to members benefit

- Developing and enforcing guidelines
- Choosing and managing moderators
- Shutting down users who disrupt and harm the community
- Involving the users and keeping the site interesting and inviting
- Generating revenue

d. Web Conferences and Video Conferences

Web Conferencing refers to a service that allows conferencing events to be shared with remote locations. Most vendors also provide either a recorded copy of an event, or a means for a subscriber to record an event. The service allows information to be shared simultaneously, across geographically dispersed locations in nearly real-time. Applications for web conferencing include meetings, training events, lectures, or short presentations from any computer. A participant can be either an individual person or a group. System requirements that allow individuals within a group to participate as individuals (e.g. when an audience participant asks a question) depend on the size of the group. Handling such requirements is often the responsibility of the group. In general, system requirements depend on the vendor. The service is made possible by Internet technologies, particularly on IP/TCP connections.

Some solutions require additional software to be installed (usually via download) by the presenter and participants, while others eliminate this step by providing physical hardware. Some vendors provide a complete solution while other vendors enhance existing technologies. Most also provide a means of interfacing with email and calendaring clients in order that customers can plan an event and share information about it, in advance.

Support for planning a shared event (web conferences) is typically integrated with calendar and email applications. The method of controlling access to an event is provided by the vendor. Additional value-added features are included as desired by vendors who provide them. As with any technology, these features are limited only by the imagination.

For interactive online workshops web conferences are complemented by electronic meeting systems (EMS) which provide a range of on-line facilitation tools such as brainstorming and categorization, a range of voting methods or structured discussions, typically with optional anonymity. Typically, EMS do not provide core web conferencing functionality such as screen sharing or voice conferencing though some EMS can control web conferencing sessions.

Other typical features of a web conference include:

- Slide show presentations - where images are presented to the audience and markup tools and a remote mouse pointer are used to engage the audience while the presenter discusses slide content
- Live or Streaming video - where full motion webcam, digital video camera or multi-media files are pushed to the audience
- VoIP (Real time audio communication through the computer via use of headphones and speakers)
- Web tours - where URLs, data from forms, cookies, scripts and session data can be pushed to other participants enabling them to be pushed though web based logons, clicks, etc. This type of feature works well when demonstrating websites where users themselves can also participate
- Meeting Recording - where presentation activity is recorded on the client side or server side for later viewing and/or distribution

- Whiteboard with annotation (allowing the presenter and/or attendees to highlight or mark items on the slide presentation. Or, simply make notes on a blank whiteboard.)
- Text chat - For live question and answer sessions, limited to the people connected to the meeting. Text chat may be public (echo'ed to all participants) or private (between 2 participants)
- Polls and surveys (allows the presenter to conduct questions with multiple choice answers directed to the audience)
- Screen sharing/desktop sharing/application sharing (where participants can view anything the presenter currently has shown on their screen. Some screen sharing applications allow for remote desktop control, allowing participants to manipulate the presenters screen, although this is not widely used.)

Web conferencing is often sold as a service, hosted on a web server controlled by the vendor. Offerings vary per vendor but most hosted services provide a cost per user per minute model, a monthly fee model and a seat model. Some vendors also provide a server side solution which allows the customer to host their own web conferencing service on their own servers.

Web conferencing technologies are not standardized, which has been a significant factor in the lack of interoperability, transparency, platform dependence, security issues, cost and market segmentation. In 2003, the IETF established a working group to establish a standard for web conferencing, called "Centralized Conferencing ". The planned deliverables of the group include:

- A basic floor control protocol. Binary Floor Control Protocol (BFCP)
- A mechanism for membership and authorization control
- A mechanism to manipulate and describe media "mixing" or "topology" for multiple media types (audio, video, text)
- A mechanism for notification of conference related events/changes (for example a floor change)

Web conferencing is available with three models: hosting service, software and appliance. An appliance, unlike the online hosted solution, it is offered as hardware. It is also known as "in-house" or "on-premise" web conferencing. It is used to conduct live meetings, remote training, or presentations via the Internet.

Videoconference (video conferencing)

A videoconference is a live connection between people in separate locations for the purpose of communication, usually involving audio and often text as well as video. At its simplest, videoconferencing provides transmission of static images and text between two locations. At its most sophisticated, it provides transmission of full-motion video images and high-quality audio between multiple locations. Videoconferencing software is quickly becoming standard computer equipment. For example, Microsoft's NetMeeting is included in Windows 2000 and is also available for free download from the NetMeeting homepage.

Digital Camera afford the user easy - and cheap - live connections to distant friends and family. Although the audio and video quality of such a minimal setup is not high, the combined benefits of a video link and long-distance savings may be quite persuasive.

The tangible benefits for businesses using videoconferencing include lower travel costs and profits gained from offering videoconferencing as an aspect of customer service. The intangible benefits include the facilitation of group work among geographically distant teammates and a stronger sense of community among business contacts, both within and between companies. In terms of group work, users can chat, transfer files, share programs, send and receive graphic data, and operate computers from remote locations. On a more personal level, the face-to-face connection adds non-verbal communication to the exchange and allows participants to develop a stronger sense of familiarity with individuals they may never actually meet in the same place.

A videoconference can be thought of as a phone call with pictures - Microsoft refers to that aspect of its NetMeeting package as a "web phone" - and indications suggest that videoconferencing will some day become the primary mode of distance communication.

5. The latest electronic learning systems

The innovation regarding the E-learning technologies is on one side the mobile learning and on the other side the collaborative open environments/workplaces.

MLearning

MLearning (Mobile learning) is the newest discovery in the field and represents the learning using mobile devices or in other definition: „Any sort of learning that happens when the learner is not a fixed, predetermined location, or learning that happens when the learner takes advantage of the learning opportunities offered by mobile technologies.

In other words mobile learning decreases limitation of learning location with the mobility of general portable devices.

Learner access to m-learning project systems and materials was via a microportal (mPortal), which consists of a series of mini web pages with navigation pointing to:

- learning materials
- mini web Page Builder tools
- a collaborative activities tool (the mediaBoard)
- peer-to-peer communication services (messages, chat, discussion and blogs)
- the learning management system
- simple help guides for the system
- links to places on the Web that may be helpful or interesting for our target audience (eg alcohol, drugs and sexual health advice services, job hunting and online learning services and dictionaries).

The mPortal also manages the 'behind the scenes' integration and security.

The Page Builder tools within the mPortal allow learners to create and edit their own mini web pages for viewing on mobile devices (and also accessible from a desktop computer) in a password-protected environment.

The pages learners create can contain a number of different elements including text, pictures, movies, animations, audio, blogs (a short version of the term 'web log', meaning a publicly accessible web-based journal), conversations and links to any web pages chosen by the learner.

Virtual Collaborative open Environments/Workplaces

A Collaborative Workspace or shared workspace is an inter-connected environment in which all the participants in dispersed locations can access and interact with each other just as inside a single entity.

The environment may be supported by electronic communications and groupware which enable participants to overcome space and time differentials. These are typically enabled by a shared mental model, common information, and a shared understanding by all of the participants regardless of physical location.

Communication comes in two forms: synchronous and asynchronous. Asynchronous communication includes email and shared file systems where information is exchanged back and forth in a non-interactive, sequential manner. The popularity of synchronous forms has increased over recent years driven by improvements in processing capabilities and the widespread availability of high speed internet. These include video and voice messaging services including shared whiteboard capabilities. Program sharing has also become available to allow remote users to share much more detailed information through CAD packages, spreadsheets, etc. and have access to these in real time.

6. Examples of good practice in implementing E-learning systems in higher education and corporate environment in Romania

In the next subchapter we will see 2 real examples of using information technology in higher education and in corporate environment

a. E-learning for corporate training and universities

The e-learning concept is frequently used in our country in these days. Now in Romania all prestigious companies and universities have e-learning platforms thus contributing to lifelong learning even from long distances from the educational source.

Some examples are:

Universities that implemented and use the e-learning system for students distance learning like Economic Studies Academy from Bucharest, Nicolae Tiulescu University, Titu Maiorescu University which uses for the moment a moodle platform but is implementing a european project financed from structural funds which main objective is the creation of a e-learning platform, Valahia University from Targoviste and so on. Being a express request from Education Ministry that each university that organize distance courses to have a e-learning platform, many universities from our country are searching modalities to have a such platform. Because the costs are in some cases bigger than the universities financial possibilities they write and implement European projects in order to finance an e-learning platform.

Another example of good practice is the E-learning system implemented at the Ecologic University from Bucharest – which will be described in the next subchapter:

In corporate environment there are some important transnational organizations and education for adults providers which had implemented for their own use or for the clients use, e-learning systems.

Online Business School program is part of the project Improving the competitiveness of SMEs in sustainable entrepreneurship (ICIMM) launched by the Consortium Romtelecom (by division dedicated to business - Romtelecom Business Solutions), Blue Point IT Solutions and OTE Academy. This program is co-financed by European Social Fund Operational Programme, Human Resources Development 2007-2013. The program is offering free online courses for professional development for managers in Romania.

Online Business School is in line with EU priorities to stimulate entrepreneurial thinking and creating a culture designed to encourage development of small and medium enterprises (SMEs).

Online Business School aims to support SMEs to improve their performance and ability to develop new markets through appropriate training of managers and promoting entrepreneurial culture.

Fig, 3. **Online Romtelecom Business School** platform. Source: Romtelecom business school - http://www.bizschool.ro/

In the long run, the program will generate a positive attitude towards entrepreneurship market will increase entrepreneurial and managerial skills of individuals to coordinate and strengthen SMEs capacity of development, generating new jobs.

The program, which will run over two and a half years, is aimed at people who occupy senior positions in SMEs in Romania. By the end of the program, participants will gain knowledge that will help to develop and complete their entrepreneurial skills to advance professionally.

b. Future without bonds - Integrated support platform for distance learning

Future without bonds is a project that has been successfully implemented at Ecological University from Bucharest - Romania. The project was financed from structural European funds for human resources development. The implementation of the E-learning platform was done in a universitary year which meant the pilot project. The platform is now used in distance learning programs for students. The platform facilities and the interface is presented in the following.

System architecture

The Proposed system architecture its on three layers (presentation layer, the logic of the application and the persistence of data in the database).

Presentation layer

Is given by the client interface of a web page. To access these pages is sufficient a web browser, standards-compliant HTML and XHTML: Internet Explorer, Firefox, Netscape etc.. In these pages will provide interface in a more user-friendly way by using AJAX technology specific controls to display information (lists of data, search results etc). Web Interface will have a color palette based on shades of green, bringing as much brand of Ecological University with users.

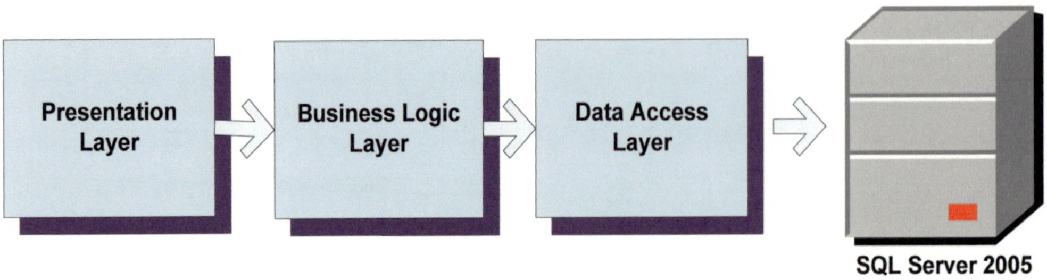

Fig. 4.The technical structure for the platform

XHTML compliant interface will, thus guaranteeing a correct view all web browsers that implement this standard.

Persistence layer

Database is provided by Microsoft SQL Server 2005. Saving data using an intermediate layer DAL (Data Access Layer), which transform the functions of the application in SQL queries or stored procedure calls. Using this layer will allow easy replacement of the port and the database on other servers, such as Oracle.
The use of such layer, represented in the figure below, will allow you to isolate code that access the database, allowing flexibility and speed in changing the database structure. Changing the database structure is the key to updating and improving the application in accordance with new requirements arise during the operation of the system.

Logic layer

Generating web pages is done by Microsoft IIS server application. This is, along with stored procedures in the database, the logic of the application.
In application, the code is written in C # language, there will be classes for each logical entity in the system: Student, Teacher, Test, Question, User, etc.. These classes have a dual role, being used to map structural or on a table in the database, and to contain specific business methods, according to object-oriented programming paradigm.
The technology that underlies the generation level of presentation is Microsoft ASP.NET 3.5. Also each web page includes code to be executed on the client, namely the web browser. Here we discuss the popular JavaScript and AJAX components that will reduce the time to view the information in the website.
Error management is through a unified system to deal with them. There are special windows for error messages, all types of incidents occurring are saved in the LOG files, grouped by day, and important actions are stored in the database along with their current time and the operator who performed the action in the system.
Using a system of auditing by saving actions in the database brings a very important advantage when you wish to study a problem arising in the system, or actions that operators did not recognize.
Clear separation between different levels of application will allow easy maintenance and a great flexibility factor to the emergence of new requirements. Both change existing pages, and create new pages will be done very quickly because the system uses *MASTER PAGE* entity type, containing all the components common to a set of interface pages.

In terms of scalability, the number of users can overcome without any problem 5000 users in the first stage, without having to commissioning of new hardware. If necessary, both computing power, storage capacity and bandwidth will be provided at no cost to the beneficiary for the entire duration of the maintenance contract.
In terms of changes in access rights, an administrator is able to set access rights for each share of the system. Each user role associated with use, and each role with a list of rights. Creation operators, assigning roles and rights at specifics roles is managed entirely by the system administrator directly from the software management module. The system is designed to allow easy definition of new rights, their definition is only needed as a constant number and scope of operation.

Technical features

Performances: Supplier shall guarantee a level of availability more than 99% because our servers are connected to the Internet through a provider with whom we have an agreed SLA more restrictive than that. Any intervention in the production application will be made only between 2:00 to 5:00, making the exception to this rule only in emergencies maximum when the application can not be used.

Multi-user operating system

The technological solution chosen meets all the criteria to support more than 1,000 simultaneous users, up to 5,000 simultaneous users, depending on the workload of the application. and Internet connection.
Ensure data consistency by using blocking routines of the business logic stored procedures. This ensure that, at short time, users can simultaneously modify the same set of information. Also this problem is partially solved by designing easy and database, with a building that are more operations such as insert, update operations are used only on user's own data set that generated this operation, avoiding such a conflict is to update data in the database.
Complex management actions will be based on cursor type tasks, but will run only at night to avoid the period of maximum load application.

Used platforms

The operating system is Microsoft Windows 2003, whose spread has proven reliability. Windows 2003 has an advanced system access, but also a mechanism for tracking errors.
Both the operating system, application and have a role-based access, authentication is done in system based on a username and password. Creating new accounts in the system, or if the password is entered incorrectly three times, will ask the user a CAPTCHA code.
Access to the Internet server is not permitted on port 80, that's why data losses caused by unauthorized entries are excluded. Both the operating system, SQL Server 2005 and are continuously updated by monitoring and Packet-sized installation and updates necessary to maintain a high level of security. Personnel authorized to administer this server connects to it using Remote Desktop Connection type applications, but only through a VPN interface, secured by additional password. When connecting to the application users need a username and password active. Both are case-sensitive. Account creation is done only by administrators and their creation is also need a valid email address and a unique registration number, thus avoiding operating errors which an account can be created several times. Passwords are not stored in the database system, retaining only the password hash code using SHA1 algorithm, making it impossible to know the user password to be used later, even by the administration.

System functionality

Intuitive and friendly interface

The user interface is intuitive, consistent and systematic, with uniform operating rules, being able to work with both mouse and keyboard to optimize massive data records.
The system must provide error messages in Romanian for:

- Data entry errors (inconsistent);
- Errors in logic to use;
- Errors from the server database management;
- Other types of errors.

Depending on the type of registered user (student, teacher, administrator) will be available only for registered user menus. It also will allow and overlapping of roles, for example based on a single account access will connect a person who teaches a course, but still the same person may participate as a student in another course. The same person may also be at the same time the system administrator.
The interface is optimally structured to allow access as quickly and as intuitive to the system functions. Are very airy windows user, the user information found on these pages just need some suggestions.
Each page have a similar structure, consisting of three main areas: header, content and footer. As you can see in the picture above, the header contains a band with its name, the current user connected, disconnect button, connect time. Also in this band will be able to make and logos of the beneficiary, the EU logo and operational program that has made financing etc.
Under this bandwidth can still be found two bands in the region header. These are current and address the current page menu, both of which are arranged one under another.
All application menu has been ordered not to occupy the horizontal surface of the display page, allowing the submenus to be displayed as a popup. This menu is generated based on access rights and the role the current user.

Error messages:

For each data field, the application will validate the data. Some data will be built in database/catalogs and the user can select from the drop-down, some will edit directly in editable fields.
Data from the drop-down will be correlations in the database and the system will generate error messages such as "*uncorrelated data ...*" , "*Required value should be selected ....*", etc..
For the data in editable fields, validation will be introduced such as: long mandatory minimum or maximum required field. The system will generate error messages like: "*Required*", "*mandatory minimum length x characters*", "*type characters are not allowed ....*".
For validation check-box type there will be validation rest of the fields and display confirmation messages/warnings, like: "*you checked ....*".
Also, there will be validations and error messages on the operating logic. This refers to the sequence of operations performed by the user. These validations will differ depending on the 4 types of users: visitor, student, teacher or administrator.
Validation will, where appropriate, before trying to save the data, for example when editing the value, or loss of focus by that field. Also the field is not properly validated, will be marked with different colors and an image that will attract user's attention. Also, when the user is with the mouse cursor over the component has not been validated, you will see a hint with description of problem.

The system will generate warning messages like "*You can not achieve the desired operation.*". Special messages will be displayed in areas where access is denied due to lack of authorization "*You do not have sufficient privileges to perform this operation.*".
All posts information, warning or confirmation message will have both text and related buttons, translated into Romanian. Therefore be used to display custom dialogs, avoiding the use of standard dialogues given operating system, whose buttons with text in English or the operating system was compiled.
For each message, along with text and buttons will also display an image suggestive of type information: exclamation mark, question mark, sign error in red etc.
If unexpected errors of all kinds, will try to explain, where possible origin of this error as clearly, accompanied by advice to contact the system administrator to resolve the problem. Errors will be studied later by the system administrator in consultation log file type.

Help system

The User's *Manual* is written in Romanian and will be represented in PDF format, its content will be anchors, allowing users to navigate through the content using mouse clicks on the chapters of the document contents.
From the application context will be able to call help, and as a result of this action will open a special page manual in PDF format system, mentioned above, but open directly to the desired chapter, based on anchors in the document.
Besides manual application, there are manual addressed to the system administrator who deals with specific problems. Course, the language is Romanian. And it will be created as a PDF document with anchors.
Both the menu Help / Help and manuals will be changed according to changes made after any new program. The system is organized into modules, each module having its pages. Below we describe in detail the functionality of each module.
*Administration:*An administrator will be able to manage at least the following entities and links between them: centers, universities, mass education (bachelor, master, postgraduate) courses, groups, years, subjects, teachers, and curriculum specialties. The management means can add, change, deletion, activation, deactivation, association.
The centers will have several colleges, each college has the form of education, and within each there are specializations, and groups.
The curriculum will be defined separately for each specialty in each year of study.
Management module is given a set of catalogs. In this case the order of definition is the following: center, faculty in the centers, forms of education in each faculty, year of study, specialization, association study subjects in each specialty groups for each year of study will inherit previously defined schedule. After that you can associate to each field of study within each group, one teacher from the list of teachers previously defined.
Teachers are defined globally, but is associated to each center for each subject in the curricula of the group. Can therefore be more teachers who teach the same material but different groups.
Administrators will have the right to define specific entities for each center separately, that there may be one administrator for each center, or an administrator can manage some or all centers.
Each director shall be entitled to a center which he also created a central rights can be transmitted by another administrator who has this right. Once an administrator has the right to that center, you can define all the entities associated with a center: faculty, groups, etc. specializations.

Teachers: A teacher will be able to upload materials in the form of files of different formats Once a teacher is assigned to a course for a particular group, it will appear in the window classes when a professor associated with connecting to the system.

The teacher may select a field and will open a window that management course where the teacher will be able to view the files already posted, to delete or add new ones by uploading to the server. The documents will be stored entirely in the database as objects of type BLOB.

The teacher will be able to define a series of questions (with one or more correct answers) and their associated answers (correct ones). Questions are defined for each subject separately. A text question is optional and an avatar and a set of answers with text and / or image. A teacher can manage the list of questions for that matter, that can add questions, modify or delete. For each question will be able to choose an image, text and X responses (each in turn with text and image). Also will check and correct answers.

Questions will begrouped by category. In a test, questions can be grouped into categories corresponding chapters of that matter.

Teachers will be able to define one or more tests for each subject of dealing. As input values for a new test we have set of possible questions, Duration, maximum, number of questions, etc.. Periods of development of the test will be defined separately for each group of students following such material.

Tests are defined for matter altogether, but we also have data-specific groups, such as date and time that will take a test. The test duration and number of questions will be defined on the field, so that each group have the same conditions of participation.

Some questions in the set will be automatically taken from previous years or groups, through selection by the teacher.

During a test, the computer will randomly pick a set of N questions (N specified by the teacher) for each student, available from the set of questions previously entered by the teacher.

The computer will randomly select a total of N questions for each student to give that test. In this way and order the questions will vary from one student to another. Also to be mixed randomly and the answers, we refer to the student display order.

Test results can be viewed and exported by teachers for each subject and group. After completing the test the teacher will be able to see a report with its results, to print them or export them in PDF format.

Teachers can define certain questions in order to drive the student government.When a teacher defines the set of test questions, he can choose by checking questions, those that are public, meaning that students can access as a sort of quiz to prepare for the exam.

The teacher will be able to see the system access history by his students (number and login, download documents, etc.) and can choose whether it will help in establishing activating the final grade. During the course you have associated a teacher, he will be able to view a report history for each student to access the system and can then take into account the historical mark the award. Activity Report will include student name, date and time of action (connecting to the system, disconnect, download documents, etc.).

Students can download their documents uploaded by teachers for school materials from the plan.After connecting a student in the system, among other things, will see the list of courses that is registered. When you choose a course will open a page with all the details of that course: title, description, teacher, etc. and also loaded the professor for that course.

Students can download/upload electronic files in default locations (essays, themes, etc). For each course, students can download materials and their various topics, as described in the previous paragraph. Also students will be able to upload the server various themes or essays. Once they are loaded, the teacher will receive a message informing the student that made a theme and will have a link to access that topic.

Students can ask teachers questions his room in private or public system.

A student will be able to view posts related to his account and his notes for each subject.

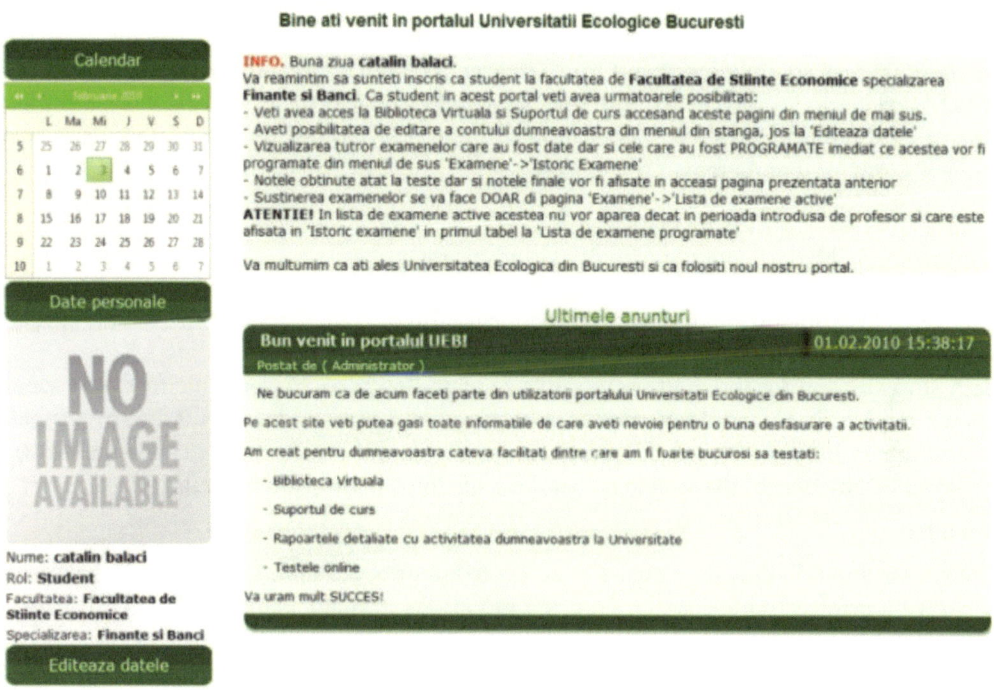

Fig. 5. **Start Web Page U.E.B.** (Ecological University of Bucharest http://www.kopernic.ueb.ro/GUI/Desktop.aspx)

Both students and teachers will have their mail box, where they can view past messages and they will be able to send and other messages in the system. The system will also have a chat, where you can discuss general topics in real-time.
At the date set by teachers, students will be able to pass the tests for materials studied, displaying to the final result.
Student input in support of the test section will be only the date and time set by the teacher, but it will resolve questions chosen randomly by the system, and finally the student will see only the result, not the right answers to questions.
In the event, while supporting tests of connection problems or other problems that make it impossible to access the student system, a top administrator rights will be able to reboot to test that a student or an entire group. The system will remain a history of these rebooting the user to reset the test, proof, date and exact time of operation are required. Optional and can store information about the host computer where to do this.
Resetting the test will be for a student or teacher the possibility to set the exact date and time when the student will again be examined. These actions are performed only by administrators, and all these actions are monitored in the system keeping all available information is absolutely important for user who executed the action (account information, which is connected station), date and time at second and subject affected by the initialization (the student group). As observation should mention that successfully completed a test by a student group or that there will be rebooted.

Virtual Library:

The system will have a module / library electronic menu.
This module will contain specialized books and other materials in electronic format could help with information platform users. Platform administrators and teachers with special rights can upload books and materials in electronic format.
Both students and visitors will users rights to view this book in electronic format. Virtual library module is a module of interest where you can upload documents in any format. Charging can be done by administrators or teachers, and access these documents can be achieved by any user of the system is that it is a visitor, student, administrator or teacher.

Reports:

The system should allow only the users access to a number of different reports. Reports can be viewed, printed to a printer or exported in various formats, PDF and Excel is required. Reports can be generated only by administrators or teachers, each of these categories have access to special reports. Any report can be viewed in web page to change the scaling factor, and be exported to PDF or Excel.
Generate report introduced a set of questions to each teacher for the part. A teacher will be able to view the set of questions for the courses they patronize, and can export them in formats like PDF or Excel.
Generate tests against reset.
Generate audit report access of the system. These reports will be available for each center administrators to have access rights.
Generate report with the results obtained by students in tests for each test / field / group / year / college / center separately.
Generate test reports / monitoring of the activities students (login, access menus, materials downloaded / uploaded in the system, etc.) These reports will be available for each center

administrators to have access rights. The teachers also will be able to access these reports only to his students.

7. Conclusion

In our information society, no one organization knows everything it needs to know collaboration creates a process for sharing information between interested parties - so that both benefit by having a more global understanding of issues and concerns. The global understanding created by collaboration fosters more accurate decision making, greater efficiencies, lower costs, and propels innovation. The on-line collaboration is applicable at any level, but specially for higher education and adults education.

In conclusion the e-learning systems are useful for any type of education, at any level. E-learning system are used also for the high school level or small children's education (eg. AEL system created by Siveco – educational software provider from Romania). The good practice example is concluding for the present work and emphasizes the importance of the information technology used in the educational processes.

As a future work we are designing a Virtual E-learning Center for adult specialization in different fields, center which will include MLearning for the people that doesn't have a PC or access to a computer but have a phone, taking into consideration the fact that today the number of phones in the world is three times bigger than the number of PC's

8. Acknowledgement

Thorough this chapter I want to acknowledge the work of all my colleagues and collaborators who participate in the implementation of the project which result is the e-learning platform, used now for distance learning of the students in Ecologic University.

9. References

Baltazar, P.H.(2010), The future of learning, FESC-UHAM

Davidson C and Goldberg D, (2010), The future of Thinking, Learning Institutions in a digital age, Chicago, the John D and Catherine MacArthur Foundation

Demiray, U et al (2010), e-Learning Practices. Cases on Challenges facing e-Learning and national development, Eskitehir, Turkey, Anadolu University

Leinenbach, J (2010), eLearning Management, Polirom

Lewin, T (2011), As on line courses grow, So does financial aid fraud, NY Times, Oct 13

Maehl, W. H. (2000). Lifelong Learning at its Best: Innovative Practices in Adult Credit Programs, San Francisco: Jossey-Bass.

Pershing J.A.(2006), Handbook of human performance technology.Principles. Practices. Potential., Pfeiffer, SF

Ravenscroft, A. (2001). Designing E-learning Interactions in the 21st Century: revisiting and rethinking the role of theory. European Journal of Education

Stacey P(2011), Teaching Science on line, Ed Tech Frontier, Oct 6.

Tremblay, E.(2010), Educating the Mobile Generation, journal of Computers in Mathematics and Science Teaching, 29(2), Chesapeake, VA.AACE

Watson, D. (2001). Pedagogy before technology: Re-thinking the relationship between ICT and teaching.Education and Information Technologies

Weller,M. (2002). Delivering learning on the Net, UK: Kogan Page

http://www.kopernic.ueb.ro/GUI/Desktop.aspx

Part 2

E-Learning for People with Special Needs

7

Designing E-Learning Collaborative Tools for Blind People

Maria Claudia Buzzi[1], Marina Buzzi[1], Barbara Leporini[2] and Giulio Mori[1]
[1]IIT – CNR, Pisa
[2]ISTI – CNR, Pisa
Italy

1. Introduction

The basic principle of e-learning is to achieve personal learning goals by acquiring skills and knowledge through computers or other network-enabled systems. The use of computers and the Internet have changed classic methods of teaching and learning, introducing the concept of distance learning as a great opportunity for studying unfettered by constraints of time and space. Although information and communication systems are helpful for implementing both the learning and teaching processes, e-learning is not merely a trivial way to transfer knowledge using electronic devices (computers, smart phones, mp3 players, etc.) while relying on the network and Web user interfaces. According to the recent concept of third-generation distance learning, the active participation of students in the formative process is an important factor in the personal learning phase (Beard & Wilson, 2002; Kolb, 1984). E-learning is a great opportunity to move from old traditional systems towards more effective and efficient methods for acquiring and transferring knowledge beyond the traditional classroom environments, adapting to the modern life and new technologies.

In addition, acquisition of new skills and knowledge is not only affected by an individual's mental schemes or beliefs, but also by their interaction, cooperation and collaboration with others (Merrill, 1991). Communication and social collaboration are crucial for generating the best learning environment. In the learner-centred model, students assume the most important role while teachers investigate and experiment more interesting and interactive ways of teaching. Another important aspect is personalization of rhythms of studying, according to student abilities.

Unfortunately, learning tools and collaborative tools in general are not always designed to be effectively used by blind users, who generally interact via an assistive technology, a screen reader, using a vocal synthesizer and only the keyboard. For instance, collaborative editing of documents could be very difficult or not usable at all for blind users if: 1) they are unaware of other users' changes; 2) the formatting toolbars and other interactive elements like menus are difficult or impossible to access; 3) the list of documents is not quickly available (Mori et al., 2011).

In this chapter we will analyze e-learning collaborative and alternative tools in the learning environment, following the new paradigm for personalized acquisition of knowledge, in order to suggest basic guidelines for making effective and improving the interaction for blind people. We will present the possibilities and advantages of e-learning, focusing on its challenging opportunities for the blind. We will describe how blind people interact with interfaces using a screen reader with a voice synthesizer (as output modality) in combination with a keyboard (as input device). In addition, we will propose suggestions for improving the design of more effective tools to facilitate collaboration and blind users' interaction and personalization. Finally, we will supply two examples of the new paradigm of learning: 1) the design of more accessible interfaces of a Web editing collaborative tool, interacting with a screen reader and 2) a Web system to personalize learning by blind students using an mp3 player.

Generally, active participation and collaborative interaction can improve the learning experience, so the full support of screen reader users in e-learning collaborative user interfaces (UIs) could also improve interaction and learning for blind people.

2. Related works

E-learning has become a hot research topic in recent years. Usability of e-learning systems and objects is a primary focus of research in this field. E-learning users can vary significantly regarding differences in learning strategies, know-how, experience, motivation to learn, user age and ability. If appropriately designed and implemented, e-learning systems are more effective and useful than classroom learning (Debevc & Bele, 2008). However, interactive learning is still difficult for persons with disabilities who use assistive technologies. Various studies focus on the usability of e-learning systems and some also include a general discussion on accessibility, but to our knowledge only a few focus on totally blind persons (especially considering collaborative tools). In (Ardito et al., 2005) the authors outlined a methodology for the rigorous evaluation of e-learning applications, but accessibility for disabled students is not analyzed. Sloan et al. proposed a holistic approach to treating accessibility. They believe that the goal of universal accessibility on the Web is inappropriate, and that instead it is necessary to explore multiple routes to equivalent experience (Sloan et al., 2006). Furthermore, Zaharias critically examined the usability of e-learning applications and proposed the student's intrinsic motivation to learn as a new usability measure (Zacharias, 2006). Developing a usability evaluation method based on a questionnaire, he carried out two large empirical studies showing the reliability of this approach. As Kelly et al. argued, rather than demanding that an individual learning resource be universally accessible, it is the learning outcome that needs to can be accessible (Kelly et al., 2005). Based on user profiles, metadata and dynamic connection to resources, the user's experience can be customized to match his/her abilities. Then an appropriate design is crucial for improving the accessibility and usability of e-learning Systems (Kelly et al., 2005).

All disabilities should be considered when designing e-learning applications. Leporini and Buzzi have discussed accessibility issues for e-learning systems (such as Learning Management Systems environments) and they have proposed empirical principles for designers developing e-learning applications in order to simplify interaction for a blind student or teacher (Leporini & Buzzi, 2007). E-learning environments should be friendly and easy to use. Furthermore, the educational material should be suitable for the abilities and skills of any user, so the same information should be provided through multiple channels, i.e. visual, auditory, tactile. De Marsico et al. defined methodological guidelines involving users with disabilities as well as pedagogical experts in the development process, believing that input from different know-how could enrich the quality of e-learning applications and provide a more satisfying learning experience (De Marsico et al., 2006). They also include two examples of building and providing Learning Objects accessible respectively to visually- and hearing-impaired students. Rodriguez et al. described a project for improving the e-learning experience for the visually impaired, based on ethno-methodology and taking into account psychosocial issues, the user context and experience (Rodriguez et al., 2006). Next they created different Learning Object formats suitable for the blind, including DAISY (Digital Accessible Information System).

Within the framework of a project aimed at providing an accessible e-learning platform for disabled and adult learners, Santos et al. (Santos et al., 2007) illustrated a methodology for developing standard-based accessible courses using two-step evaluations. However, for the totally blind more specific UI features are necessary than those in this study, such as providing a page overview, full control of interface elements and easy and rapid navigation via keyboard.

Cooperative environments and tools are particularly interesting and useful in the educational field, where knowledge is assembled cooperatively. Some studies focus on the accessibility and usability of e-learning systems for blind people but to our knowledge only a few specifically involve a study concerning collaborative environments and tools.

Khan et al. (Khan et al., 2010) performed a usability study in the educational environment ThinkFree, a collaborative writing system, with four novice and four experienced users. Specifically, authors compared ThinkFree to Google Docs by means of a user test with Think Aloud protocol, a post-test questionnaire to collect user feedback and interviews to validate the gathered results. Although ThinkFree proved effective for the proposed tasks, efficiency and availability of resources were more limited than in Google Docs.

Schoeberlein et al. (Schoeberlein & Yuanqiong, 2009), revising recent literature on groupware accessibility and existing solutions, have highlighted the need for future research. Authors observed that most articles address the needs of a specific category of disabled persons. In particular, visually-impaired people with reduced or no visual perception experience objective difficulties when interacting with a complex layout via screen reader, and they are frequently studied.

Recently Kobayashi developed a client application (Voice Browser for Groupware systems VoBG) for enabling visually impaired persons inexperienced in computer technology to interact with a groupware system that is very popular in Japan (Garoon 2). The VoBG browser intercepts Web pages generated by the groupware server, parses their HTML code and simplifies on-fly their content and structure in a more understandable format for target users (Kobayashi, 2008).

Thiessen gave an example of using WAI-ARIA to design and implement a chat, highlighting some limitations of live regions (Thiessen & Chen, 2007). However, this problem is common with emerging standards, since browsers and assistive technologies need to conform to the new specifications, and this takes some time before reaching stable implementations.

Different studies exploring singular aspects of educational and collaborative environments should be integrated towards a new concept of learning adaptable to all the categories of students, including people with special needs.

3. Background: A new paradigm of learning

Analyzing the rising trend of information and communication technologies, the emergence of new devices with new interfaces and web 2.0 technologies has changed our way of living, the way of communicating, operating and delivering knowledge. As a consequence, a new paradigm occurs in transferring the knowledge from teachers to students, and vice versa. Before trying to analyze this new learning paradigm, it is necessary to understand the different impact of studying activities on the efficiency of learning.

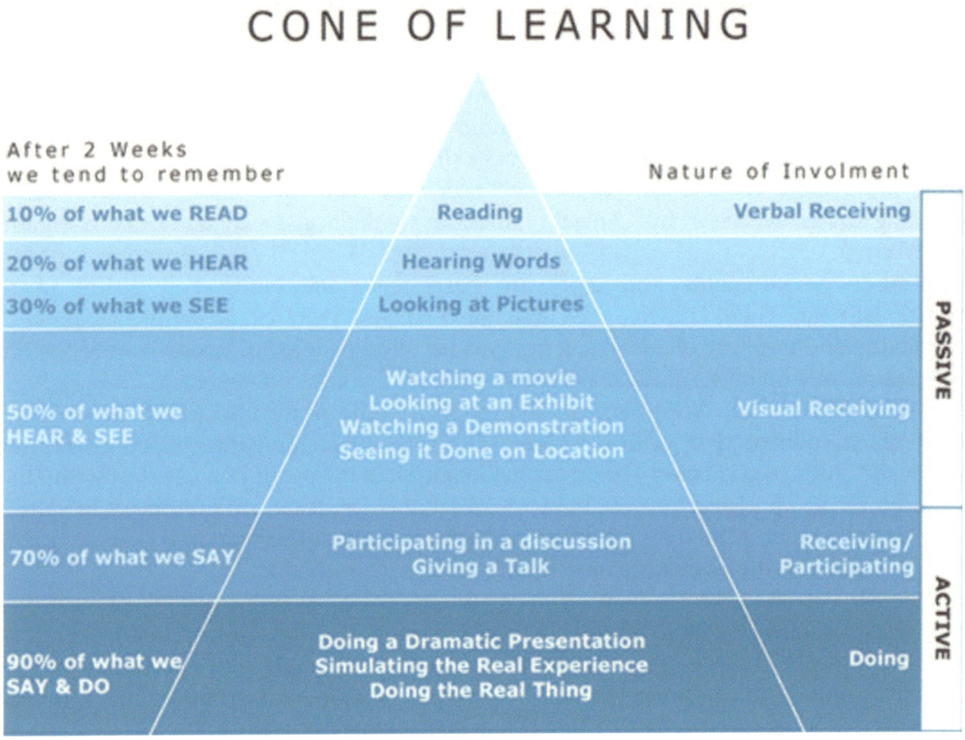

Fig. 1. Cone of learning (Dale 1969).

3.1 Cone of learning

Edgard Dale, an educationalist at Ohio State University (Dale, 1969), conducted his research on the impact of audio and visual material, to investigate the learning effects of direct experience vs. pure abstraction or simple academic theory. Dale got interesting results from his experiences with students. He tried different methods on different student groups, and he tested their knowledge after two weeks. Groups of students that learned from just reading remembered only 10% of the information, while the group that learned from watching and hearing a demonstration remembered 50% of content, and the group that actually practiced a real experience, remembered the 90%. Dale's research emphasized a *"Cone of learning"*, distinguishing the learning methods in passive and active categories. Graphical results of the Cone of Learning are shown in Fig. 1.

Nevertheless the validity of the Cone of Learning depends on the subject's personal abilities. This is especially critical for persons with disabilities, especially subjects with learning disturbances or pathologies. Furthermore there is the tendency of individuals to have a certain resistance to change, not easy to overcome. In the following section we will present the main reasons.

3.2 Need for new educational learning methods

Social and cultural changes are not always simple, especially when they involve many actors and consistent shifts in their habits and their way of thinking. The aim to improve learning efficiency at different levels of the Cone of Learning can have great impact on teachers who have to prepare learning material in an alternative multimedia style (instead of mainly textual), with considerable effort. This effort and consequent tasks increase still more for teachers with some sort of physical disability who address the same problems as students with special needs. Other general and cultural obstacles for applying the Cone of Learning are (Potts & LaMarsh 2004; Birenbaum et al. 2006): 1) despite the fact that world knowledge increases exponentially so fast, and quick adaptation is necessary, most academic institutions continue to rely on older educational methods; 2) Higher education is not yet using technology to its best advantage and rapid industry development is infrequently in correlation with the education programs; 3) there is a gap between the knowledge that is taught in the university or in the educational institutes and that required to students in the actual jobs. In the same paper, Birenbaum, states that in various European countries current assessments focus on *"teaching for assessment and not teaching for learning"*; this practices is limited in scope and fails too many learners because they ignore individual learner differences.

An interesting journal (Bisoux, 2007) interviewed five experts in online education, showing how they stress many common points about the incomplete diffusion of e-learning:

1. not understanding the advantages that online technology affords
2. little interest in discovering how students really use technology and how online pedagogical structures operate
3. lack of training to use that technology to best advantage
4. difficulty understanding that the Web is not yet a simple one-way channel of delivery but an immersive environment where users-learners create and share information
5. collaborative interactive e-learning environments help students *"learn to be"*, not just watch and listen. At present, the situation has changed little.

According to the difficulty applying the Cone of Learning, there is a need to change traditional teaching methods, adapting to the new rapidly changing situation and exploiting Dale's different levels of learning delivery. Past teaching methods implied hierarchical transfer of knowledge from teachers or professors to the students, who passively accepted the given information. Students often repeat or mechanically reproduce information with the only goal of passing the exam or being promoted at the end of the year. This way of teaching is mere mechanical transmission of information, often reflecting the teacher's interests and area of expertise, and not considering the real interests of the students. Modern educational methods should offer students the possibility choosing topics of interest so they can further explore what they really like (in addition to the basic institutional program). Considering the huge amount of available data on the Web and media in this "epoch of information", new generations of students are multitasking and able to acquire information about their interests faster than in the past. Google-like multimedia information systems delivery contrast with traditional educational passive methods. Students want to be active participants in the learning process, reproducing knowledge based on experience. Introducing this kind of interactive learning, students will be able to understand better and remember much longer (Tomasegovic et al. 2011).

Introducing a more interactive way of learning can change the vertical hierarchy between teachers and students to a horizontal one, improving teacher-student interaction and relations. Active interaction is a concept that is strictly integrated with the idea of personalization. Active interaction improves the "feeling" of the students of being the primary participant in the learning process, while personalization gives them the opportunity to learn "anytime, anywhere" following self-based rhythms of study to fulfil their needs. Students feel more involved in the learning process and teachers can improve their educational skills, designing new learning methods to help students developing their talents and capabilities. Traditional educational methods valued individual effort, while the new learning paradigm focuses on emphasizing interaction between students with the objective of also favouring the communication and socialization skills, which are very important in the learning but also in the working environment. Students are often involved in group or working teams, because cooperation and collaboration are fundamental to a learning experience based on concrete experience.

4. Collaboration

Human-Computer Interaction (HCI) is a research field aiming at improving interaction of users with applications and electronic devices. Its aim is to do so by developing new user interfaces (UIs) that make interaction more natural and devices easy-to-use for any individual. A key concept for HCI is usability: according to the ISO definition, an interface should allow the user to achieve a target goal (effectiveness) in the best (efficient) and fully satisfying way (ISO 9241-11, 1998). The evolution of the working style of human beings, and improved technology regarding communication and interaction mechanisms have profoundly changed the classic concept of HCI towards a new HCHI (Human-Computer-Human Interaction), in order to work in collaboration with other people. These changes have introduced the Computer-Supported Cooperative Work (CSCW) discipline. The user interacts not only with the system (a typical area of HCI) but also with other users throughout the system, performing cooperative tasks (typical area of CSCW). The term **groupware** is especially used for this technology (usually with use of computers) to facilitate a task shared among many persons. In order to get high quality groupware applications, special features regarding CSCW should be taken into account: collaboration, coordination, communication, information sharing and cooperation (Poltrock & Grudin, 1994, 1999, 2005). While **cooperation** is used for small groups of users who share key objectives and cooperate among themselves, **collaboration** is used for big groups (such as big organizations) that collaborate together even when they have different goals (possibly even coming into conflict). The main difference is that the term "cooperation" is used for people working closely together (Grudin, 1994). **Coordination** is fundamental in any organization working in a unifying way to increase quality and reduce costs (Poltrock & Grudin, 1999). **Communication** brings people into contact through frequent, unplanned, high-quality and real-time interaction (Greenberg, 1989). Data, information, documents in general are shared (**information sharing**), elaborated, modified in a virtual software environment to ease interaction and improve knowledge between collaborators (Poltrock & Grudin, 1999).

Although active cooperation between students is fundamental and facilitates the training process during practice, sometimes individual learning is preferable, especially regarding theoretical aspects (Prince et al., 2005; Stahl, 2005). Calibration and combination between an individual's learning phase (following personal rhythms) and the active collaboration phase with other participants, is an important aspect discussed in academic and research literature (Kayes, et al., 2005). Sometimes an approach to teaching and learning combines traditional face-to-face classroom methods with more modern computer-supported activities (*blended learning*), because this strategy creates a more integrated approach for both instructors and learners.

Active interaction with other students (following a common goal), listening to different points of view or suggestions from a teacher (to clarify obscure concepts and other issues in the studying phase) is a kind of collaboration that provides concrete benefits for the personal learning process.

However, collaboration can also be influenced by different ways of content delivery. For example, the off-line or on-line modes of learning produce a completely different user experience. In fact, Computer Based Training (CBT) consists of only self-paced learning activities, usually delivered by CD-ROM, while Web Based Training (WBT) is delivered via Internet using a web browser, allowing more interaction with the external world. Sometimes a "live" collaborative experience is also preferable: for example visiting an exhibition can be more effective than obtaining cultural information from a Web site or multimedia CD (Ghiani et al., 2009).

Between collaborative features, **awareness** is fundamental (especially using collaborative computer-supported tools) since it represents a user's perception of the other users in the system. A participating user interacting with other users on an interface should know who is performing (or performed) an action, when, where and specifically what. Collaboration in e-learning environments allows easier acting in time and space, really affecting the way people interact. Combination of other additional special features of time and space (typical of a groupware application), produces four categories of collaborative tools (time-space matrix):

1. same time/same places (in which decision rooms, single display groupware, shared table/wall display, etc. are typical e-learning tools);
2. same time/different places (using video conferencing, instant messaging, chats, shared screen, etc.);
3. different times/different places (using email, bulletin boards, group calendar, wikis, etc.);
4. different times/same places (using team rooms, shift work groupware, project management, etc.).

Collaborative environments should keep in mind many learning styles and interaction needs of different kinds of people, including people with special needs, so the design of accessible and usable interfaces is crucial.

5. Importance of accessible and usable interfaces

Knowledge and information can be properly expressed heterogeneously using text, audio, videos, etc. (depending on the educational content), so interfaces of e-learning tools can present many multimedia elements (enriched user-interfaces) involving multi-sensorial channels (visual, auditory and kinaesthetic) (Fleming, 2001; Hawk & Shah, 2007; Kayes et al., 2005; Stahl, 2005). Unfortunately, visual and multimedia interaction can be a problem for users with visual disabilities.

E-learning environments should be usable by anyone. For this reason, it is important to also verify the accessibility and usability of e-learning collaborative tools for people with special needs. Accessibility and usability should always be considered during the design of a user interface allowing universal access to anyone. Accessibility permits users to reach on-line application content, while usability provides simple, efficient and satisfying navigation and interaction.

Guidelines for designing usable and accessible Web interfaces have been proposThe W3C Web Content Accessibility Guidelines (WCAG, 2008) are general principles for making Web content more accessible and usable for people with disabilities. The WCAG (2.0) are organized into four principles: clear perception of content information (content perceivable), complete interaction with an interface in its functions (interface elements operable), comprehension of meaning (content understandable), and maximizing the interface's compatibility with new assistive technologies and devices (content robustness).

6. Blind user interaction

Facing many kind of disabilities can require different and individual strategies. In the research literature, of all the various sensorial disabilities (low vision, motor, auditory) blindness presents the most difficulties when completing a task (Craven & Brophy, 2003; Ivory et al., 2004; Petrie et al., 2004). For this reason, we focus our attention only on blind users, who have no sight at all, without other kind of disabilities (motor, auditory, etc.).

There is a tendency to assume that people who become blind manage better with blindness than people who were born blind, because they have more references and memories. However, this tendency can depend on individual learning and life experiences (Chambel et al., 2009).

Blind people interact with a user interface using an assistive technology, the screen reader with a voice synthesizer or a Braille display. The latter is expensive and slow, so it is rarely used. A screen reader is a software that describes aurally (if a voice synthesizer is used) and sequentially the content of a user interface; blind users mostly navigate via keyboard since it is considered faster than a vocal input. This kind of interaction and perception can be difficult and frustrating for blind people because:

a. content serialization produces an overload of vocal information in sequence
b. a blind user has no overall perception of the whole interface
c. the screen reader announces information mixing content and structure (related to description of interactive elements)
d. the screen reader can announce information in the wrong order, depending on the HTML code (for instance a table's content is generally organized in columns but it is read by rows).

All these problems cannot be completely resolved by the W3C Web Content Accessibility Guidelines alone because they are general principles for making Web content more accessible and usable for all people with disabilities. To fill this gap, the WAI group is working on the Accessible Rich Internet Applications specification (WAI-ARIA) that specifically aims to make dynamic web content and applications (developed with Ajax, (X)HTML, JavaScript) more accessible to blind people.

6.1 Accessible Rich Internet Applications (WAI-ARIA) suite

Usually, certain functionalities used in websites are unavailable to some users with disabilities, especially people who rely on screen readers and people who cannot use a mouse. Typical difficulties of blind interaction using a screen reader with a vocal synthesizer can be resolved by using the WAI-ARIA suite (WAI-ARIA, 2011), which favours effective interaction with the Rich Internet Application; among other things, WAI-ARIA permits drag & drop via keyboard, the definition of standard roles for graphical widgets of the user interfaces and also allows developers to define the main regions of a user interface to allow a blind person to move quickly to the desired area instead of being forced to interact with the UI sequentially. The challenge is considerable regarding one of the most notorious problem for Web developers and users: different behaviours of different browsers. In addition, it is necessary to also consider different supports of browsers for different versions of screen readers. For our tests, we used a common commercially available screen reader, JAWS for Windows (JAWS, 2011), in versions 10, 11 and 12.

Although considering all these aspects is not an easy task, we can suggest some basic characteristics for collaborative learning tool interfaces and applications, focusing on facilitating interaction and learning experience for blind users.

7. Appropriate learning tools

Designing appropriate learning tools for any kind of users is not a trivial task. In general a good embedded e-learning tool or platform should take into consideration the following aspects:

a. **personalization** (considering a student's knowledge level, objectives, time and pace)
b. **learning by doing** (through practical activities, simulations, virtual laboratory, etc.)
c. **active participation and collaboration with other students** in the Virtual Learning Environment (sharing resources with other students, teachers, tutors or mentors).

We believe that for blind users, extra aspects should also be addressed at three levels:

1. **Making accessible and usable interfaces for blind students**: this feature will also facilitate and simplify the interaction of other users;
2. **Increasing the accessibility of awareness information on other collaborators**: every user (especially the blind) want to know who is collaborating, what, when and where she/he is doing something, and desire to be updated on her/his and others' status;
3. **Providing educational content in different sensorial channels**: interaction and integration between blind students and students without disabilities will develop perception of less exploited internal sensorial representations in everyone.

In addition, considerations on the use of different sensory channels are indispensable for understanding their effects on learning and delivering educational content.

7.1 Importance of enriching sensory learning experience

Most common and important communication media in our society are based on sight (television, graphical advertisements, 3D movies, illustrated magazines, Web, etc.). Many studies confirm visual sensorial channels as the most used by humans and the fastest way to acquire information. Obviously, this way of communicating is unavailable to blind users. The exclusion of printed educational material (books, magazines, journals, etc.) is a major challenge for blind students using digital content in the educational environments when there is reference to visual material (photos, diagrams, videos, etc.) in the didactic content. Nevertheless, a person's predominant internal sensorial perception (visual, auditory and kinaesthetic) has an impact on her/his interaction with the external environment and on the way new information is elaborated. An important study by UCLA Professor of Psychology Albert Meharabian (Meharabian, 1971), expert in communication, asserts that especially in the beginning of communicating new concepts, the impact of verbal communication (words) accounts for 7%, non-verbal communication (tone of voice, intonation, speed, etc.) accounts for 38%, and paraverbal (body language) accounts for 55% of overall communication. Independently of the precision of these percentages, it is clear that this predominant visual gap for the blind should be compensated for in a different way. A solution to this aspect could be the exploitation of senses other than vision (hearing, touch, sense of smell and taste), using them in a single modality or in a proper input/output combination (otherwise, a bad combination can decrease attention during learning). Perceptibly, the senses of smell and taste do not appear important for learning activities (excepting in particular contexts in which particular sensors are used), but hearing and touch can be exploited in a more sophisticated manner in many applications. For example the quality of voices and their characteristics (tone, speed, etc.), targeted use of sounds, use of non-invasive haptic devices, use of appropriate tactile effects or use of sensors for recognizing human gestures, etc., are all elements that can enrich the learning experience of multi-sensorial educational material.

Sight is the predominant sensorial channel and can quickly deliver more information than touch and listening (Ghiani et al., 2011; Chittaro, 2010). However, in terms of acquiring information, touch requires more time than listening to be familiarized during decoding of the information; so touch is usually used in combination with audio and graphics. When designing applications for the blind, audio is preferred for delivering crucial information, while touch is used to integrate particular feedback effects or to emphasize repetitive notifications (being less annoying than using the auditory channel).

However, design of an interface for a specific sensorial channel can also have effects on learning. For example graphical or vocal interfaces have substantial differences. Although audio has many advantages (see section 8.2), interaction with a vocal interface presents different and limiting characteristics compared to a graphical one. Using a metaphor, sight can transfer more information "in parallel", while listening is "sequential" (Pitt & Edwards, 2003). A graphical interface can present an overview of the content, while audio interaction has to face volatile human memory. Ability to memorize during interaction with a vocal interface is limited to few seconds, so a user can be easily distracted or disoriented about her/his status, often requiring feedback from the system. Thus designing learning applications using alternative sensorial channels other than sight has particular requirements.

Blind students also present different styles of learning, even if they have a tendency to be more audible and sometimes kinaesthetic in regard to touch. Thus, different approaches of learning should be adapted to the individuals. Designing learning application for students with special needs can benefit other students as well, but sometimes it is necessary to consider particular situations. For example, a too-meticulous description of a diagram can become boring for a sighted person, beyond a certain level of detail, while it can be essential for a blind person. (Chambel et al., 2009). It is important to be aware that proper collaborative learning tools should offer different choices of suitable educational material, fulfilling the needs of different kinds of students interacting together or studying alone.

Although personalization of learning "anytime, anywhere" is an important aspect of the new learning paradigm, sometimes it is also necessary to consider the effects on interaction when a student (blind or without disabilities) moves, instead of sitting at a desk (Chittaro, 2010):

- **Perceptual**: conditions of the environment can change (illumination, noise, temperature, vibration, motion, etc.). For example, exploitation of the auditory channel can be difficult in a noisy environment.
- **Motor**: mobile conditions can impair the ability to fine-control voluntary movements. For example, vibrotactile devices can be less effective during acceleration or deceleration in a vehicle.
- **Social**: sometimes certain kind of interaction are restricted by the social rules. For example the use of gestures near strangers can be embarrassing, or using sound at a conference not well-tolerated.
- **Cognitive**: mobility can limit one's attention to the device or to the application content. For example, paying attention to the announcement changes in the airport or listening to an audio device while properly responding to other people can be source of distraction. Also, interaction with an audio device in the street even for a sighted user can be a risk for her/his safety.

It is clear that the proper combination of multi-sensorial channels in a proper manner together with knowledge acquisition by real experience are important factors for more efficient learning: Dale's Cone of Learning confirms this, as shown in Fig. 1 (Section 3.1).

8. Examples of learning tools

In this section we present two examples of possible learning tools. The first example is a preliminary prototype related to the design and development of more accessible interfaces of a Web collaborative editing tool (Google Documents) that improves the interaction of blind users operating with the JAWS screen reader (Mori et al., 2011); the second example is not properly a collaborative tool (in the strict meaning of term), but could be used by teachers and students to facilitate delivery of educational material, i.e., provided with the tool of the previous example. We designed and developed an experimental accessible Web system transforming digital documents to audio podcasts loadable on an mp3 player. In this example, we want to emphasize three important concepts of the new learning paradigm: a) the importance of using different sensorial channel for blinds and sighted users (for example, belonging to and cooperating together in the same class); b) the importance of personalized learning ("anytime, anywhere") beyond the classroom limits; c) the importance of using tools that can facilitate teachers and students. This second example shows a Web tool transforming digital documents (for example edited with Google Documents), in audio podcasts that can be loaded on a personal mp3 player (Mori et al., 2010). Audio podcasts exploit the auditory sensorial channel of the students, in order to facilitate personalization of studying following self-based rhythms. The concept of learning "anytime, anywhere" beyond the class limits is a key concept for all students, and also helps teachers improve their way of teaching. The tool of the second example could be useful for any student and specifically is really useful for blind students in which the going-over phase is critical.

8.1 Design and development of accessible interfaces of Google Documents

Google Docs is a collaborative web-based word processor, spreadsheet, presentation, form, and data storage service offered by Google (Google Docs, 2007). Google Documents is the Google Docs application focused on collaborative editing and word processing. This application allows users to edit text documents at the same/different times and places. It is an online collaborative word processor.

In a preliminary study, we analyzed interaction with Google Docs via JAWS (version 10, 11 and 12) on both the Microsoft Internet Explorer (IE) and Mozilla Firefox browsers in order to understand the problems encountered by blind people when writing a document collaboratively, focusing on the login, document list and text editing Web pages. The design and implementation of a modified version of these Google Docs interfaces aimed to incorporate accessibility criteria enhancing user experience while maintaining the same appealing "look & feel" (Mori et al., 2011).

The main accessibility problems detected by our inspection (in February 2011) via screen reader can be summarized as follows:

a. Many interactive elements cannot be detected by a screen reader nor be accessed via keyboard (since they are not standard (X)HTML elements and their labels are announced by the screen reader as simple text), making some tasks impossible to complete.
b. Blind users have difficulty orienting themselves during interaction, listening to the interface contents sequentially, with no possibility of quickly moving from one part of the interface to another or using main editing functions (such as creating or accessing a document) or the document list.
c. Lack of a summary attribute for table used as layout purposes for the list of documents in the Main page does not quickly provide useful information on its content, and this requires and extra effort for blind users who have to read all cells sequentially to understand the content of the table (see area 5 of Fig. 2).
d. The editor is not practically accessible. The main menu (file, edit, view, insert, format, etc.) and the style formatting toolbar (font type or size, etc.) are inaccessible because they cannot be reached via keyboard, while bold, italic or underlined functions can only be used through keyboard shortcuts (CTRL+b, CTRL+i, etc).
e. Some dialogue windows are not accessible at all and messages notifying the presence of other users are not announced by the screen reader, against the awareness principle (Fig. 3).

The modified pages of Google Docs have been created saving the original pages and ridding them of useless code (such as Javascript and functions responsible for dynamic behaviour of interface elements). Creating the modified pages starting from the original Google Documents pages was preferred instead of creating them from scratch, permitting a better maintenance of the same "look & feel". Fig. 2 shows the Main ("All items") page of the modified UI.

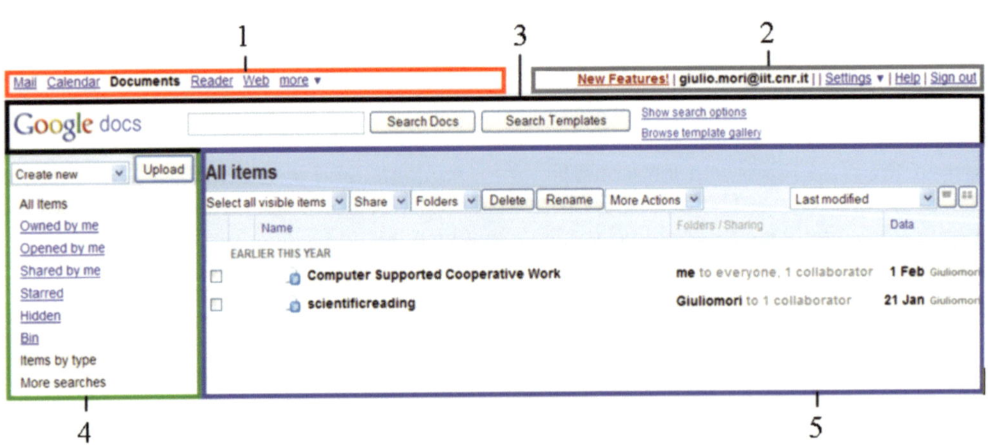

Fig. 2. Modified Google Docs "All items" page, divided into five areas.

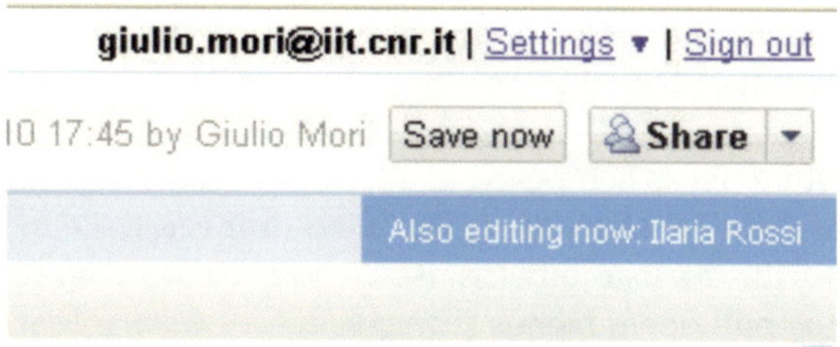

Fig. 3. Graphical notification of another collaborator online.

Previously listed accessibility problems have been fixed as described below:

a. Interactive elements (buttons, links, pull down menus, etc.) in the modified interfaces have been substituted with standard (X)HTML widgets, producing more accessible effects, because they has become reachable via keyboard, allowing JAWS to announce them.

b. Each modified page has been divided into a number of areas to facilitate user navigation, permitting a blind user to jump quickly from one point to another and avoid listening to all the content sequentially. Areas are not visible to the users, but are marked by WAI-ARIA landmarks roles allowing a blind user to move quickly to a different area (by pressing a special shortcut that provides a list of areas navigable via arrow keys). Fig. 2 shows five areas of the Main page of Google Documents. Standard WAI-ARIA landmarks use prefixed labels to indentify the name of an area such as *banner, contentinfo, search, navigation* and *main*, which are not very significant for the user and for her/his orientation. WAI-ARIA also permits the use of regions with personalized labels; these labels are correctly announced by Version 12 of JAWS, but unfortunately at the time they were not properly supported by the previous versions (only the name "region" was announced). To solve this problem, we used a trick introducing hidden labels, which are like a sort of bookmark in the interface (Fig. 4).

Fig. 4. Implementation of hidden labels.

Each area is a (X)HTML *div* element that contains a label; the *New label of Region* is an (X)HTML heading *h2*, that is not visible in the layout of the page because a CSS script moves it outside the screen. This solution allows a blind user (pressing the "h" key for retrieve headings) to jump from one heading to another. Finally, the blind user can move from one area to another by either: 1) activating landmarks by pressing a special key combination on the keyboard (showing a navigable list via arrow keys), or 2) pressing the "h" key to jump to the next hidden label (by adding the shift key, it is possible to reach the previous one).

c. The "summary" attribute has been added to the tag *<table>* to clarify its content. Usually the "t" JAWS key quickly permits to move to the next table, so a descriptive summary can facilitate navigation and understanding. However, in case the user wants to explore the content of the table, JAWS allows her/him to jump easily from one row to another.

d. The modified editor page is composed of a toolbar and a text area (Fig. 5) and it is now accessible and reachable via keyboard. The blind user can write in the text area and can quickly access to the toolbar buttons (*save, bold, italic, underlined, left, center, right, justified*) and to the pull down menus (*Paragraph, Font Family, Font Size)* by pressing the "h" key related to the hidden label inserted before the toolbar.

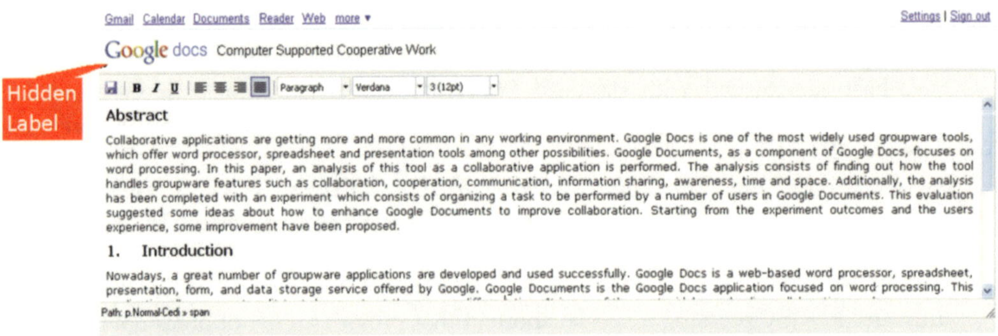

Fig. 5. Modified page of the editor.

Accessibility of the editor has improved because we used an existing accessible ready-to-use editor online, the TinyMCE editor (an Open Source Javascript-based HTML WYSIWYG editor) (TinyMCE, 2011) that works correctly with both Mozilla Firefox and Microsoft IE;

e. Real time and informative messages can be solved using server side Ajax code, since WAI-ARIA has been designed for dynamic content and advanced user interface controls that exploit this technology.

This experience has shown the importance of designing accessible and usable interfaces for cooperative or learning tools in general. Unfortunately, this experience has also shown various compatibility issues during interaction and different behaviors that occur using IE and Firefox browsers. Compatibility between browsers is a real actual hard challenge for designing and developing Web UIs.

8.2 A Web tool transforming digital documents to structured audio podcasts

This second example shows a Web tool transforming digital documents (for example, edited with Google Documents) to structured audio podcasts that can be loaded onto a personal mp3 player (Mori et al., 2010). Audio podcasts exploit the auditory sensorial channel of the students, with the objective to facilitate personalization of studying following self-based rhythms. A podcast is a digital file (audio or video) distributed on the Internet through Web Syndication. Audio podcasts are a great tool for learning and offer many advantages:

a. a student can listen to educational material while doing other things (running, driving, ironing, etc.)
b. extends classroom limits, because a student can listen to the recorded lesson files again, at any moment or location
c. students are less anxious because they can listen to the lesson even when they miss a class
d. a student can personalize her/his pace of studying

e. audio requires less resources than video to create and reproduce
f. teachers can improve their teaching methods by listening to audio podcasts of the lessons again.

When reading a book such as a novel, one is forced to be sequential in order to understand the plot; otherwise, in the case of educational books or documents (like manuals, paper, technical reports, transcription of lessons, etc.) continuous reading is not always the most appropriate for effective learning; usually this kind of educational material is structure-based in sections and paragraphs: this kind of structure facilitates exploration and internal searches, so that student can read only the parts of interest.

In a preliminary questionnaire (Leporini et al., 2009), blind and visually impaired users stated they preferred listening to a document in form of audio podcasts with a personal mp3 player, instead of reading it by a screen reader or a magnifier on a computer (this was a confirmation of the desire for a certain freedom in personalizing learning). Many studies have shown that short podcasts (max 10-15 min) are more effective for learning than a single long unit. Long podcasts may decrease attention, thus reducing comprehension (Cebeci & Tekdal, 2006; Ormond, 2008). When podcasting is used for educational purposes, well-structured short podcasts (following the structure of a document - i.e., converting each section into one podcast) facilitate exploration and internal searches. Educational audio podcasts can be produced by recording live events but this requires time, costs and resources; in alternative software text-to-speech converters (like Text2mp3, DSpeech, etc.) can break a document down into several mp3 files based on a time division (e.g., 5/10/15 minutes) or on a manual "break string" inserted by the user in the document, but time division cannot be as effective as a structured one.

From the previous considerations, we designed and developed an experimental web-based prototype that receives a document (.doc,.docx,.rtf,.txt) and provides a set of audio files reflecting the document's internal structure (one file for each document section). Fig. 6 shows the architecture of the system. An example of application is the following: a teacher (or a student) can upload a document (for instance, created with Google Documents) of the daily lesson (or personal notes) using the input interface of the system. The system tries to identify titles of sections, splits the document according to the sections detected and converts each section into an audio file using a Text-To-Speech module (TTS); the mp3 files (one per section) can be downloaded by students from an accessible Web page. Input and output Web interfaces are accessible based on WAI-ARIA and can also be accessed by blind students with a screen reader. Blind students are also provided with .talk files, used by the firmware Rockbox (Rockbox, 2001) that allows the blind to be guided vocally on an mp3 player during navigation of files and folders. Talk files are obtained transforming each title of sections in audio streaming.

The system emphasizes titles of sections aurally using a different gender of voice, while it uses the voice chosen at the beginning for the podcast content (Fig. 7).

The system also highlights bold phrases inside a paragraph of each section (to better deliver the author's emphasis) by inserting in the podcast an ascending sound at the beginning of each bold phrase and a descending sound at the end. The system also identifies tables inside the document, converting each one into a single separated podcast, since listening to a table (especially if very big) is frustrating for a blind person. When a blind student uses an mp3 player, she/he can easily skip from one mp3 file to another (using the buttons track forward/previous) to learn whether the content of each podcast is interesting (because each

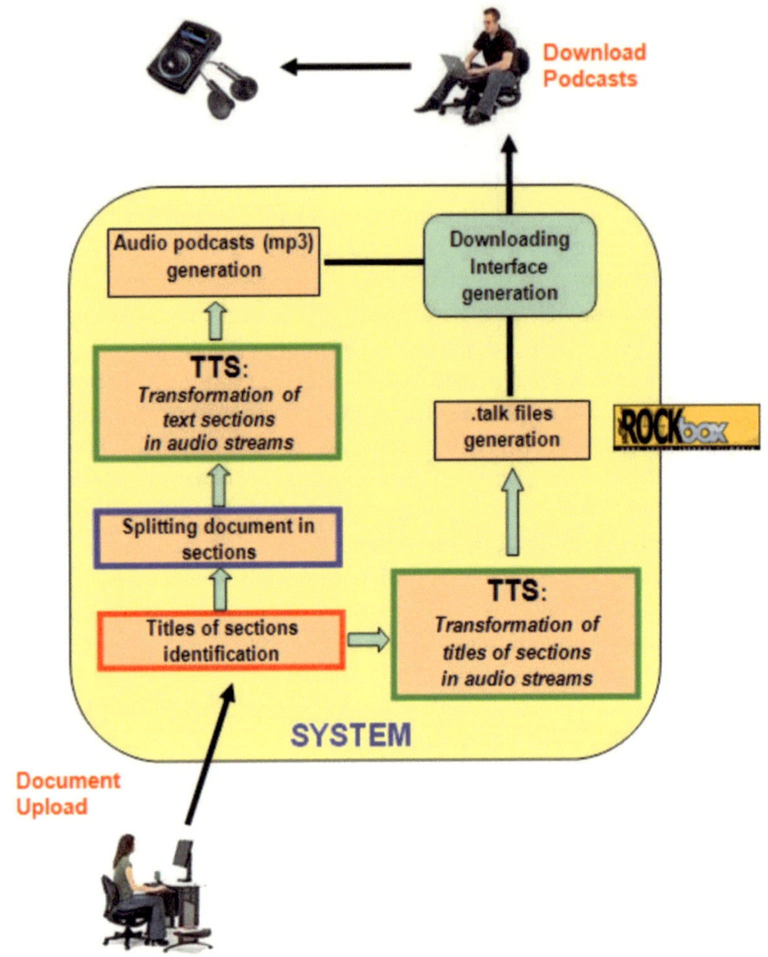

Fig. 6. Architecture of the web-based system for generating structured audio podcasts.

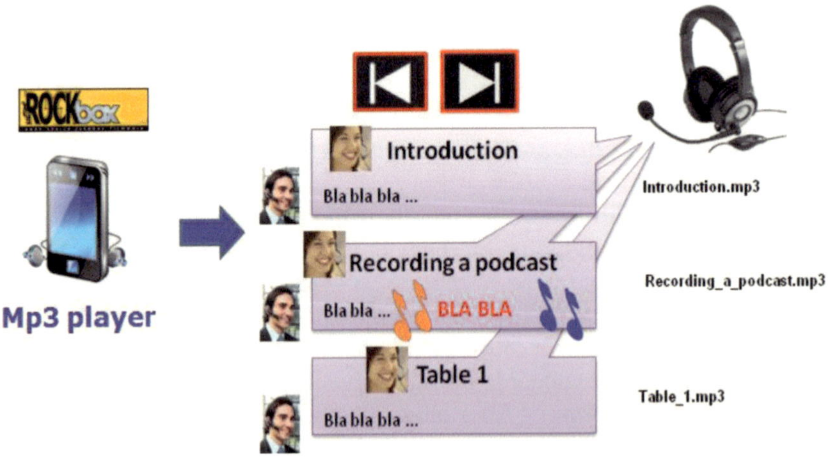

Fig. 7. Interaction of blind user on an mp3 player equipped with Rockbox firmware.

audio podcast contains the title in the first few seconds). This is especially helpful when listening to new audio educational material in order to understand content and search for the most important sections, or for the going-over phase, which is critical for blind students. This experience has confirmed for us the importance of using alternative learning tools to personalize the pace of studying beyond classroom limits, facilitating education for any kind of student and teacher.

9. Conclusion

New learning paradigms are based on collaboration, experience, and personalized acquisition of knowledge according to student ability and skills. Collaboration is a key element of learning, so the availability of usable tools supporting and favouring student cooperation is a critical factor for achieving easy and rapid results. New technologies and the Internet offer a fertile ground for foraging this growth.

In this chapter we have discussed features of collaborative e-learning tools and suggested basic guidelines for enhancing their usability for blind people. We first have discussed the potential of e-learning, focusing on the great opportunities it offers for the blind. After describing the interaction mode of the blind people, we have proposed basic general suggestions for improving the design and personalization of collaborative tools. Two examples have been presented to clarify the concepts introduced: 1) the design of accessible interfaces of Google Docs, a popular collaborative Web editing tool, optimized for interacting via screen reader and 2) the design of a Web tool for converting digital documents to structured audio podcasts to support personalized learning, especially for the blind.

Active participation and collaborative interaction can improve the learning experience for anyone. Personalization is crucial for those with cognitive and learning disabilities, tailoring education to each student's ability.

However, new tools alone are not enough to deliver effective and usable customized learning units. The great challenge actively involves teachers who must know and creatively apply new technologies, systems, applications and tools to improve the learning process, making them also available on mini-computers, laptops and mobile devices (smart phone, mp3 players, play devices, etc.). When designing learning tools, teachers should also keep in mind student abilities, interests and capabilities in order to bring them to their full potential.

In conclusion, further research in this direction is needed. Future studies would investigate several topics: the accessibility, usability and adaptability of e-learning systems on mobile computing and handheld devices, the customization of user interfaces to personalize the learning experience, the delivery of educational units with different sensorial channels, and the design and creation of new collaborative learning objects and applications. Moreover, educational-centred topics such as pedagogical and teaching strategies, behaviour analysis and new assessment methodologies should also be addressed.

10. References

Ardito, C., Costabile, M., De Marsico, M., Lanzilotti, R., Levialdi, S., Roselli, T. & Rossano, V. (2005). An Approach to Usability Evaluation of e-Learning Applications. *Universal Access In the Information Society*, Vol. 4, No. 3, pp. 270-283, ISSN: 16155289

Beard, C. M., & Wilson, J. P. (2002). *The Power of experiential learning: a handbook for trainer and educators,* (first edition), Kogan Page, ISBN 0 7494 3467 8, London, UK

Birenbaum, M., Breuer, K., Cascallar, E., Dochy, F., Dori, Y., Ridgway, J., Wiesemes, R. & Nickmans, G. (2006). A learning integrated assessment system. *Educational Research Review*, Vol. 1, No. 1, 24 April 2006, pp. 61-67

Bisoux, T. (2007). The Evolution of E-learning, In: *BizEd*, January/February 2007, pp. 22-29, Available from: http://www.aacsb.edu/publications/archives/janfeb07/p22-29.pdf

Cebeci, Z., & Tekdal, M. (2006). Using Podcast as Audio Learning Objects. *Interd. Journal of Knowledge and Learning Objects*. Vol. 2, pp. 47-57

Chambel, T., Antunes, P., Duarte, C., Carriço, L. & Guimarães, N. (2009). Reflections on Teaching Human-Computer Interaction to Blind Students, *Proceedings of Creativity and HCI: From Experience to Design in Education, Vol. 289, pp.* 123-142

Chittaro, L. (2010). Distinctive aspects of mobile interaction and their implications for the design of multimodal interfaces, *Journal on Multimodal User Interfaces*, Vol. 3, No. 3, pp. 157-165

Craven, J. & Brophy, P. (2003). Non-visual access to the digital library: the use of digital library interfaces by blind and visually impaired people. In: *Technical report, Manchester: Centre for Research in Library and Information Management - CERLIM*, 08.03.2011, http://www.cerlim.ac.uk/pubs/index.php

Dale, E. (1969). *Audio visual methods in teaching* (third edition), Holt, Rinehart & Winston, New York

De Marsico, M, Kimani, S, Mirabella, V, Norman, K. L. & Catarci, T. (2006). A proposal toward the development of accessible e-Learning content by human involvement. *Journal Universal Access in the Information Society*. Vol. 5, No. 2, August 2006, pp. 150-169

Debevc, M. & Bele JL. (2008). Usability testing of e-learning content as used in two learning management systems, In: *European Journal of Open, Distance and E-Learning*, 08.03. 2011, Available from: http://www.eurodl.org/materials/contrib/2008/Debevc_Bele.htm

Fleming, N. D. (2001). *Teaching and learning styles: VARK strategies*, ISBN 0-473-07956-9, Christchurch, New Zealand

Ghiani, G., Leporini, B. & Paternò, F. (2009). Vibrotactile feedback to aid blind users of mobile guides, Journal of Visual Languages and Computing, Vol. 20, No. 5, October 2009, pp. 305-317

Google Docs, In: Google Documents, Available from: http://www.docs.google.com

Greenberg, S. (1989). The 1988 conference on computer-supported cooperative work: Trip report, *Canadian Artificial Intelligence ACM SIGCHI Bulletin*, Vol. 20, No. 5, pp. 49-55, July 1989

Grudin, J. (1994). CSCW: History and Focus. University of California, *IEEE Computer*, Vol. 27, No. 5, pp. 19-26

Hawk, T. F. & Shah A. J. (2007). Using Learning Style Instruments to Enhance Student Learning, *Decision Sciences Journal of Innovative Education*, Vol. 5, No. 1, January 2007, pp. 1-19

International Organization for Standardization (ISO) 9241-11. (1998). Ergonomic requirements for office work with visual display terminals (VDTs) - Part 11: Guidance on usability, In: UU Department Information Technology, Available from: http://www.it.uu.se/edu/course/homepage/acsd/vt09/ISO9241part11.pdf

Ivory, M. Y., Yu, S. & Gronemyer, K. (2004). Search result exploration: a preliminary study of blind and sighted users' decision making and performance. *Proceedings of Extended abstracts of CHI 2004*, pp. 453-1456, ISBN:1-58113-703-6, Vienna, Austria, April 24-29 2004

JAWS Screen Reader. (2011). In: Freedom Scientific, 08.03.2011, Available from: http://www.freedomscientific.com/products/fs/jaws-product-page.asp

Kayes, A., Kayes, D. C. & Kolb, D. A. (2005). Experiential Learning in Teams, *Simulation and Gaming*, Vol. 36, No. 3, pp. 330-354

Kelly, B., Phipps, L. & Howell, C. (2005). Implementing a holistic approach to e-Learning accessibility. *Proceedings of ALT-C 2005, International Conference of the Association for Learning Technology*, In: UKOLN, 08.03.2011, Available from: http://www.ukoln.ac.uk/web-focus/papers/alt-c-2005/accessibility-elearning-paper.doc

Khan, M. A., Israr, N. & Hassan, S. (2010). Usability Evaluation of Web Office Applications in Collaborative Writing. *Proceedings of ISMS, First International Conference on Intelligent Systems, Modelling and Simulation*, pp. 147-151, ISBN: 978-0-7695-3973-7, Liverpool, England, January 27 – 29, 2010

Kobayashi, M. (2008). Voice Browser for Groupware Systems: VoBG - A Simple Groupware Client for Visually Impaired Students. *Proceedings of ICCHP 2008, International Conference on Computers Helping People with Special Needs*, pp. 777-780, ISBN: 978-3-540-70539-0, Linz, Austria, July 9-11, 2008

Kolb, D. (1984). The Process of Experiential Learning, Chapter 2 in: *The experiential learning: Experience as the source of learning and development*, pp. (20-38), Prentice Hall, ISBN 0-13-295261-0, New Jersey, USA

Leporini, B. & Buzzi, M. (2007). Learning by e-Learning: Breaking Down Barriers and Creating Opportunities for the Visually-Impaired. *Proceedings of UAHCI'07, International Conference on Universal Access in Human-Computer Interaction: applications and services*, pp. 687-696, ISBN: 978-3-540-73282-2, Beijing, China, July 22-27, 2007

Leporini, B., Buzzi, M. C., Buzzi, M. & Mori, G. (2009). Automatically Structuring Text for Audio Learning, *Proceedings of UAHCI 2009 International Conference Universal Access in Human-Computer Interaction. Applications and Services, part III*, Volume 5616, pp. 73-82, ISBN: 978-3-642-02712-3, San Diego, CA, Inuted States, 19-24 July 2009

Mehrabian, A. (1971). *Silent Messages* (1st ed.), ISBN 0-534-00910-7, Wadsworth, California: Belmont

Merrill, M. D., (1991). Constructivism and Instructional Design. *Educational Technology*, Vol. 31, No. 5, May 1991, pp. 45-53, ISSN-0013-1962

Mori, G., Buzzi, M. C., Buzzi, M. & Leporini, B. (2010). Structured Audio Podcasts via Web Text-to-Speech System, *Proceedings of WWW 2010, international Conference on World Wide Web*, ISBN: 978-1-60558-799-8, Raleigh, North Caroline, United States, April 26-30 2010

Mori, G., Buzzi, M. C., Buzzi, M., Leporini, B., & Penichet, V. M. R. (2011). Making "Google Docs" User Interface More Accessible for Blind People, *Proceeding of ADNTIIC 2010, International Conference on Advances in New Technologies, Interactive Interfaces, and Communicability*, pp. 14-17, ISBN: 978-3-642-20809-6, Huerta Grande, Cordoba, Argentina, October 20 – 22, 2010

Ormond, P. R. (2008). Podcasting enhances learning. *Journal of Computing Science in Learning*, Vol. 24, No. 1, pp. 232-238

Petrie, H., Hamilton, F. & King, N. (2004). Tension, what tension?: Website accessibility and visual design. *Proceedings of the International Cross-disciplinary Workshop on Web Accessibility (W4A)*, No. 76, pp. 13 – 18

Pitt, I. & Edwards, A. (2003). Design of Speech-based Devices, Springer, ISBN 978-1-85233-436-9

Poltrock, S. & Grudin, J. (1994). Computer Supported Cooperative Work and Groupware, *Proceedings of CHI 1994 Conference Companion on Human Factors in Computing Systems*, pp. 355-356, Boston, Massachusetts, United States, April 24-28, 1994

Poltrock, S. & Grudin, J. (1999). CSCW, groupware and workflow: experiences, state of art, and future trends, *Proceedings of CHI 1999 Extended Abstracts on Human Factors in Computing Systems*, pp. 120-121, ISBN:1-58113-158-5, Pittsburgh, Pennsylvania, United States, May 15-20, 1999

Poltrock, S. & Grudin, J. (2005). Computer Supported Cooperative Work and Groupware (CSCW), *Proceedings of Interact 2005*, Rome, Italy, September 2005

Potts, R. & LaMarsh, J. (2004). *Master change, maximize success*, Chronicle Books, ISBN 0811841707, 9780811841702, San Francisco

Prince, K. J. A. H., Van Eijs, P. W. L. J. & Boshuizen, H. (2005). General competencies of problem-based learning (PBL) and non-PBL graduates, *Medical Education*, Vol. 39, No. 4, April 2005, pp. 394–401, Wiley Online Library, ISSN 0308-0110

Rockbox Open Source firmware, In: Rockbox, Available from: http://www.rockbox.org/

Rodriguez, E.P.G., Domingo, M.G., Ribera, J.P., Hill, M.A. & Jardi L.S. (2006). Usability for All: Towards Improving the E-Learning Experience for Visually Impaired Users. *Proceeding of ICCHP 2006, International Conference on Computers Helping People with Special Needs*, pp. 1313-1317, ISBN: 3-540-36020-4, Linz, Austria, July 9-11, 2006

Santos, O. C., Boticario, J. G, Fernández del Viso, A., Pérez de la Cámara, S., Sánchez, C. R., Gutiérrez y Restrepo E. (2007). Basic Skills Training to Disabled and Adult Learners Through an Accessible e-Learning Platform, *Proceedings of UAHCI'07, International Conference on Universal Access in Human-Computer Interaction: applications and services*, pp. 796-805, ISBN: 978-3-540-73282-2, Beijing, China, July 22-27, 2007

Schoeberlein, J. G. & Yuanqiong, W. (2009). Groupware Accessibility for Persons with Disabilities. *Proceedings of UAHCI '09, International Conference on Universal Access in Human-Computer Interaction*, pp. 404-413, ISBN: 978-3-642-02712-3, San Diego, CA, USA, July 19-24, 2009

Sloan, D., Heath, A., Hamilton, F., Kelly, B., Petrie, H. & Phipp, L. (2006). Contextual web accessibility - maximizing the benefit of accessibility guidelines. *Proceedings of W4A '06, International cross-disciplinary Workshop on Web Accessibility*, ISBN:1-59593-281-X, Edinburgh, Scotland, UK, May 22-23, 2006.

Stahl, G. (2005). Group cognition in computer-assisted collaborative learning, *Journal of Computer Assisted Learning*, Vol. 21, No. 2, Apr 2005, pp. 79–90 (2005), ISSN-0266-4909

Thiessen, P. & Chen, C. (2007). Ajax Live Regions: Chat as a Case Example. *Proceedings of W4A '07, International cross-disciplinary Conference on Web Accessibility (W4A)*, pp. 7-14, ISBN:1-59593-590-8, Banff, Canada, May 07–08, 2007

TinyMCE Editor. (2011). In: TinyMCE, 08.03.2011, Available from: http://tinymce.moxiecode.com/

Tomasegovic, T., Zitinski Elias, P. Y., Baracic, M., Mrvac N. (2011). E-learning and Evaluation in Modern Educational System, *US-China Education Review*, Vol. 8, No. 2, February 2011, pp. 198-203, ISSN 1548-6613

W3C. (5 Dec 2008). Web Content Accessibility Guidelines 2.0. In: W3C, 08.03.2011, Available from: http://www.w3.org/TR/WCAG20/ (5 Dec 2008);

W3C. Accessible Rich Internet Applications (WAI-ARIA) 1.0, In: *W3C Candidate Recommendation 18 January 2011*, 08.03.2011, Available from: http://www.w3.org/TR/wai-aria/

Zaharias, P. (2006). A usability evaluation method for e-learning: focus on motivation to learn. *Proceedings of CHI EA 2006 extended abstracts on Human Factors in Computing Systems*, ISBN:1-59593-298-4, Montreal, Québec, Canada, April 22-27, 2006

Part 3

Case Study

8

How Can We Explain the Relationship Between Quality Interaction and Quality Learning in E-Learning? A Maximum Variability Study in Four-Cases

Ana Elena Schalk Quintanar
Phd. In Education
Chile

1. Introduction

In this chapter, part of a research project developed over three years (2005-07) is presented. Its main objective consisted in describing the relationship between the quality of interaction in asynchronic discussion forums and the quality of learning achieved in experiences of e-learning formation. The current work identifies the way in which interaction actually contributes to the quality of learning. This is achieved on the basis of a descriptive research where the emphasis is on a positive relationship between the quantity and quality of the discourse of the participants, and the quality of the learning achieved and reflected in the different instances of the evaluation. All of this allows questions which motivate further investigation of this relationship in greater depth.

Whether e-learning theory sustains interaction is very important for quality learning, but up to now we have not known how to boost the value of constructing knowledge and learning with others in e-learning experiences. The results of the research were expected to explain if a relationship between interaction and learning exists and how it can be described.

The evidence collected allows us to recognize and to confirm the importance of facilitating cognitive discussions to build relevant and significant learning for students.

Although three of the four cases confirm the fundamental theory, the fourth opens new perspectives to be developed in the future as a research line.

1.1 Background

The current work comes on top of that which started to analyse and value the relevance of education via IT in the 1990s. Mason (1990) offered a framework for understanding communication through computers. In this framework synchronic and asynchronic communication are distinguished. Other investigative proposals have also appeared (Schotsberger, 2001; Van Dijk, 2000) which have analysed the discourse in depth from different viewpoints. This has shown us that it is not the *quantity* but the *quality* of interactions that makes it easier to investigate and try to comprehend the ways in which the learning process is developed through the interaction and exchange of ideas in computer-assisted communication.

Gunawardena, Lowe and Anderson (1997) undertook the task of defining an instrumental model which could be used to examine the construction of knowledge. Based on Vigotsky´s theory and using phases of discussion productively to determine the weight of the constructed knowledge, this analytical model offers relevant elements that allow the understanding of the construction process, both in teaching and in learning, in collaborative environments. This is because of its focus on interaction as a vehicle of knowledge construction and its ability to detect the construction of knowledge that emerges in a conference, quite apart from its consideration of the learning context with a relative strength in this model.

In turn, Rourke, Anderson, Garrison and Archer (2001) identified three elements of the investigative community. The first was social presence in discourse. The other two were cognitive and teaching presence. The researchers emphasized the relevance of the first element as essential to motivate students in their learning process. This social dimension was configured in three categories: affective responses, interactive responses and coherent responses.

Later on, Garrison, Anderson and Archer (2003) identified cognitive presence in a model of the investigative community. This presence reflected higher-order knowledge and an achieved application generally supported by literature and research related to critical thinking. They implemented four stages, initiation, exploration, integration and resolution, as moments of the cognitive dynamics. Another prominent contribution of this work was to use the complete message as the analysis unit. This decision regarding the analysis unit was tested by two reliability indexes: the Holsti and the Kappa coefficients, high-quality results being obtained in both cases. This resulted in future investigations related to the discourse analysis in asynchronic environments and the standardization of the complete message as the analysis unit.

At the same time, Anderson, Rourke and Garrison (2001) developed a proposal to analyse the presence of teaching in the frame of the investigative community.

They considered the following teaching roles: experience design, facilitation and co-creation. They also determined that for the production of a socially active environment, the teacher or tutor's mastery of the subject would allow the students to have access to direct instruction. Its reliability was proven by the Kappa's indexes, a high coherence level being obtained.

Along with these contributions, other works that identified the way in which communication between participants occurred were developed. They determined three specific dynamics: participation, interaction and interactivity. Participation is not interaction and the concepts must be distinguished. The first one refers to the number of messages that one person leaves in a discussion forum. The second one shows how those messages are answered by other people, generating a developing communicative activity. In 1992, Henri was one of the first to analyse the interaction quality of online forums. He differentiated between participative and interactive dimensions (Henri, 1992). He defined participation as the number of meaning units in a concrete forum. On the other hand, there is a fine distinction between interaction and interactivity.

Interactivity is the key variable in communication situations: it conveys the degree to which communication transcends reaction. It is a process variable, characteristic of communication situations. Interactivity is not a characteristic of the informational environment, since it has to do with the way in which messages follow a sequence and interrelate with each other and with previous messages (Perera, V; & Clarés, 2006).

On the basis of these investigative contributions, this study follows the line of knowledge production covered by investigators such as Marcelo (2002), Marcelo and Perera (2004) Torres (2002) and Perera (2007), who developed investigative works related to analysis of the discourse in Spanish-speaking asynchronic forums.

This work focuses on the integration of three relevant elements that interrelate with each other in a virtual learning experience. These elements are: the quantity and quality of interactions, learning results for the different units of formation and the quality of the final work, which should report the implementation of the expected learning process.

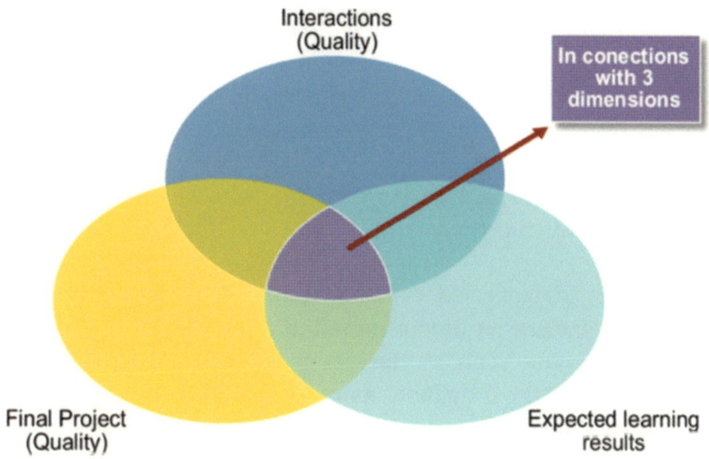

Fig. 1. Research Variables

Throughout this research it was considered that the combination of the e-learning elements would, on the one hand, make it possible to argue for the importance of participation, interrelation and collaboration on the net in order to achieve the expected learning progress, progress believed to go beyond the contents themselves and to be the basis for the development of actual competences. On the other hand, it should make it possible to provide scientific knowledge for the necessary modifications to increase the quality of the activity, considering that this is an aspect frequently challenged in virtual formation.

When this investigation refers to the "expected" learning results (and those proposed as goals but those obtained by the student throughout his/her learning process), they have a direct relation with the *mobilization of executed actions* and not only with understanding and repetition of concepts and learned subjects (declarative knowledge). Nor are they related to the mere ability to reproduce established procedures (such as, for example, any of the working actions of a technological platform).

These learning results refer to the integration of both declarative and procedural elements in an expected performance, which requires strategic learning results to be reflected in the valuation of concrete opportunities, decision-making related to knowledge and procedure and the design of possible alternatives for the solution of significant situations and their timely execution (Schalk, 2006).

1.2 Main question

Given the presentation of the core point where the three elements considered in a virtual formation experience are set out, the current investigation raises two questions: is there a relation between the quantity and quality of the participations and interactions that take place in the asynchronic discussion forums, and the quality of the expected learning results in the selected e-learning experiences? How does this relation become evident?

1.3 Secondary questions

From the previous question, the following are derived:

- What is the configuration of the quantity, dimension and category of participations for every case?
- Is it possible to establish a direct relation between the number of interventions and their quality and the results of the learning processes in every module within the context of the defined cases?
- Is it possible to prove a relation between the achievement level of the evaluation criterion considered in the final work project and the discourse quality previously analysed?

This study is based on the collected evidence from previous investigations of discourse analysis in asynchronic communication forums and on a number of studies of the learning experience using approaches such as the design model and didactics and evaluation. Consequently, the current investigation aims to find enough evidence to allow full understanding of the relation between interaction (in its three dimensions: social, cognitive and learning-wise) and the learning quality in a virtual modality. If such a relation exists, this investigation hopes to explain it.

If the study is successful it will allow deeper understanding of how students learn in a forum (asynchronic communication) and how this activity is related to the achievement of the expected learning results in virtual modality courses.

Finally, this study intends to contribute possible answers to the question still asked by many researchers as to how one can boost the value of constructing knowledge and learning with "others" in e-learning (De Wever, Schellens, Valcke, & Van Keer, 2006) (Fainholc, 2006; Marcelo & Perera, 2007).

2. Development of the research

2.1 Material, sample and methods

During 2005 and 2006 a preliminary investigation was carried out. It served as a first approach to analyse the relation between two variables (Schalk, 2007): the quantity and quality of interactions and the quality of expected learning results. From this it was concluded that there was a positive correlation between the discourse quantity and quality in discussion forums and the learning results in formation modules.

In order to study this phenomenon more deeply, the following sample was selected. It is constituted by post-degree formative activities.

- Analysis Group 1: Version October, 2005 to June, 2006. (Expert 2005)
- Analysis Group 2: Version October, 2006 to June, 2007. (Expert 2006)
- Analysis Group 3: Version October, 2006 to June, 2007. (SAE Course)

- Analysis Group 4: Version October, 2006 to June, 2007. (Master's degree)

All these courses were offered by Seville University between the academic years 2005 and 2007. The academic certification comprised "Expert" had a duration of 280 formative hours; and for "Master's degree" had a 340 hours in the second year along with the attached requirement of having approved the Expert level.

The total number of participants from all courses was 171, including students, guest teachers, tutors and curriculum directors distributed as follows: the 2005 Expert version had 63 participants; the 2006 version, 51; the SAE Expert version, 31; and the Master's degree version, 26. The number of analysis units increased to over 10,000.

Case methodology was used. Four cases of highest variability were formed. As shown below, a chart was drawn to describe every case.

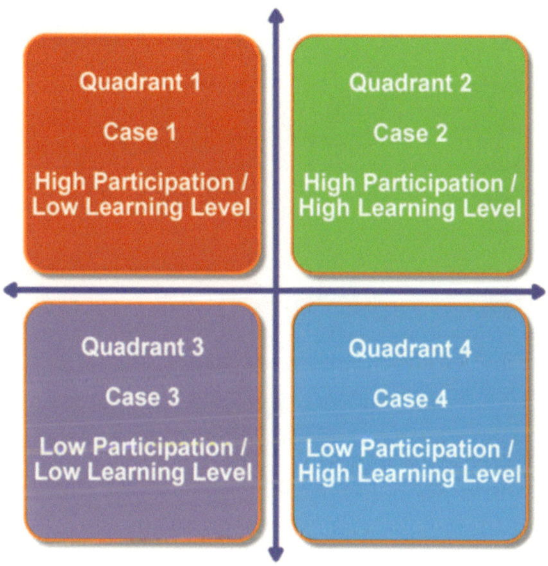

Fig. 2. Four Cases of Highest Variability

The horizontal variable (X axis) represents the evaluation variable (reflection of expected learning results) and the vertical variable (Y axis) represents the participation variable.

- Quadrant 1: students who showed a high participation level and a low evaluation level.
- Quadrant 2: students with a high evaluation and high participation.
- Quadrant 3: students with low participation and low learning results.
- Quadrant 4: students with low participation but high learning results.

The following criteria were set for the selection of students to form the cases:

1. To have all the evaluations of the 13 learning units.
2. All student interventions in forums and the respective discourse analysis to be based on the three dimensions of the discourse analysis model (social, cognitive and educational) (Rourke et al., 2001).
3. All intervention dynamics to contain the three elements of participation, interaction and interactivity.
4. Accredited evaluation of the final coursework, the said evaluation to be determined by 13 criteria: enable the core part of the course's, the communication areas, titles of the

subjects, introduction to the subjects, development and design of icons, agenda's, access to the subjects, resources', development of contents (two full units), and including the contents, the box of activities, and the right block and left block.

5. Application profile of every student in every case available.
6. Results of the self-evaluation tool applied six months after the formative period.
7. Students classified in one of the four quadrants in its most extreme value

A total of 21 students met these criteria and therefore qualified as members of every one of the cases.

Those who clearly had the most valued characteristics were selected, and students who had intermediate values in some of the variables were omitted, so the highest variability condition was fulfilled. The following tables present the codes of students selected.

CASE 1			
Participant code	x514	xs02	x617
CALIF	8,122	6,86	5,08
INTERV.	166	30	82

Table 1. Participants of Case 1

CASE 2			
Participant code	xs15	x642	x609
CALIF	9,31	9,261	9,33
INTERV.	77	46	51

Table 2. Participants of Case 2

CASE 3			
Participant code	x608	x626	x606
CALIF	7,928	5,65	7,66
INTERV.	33	18	11

Table 3. Participants of Case 3

CASE 4			
Participant Code	x607	x621	xs11
CALIF	8,217	8,45	9,36
INTERV.	13	25	21

Table 4. Participants of Case 4

Since each case had three participants who fulfilled the criteria, a second exercise was carried out to determine who could fulfill the "highest" possible value in each quadrant. That was the main condition of the method research type (maximum variability), that is, the students selected were those who had the highest values of conditions and criteria.
Therefore, the cases were classified as follows:

CASE 1		
Participant code	xs02	x617
CALIF	6,86	5,08
INTERV.	30	82

Table 5. Final Participants of Case 1

CASE 2		
Participant code	xs15	x609
CALIF	9,31	9,33
INTERV.	77	51

Table 6. Final Participants of Case 2

CASE 3		
Participant code	x626	x606
CALIF	5,65	7,66
INTERV.	18	11

Table 7. Final Participants of Case 3

CASE 4		
Participant Code	x621	xs11
CALIF	8,45	9,36
INTERV.	25	21

Table 8. Final Participants of Case 4

2.2 Case analysis method: Criteria

In this stage of the investigation an analysis of the cases by group was carried out to identify every possible interrelation between:

- Discourse dimensions for every participant (Rourke et al., 2001), that is, social, cognitive and didactic or learning dimensions.

- Dynamic of intervention according to the distinctions of participation, interaction and interactivity.
- Evaluations of each one of the modules.
- Final work (fulfilling all 13 evaluation criteria)
- Self-evaluation (post-formation)

The aim was to check in the databases that every case had elements that were similar and different which could offer relevant evidence to answer the research questions. Furthermore, it was deemed relevant to identify how the variables behaved under specific conditions in every case.

3. Conclusion

The first case, which relates high participation to a low level of learning, confirms what other studies have already revealed, namely that a high turnout does not necessarily reflect a high level in the achievement of expected learning outcomes, and that the quality of the discourse will therefore play a key role in such achievement.

Case 2 allows us to claim that a high turnout, translated into unintended interactions with learning objectives, reflects a high level of impact on the achievement of expected learning outcomes, and that the quality of learning plays a key role. It would then be a fundamental task of the tutor´s work to help of the students to develop a digital proficiency that allows them to learn in this modality.

Case 3 details the relationship between variables, where despite the apparent similarity of the quality of the discourse to the features of Case 1, which tends toward explicit interaction and a low presence of structuring and applications in its interventions, it can be inferred that the lack of participation and interaction produces a low learning level, so the relationship between quality of discourse and quality of learning is evidenced.

Finally, as noted before, the case that offers greater possibilities for further investigating the relationship between discourse quality and quality of learning is the fourth one. What we can conclude from this is that the greater the presence of the cognitive dimension, the greater the evidence of the relationship between interaction and learning expectancy, this being the first perspective which opens up possibilities for research development.

New questions also arise. In the fourth case, the students´ situation was different. We could not find if: did they have a previous set of skills that enabled them to meet the evaluation criteria? Do the clarity of design and the pedagogical model underpinning the selected courses permit self-learning, so that the interaction is not required for the achievement of learning? Did the way in which they were supplied with the forum discussions by tutors directly or indirectly influence the promotion of student participation, without it being detrimental to the quality of their learning? This analysis of experiences shows us that we still have some distance to cover between individual learning (self-study) and collective learning (social constructivism), and need to design courses that give more value to the process and interactive activity followed by the student.

Without a doubt, continuing investigation of the relationship of the variables quality of learning and quality of discourse , in e-learning, is required to discover why it is that students with very few interactions in e-learning courses achieve high levels of individual learning (learning through self-instruction), when the definition of this mode and the pedagogical model of the courses analysed are based on collaborative learning, the value of community learning and the social construction of personal knowledge for the knowledge and learning society.

4. References

Anderson, T., Rourke, L., & Garrison, D. (2001). *Assessing teaching presence in asynchronous, text-based computer conferencing*. Retrieved from www.aln.org&alnweb/journal/

De Wever, B., Schellens, T., Valcke, M., & Van Keer, H. (2006). *Content analysis schemes to analyse transcripts of online asynchronous discussion groups: A review* (Vol. 46). London: Science Direct, Elsevier.

Fainholc, B. (2006). *La interactividad en la educación a distancia*. Buenos Aires: Paidós.

Garrison, D., Anderson, T., & Archer, W. (2003). *E-learning in the 21st Century*. Great Britain: RoutledgeFalmer.

Gunawardena, C., Lowe, C., & Anderson, T. (1997). Analysis of a global online debate and the development of an interaction model for examining social construction of knowledge in computer conferencing. *Journal of Educational Computing Research, 17*, 397-431.

Henri, F. (1992). Computer conferencing and content analysis. In A. Kaye (Ed.), *Collaborative learning through computer conferencing* (pp. 117-136). Berlin: Springer-Verlag.

Marcelo, C. (2002). *Aprender con otros en la red. Investigando evidencias.* Paper presented at the Virtual Educa 2002.

Marcelo, C., & Perera, V. H. (2004). El análisis de la interacción didáctica en los nuevos ambientes de aprendizaje virtual. *Bordón, 56*(3 & 4), 533-558.

Marcelo, C., & Perera, V. H. (2007). Comunicación y aprendizaje electrónico. La interacción didáctica en los nuevos espacios virtuales de aprendizaje. *Revista de Educación, 323*, 381-429.

Perera, V. (2007). *Estudio de la Interacción didáctica en e.learning*. Seville: Universidad de Sevilla.

Perera, V., & Clarés, J. (2006). Análisis de la interacción grupal para la construcción del conocimiento en entornos de comunicación asincrónica. *Complutense de Educación, 17*, 155-167.

Rourke, L., Anderson, T., Garrison, D., & Archer, W. (2001). Methodological Issues in the content analysis of computer conference transcripts. *International Journal of Atrificial Intelligence in Education, 12*, 8-22.

Schalk, A. (2006). Modelo pedagógico para formación de adultos en el desarrollo de competencias. *Revista de Facultad de Ciencias Administrativas de la Universidad Nacional Mayor de San Marcos.*

Schalk, A. E. (2007). *El valor de la Comunicación e interacción asincrónica en una experiencia de formación virtual: análisis del discurso, desarrollo de competencias y calidad del producto final con los aprendizajes esperados Programa de Experto y Master en e.learning de la Universidad de Sevilla.* Paper presented at the XIX Encuentro Nacional y V Internacional de Investigadores en Educación. Retrieved from http://www.rmm.cl/usuarios/pponce/doc/200711141622570.programaencinvestig2007.doc

Schotsberger, P. (2001). *Classifying forms of synchronous dialogue resulting from web-based teacher professional development*. Orland, FL. Comunicar. No. 35.

Torres, J. (2002). *El análisis de la comunicación asincrónica en la formación a través de internet: construcción y validación de un sistema de categorías.* Seville: Universidad de Sevilla.

Van Dijk, T. A. (2000). El discurso como interacción social. Gedisa. *El discurso como interacción social. Estudios sobre el discurso II:Una introducción multidisciplinaria.* (Vol. II, pp. 213-262). Barcelona